The Living Dead

The Living Dead

A Study of the Vampire in Romantic Literature

James B. Twitchell

Duke University Press   Durham, N.C.   1981

Copyright © 1981, Duke University Press

Printed in the United States of America

Library of Congress Cataloging in Publication Data

Twitchell, James B   1943–
  The living dead.

  Includes bibliographical references and index.
    1. English literature—19th century—History and
criticism. 2. American literature—19th century—
History and criticism. 3. Vampires in literature.
4. Romanticism I. Title.
PR469.V35T85 1980   820'.9375   79-54290
ISBN 0-8223-0438-4

For Mary

Contents

Preface

I couldn't care less about the current generation of vampires: personally I find them rude, boring, and hopelessly adolescent. However, they have not always been this way. In fact, a century ago they were often quite sophisticated, used by artists as varied as Blake, Poe, Coleridge, the Brontës, Shelley and Keats, to explain aspects of interpersonal relations. However vulgar the vampire has since become (as any twelve-year-old can explain), it is important to remember that along with the Frankenstein monster, the vampire is one of the major mythic figures bequeathed to us by the English Romantics. Simply in terms of cultural influence and currency, the vampire is far more important than any of the other nineteenth-century archetypes—more important than all the Wandering Jews, Don Juans, Reclusive Poets, Little Nells; in fact, he is probably the most enduring and prolific mythic figure we have. This book traces the vampire out of folklore into serious art until he stabilizes early in this century into the character we all too easily recognize.

But this book is really not about vampires; it is about Romanticism and what many major English and American artists found so intriguing in the myth. There are certain occupational hazards in attempting this kind of study: one must sacrifice depth for breadth, practice certain economies of scale, and always run the risk of mistaking and oversimplifying. Unfortunately, or fortunately, as the case may be, one of the central works, *Varney the Vampyre*, has been almost lost to us, and in this case I have taken the liberty of summarizing the plot, but in other cases I have treated only accepted masterpieces. Due to the exigencies of space, I have had to overlook the rich Continental tradition of vampire stories in the nineteenth century (Maupassant's *The Horla*, Tieck's *Wake Not the Dead*, Hoffman's "Aureila" from *The Serapion Brethren*, Nodier's *Smarra*, Alexis Tolstoy's *The Family of the Vour-dalak*, many ballads in Mérimée's *La Guzla*, Baudelaire's "Metamorphoses of the Vampire," Gautier's *Clarimonde*, Turgeniev's *Clara Militch*, Jan Neruda's *The Vampire*) as well as the vampire's rather startling rebirth in the contemporary novel, on Broadway, and in Hollywood. Occasionally, however, I could not stop myself and have wandered into the twentieth century (James's *The Sacred Fount* and D. H. Lawrence's *The Rainbow* and *Women in Love*), but I did so only because I consider these treatments of the myth quintessentially Romantic.

This book has been great fun to write, and I am thankful to the Florida Humanities Council for their grants and to *Ball State University Forum, Studies in the Novel, Studies in Short Fiction, Tennessee Studies in Literature, Southern Humanities Review*, and *Research Studies* for their permission to use bits and pieces of

x   *The Living Dead*

articles. I am also indebted to four years of students who have suffered me this strange interest, to my graduate instructors Jonathan Trobe, Richard Freeman, and Arthur Sandeen as well as to Professors Aubrey Williams, Leonard Woolf, and especially Devendra P. Varma for encouragement and instructive comments.

The Living Dead

1. Introduction

> "Rubbish, Watson, rubbish! What have we to do with walking corpses
> who can only be held in their grave by stakes driven through their
> hearts? It's pure lunacy."
>
> "But surely," said I, "the vampire was not necessarily a dead man? A
> living person might have the habit. I have read, for example, of the old
> sucking the blood of the young in order to retain their youth."
>
> "You are right, Watson. It mentions the legend in one of these refer-
> ences. But are we to give serious attention to such things? This agency
> stands flat-footed upon the ground, and there it must remain. The
> world is big enough for us. No ghosts need apply."
>
> —Sir Arthur Conan Doyle, *The Adventure
> of the Sussex Vampire*

Sherlock Holmes may have no time for vampires, but his friend Dr. Watson quite obviously does. As a matter of fact, Watson's mention of the "old sucking the blood of the young in order to retain their youth" hints that his knowledge may be extensive. For he knows that vampires are not always foamy-mouthed fiends with blood dripping from extended incisors, but rather can be participants in some ghastly process of energy transfer in which one partner gains vitality at the expense of another. Presumably the doctor knows this because he has done his reading, and it is that reading—not in the medical but in the fictional literature of the nineteenth century—that this book will examine.

While critical attention has been paid to other mythic figures in Romanticism such as Prometheus, Don Juan, and the Wandering Jew, the vampire has been overlooked. Partly this is because his current commercial popularity is almost invariably vulgar: vampire dolls, vampire teeth, vampire cartoons, vampire costumes, and "vitamin enriched" vampire cereal (*Count Chocula*), to say nothing of a spate of vampire television shows, movies, and comic books, have made him more a subject of parody than of serious study. However, the contemporary moon-faced, sunken-eyed, cadaverous vampire licking his chops at the sight of an unprotected virgin is as far removed from his Romantic lineaments as is the Frankenstein monster with bolts through his forehead and huge stitches down his cheeks from the creature Mary Shelley created.

Ironically, the vampire has also been overlooked because most of the early criticism, while often perceptive, was decidedly eccentric. Here is a case of iatrogenic criticism, for the doctor/critic has often done his subject more harm than good, causing more confusion than clarification. The three prominent early critics of the vampire, all writing in the 1920s, were D. H. Lawrence, Montague Summers, and Mario Praz, and each had a profound influence on the shape of criticism to come. Lawrence's comments on Poe in *Studies in Classic American Literature* were rhapsodic about the vampire myth's ability to explain neurotic love. In *The Vampire: His Kith and Kin*, Montague Summers, a controversial Jesuit, was critically hampered by his own literal belief in vampires, which caused many problems, not the least of which was his mistaking a popular "penny-dreadful" for a scholarly dissertation on vampires; while Praz, in *The Romantic Agony*, was overly concerned with making the vampire fit into a DeSadean interpretation of Romanticism.[1] Although these works often sparkle with brilliant insight, they more often illuminate the critic than the vampire. The situation is now changing, as there have been in the last decade a number of book-length studies of the vampire myth, but there is still no extended appraisal of the vampire in literature.[2]

What Summers neglected and what Lawrence and Praz overstated was the psychological use of this mythic figure as an analogy to explain human interactions. For the vampire in Romanticism had a more profound use than making the reader's skin crawl or showing how daring the artist could be. Admittedly, writing schauerromans exploiting gothic sensibility was fashionable, and, admittedly, the vampire story was an aberration of Romantic eroticism, as Praz implies, but the myth was also often used in serious attempts to express various human relationships, relationships that the artist himself had with family, with friends, with lovers, and even with art itself. In the works of such artists as Coleridge, Byron, Shelley, Keats,

1. D. H. Lawrence, "Edgar Allan Poe," from *Studies in Classic American Literature*, in *Selected Literary Criticism*, ed. Anthony Beal (1932; rpt. New York: Viking Press, Compass Books, 1966); Montague Summers, *The Vampire: His Kith and Kin* (1928; rpt. New Hyde Park, N.Y.: University Books, 1960; and Mario Praz, *The Romantic Agony* (1933; rpt. and rev., London: Oxford University Press, 1970).

2. The best place to learn about the Romantic vampire is in Thomas Pecket Prest's (or James Malcom Rymer's, for the authorship is disputed, *cf.* E. F. Bleiler's "Introduction" to the Dover Edition) *Varney the Vampyre or, The Feast of Blood* (1847; rpt. New York: Dover Publications, 1972). This book has all the myth and more in two volumes. Arno Press also has an edition under the editorial direction of Sir Devendra P. Varma in three volumes (New York: Arno Press, 1970). Both editions are hard to use, as they are reprints of the original periodical publication, but *Varney* is invaluable as a source of vampire lore. The pioneering scholarly work on vampires was Dom Augustin Calmet's *Traité sur les Apparitions des Esprits, et sur les Vampires* (1746). Montague Summers's *The Vampire: His Kith and Kin* is primarily based on Calmet's work, and has itself been followed by a spate of derivative works, including Gabriel Ronay, *The Truth about Dracula* (New York: Stein and Day, 1974); Douglas Hill, *The History of Ghosts, Vampires and Werewolves* (New York: Harper and Row, 1973); Leonard Wolf, *A Dream of Dracula: In Search of the Living Dead* (New York: Popular Library, 1972); Tony Faivre, *Les Vampires* (Paris: Eric Losfeld, 1962); Anthony Masters, *The Natural History of the Vampire* (London: Mayflower Books, 1974); Nancy Garden, *Vampires* (New York: J. B. Lippincott Co., 1973); Margaret L. Carter, *Shadow of a Shade: A Survey of Vampirism in Literature* (New York: Gordon Press, 1975); Raymond T. McNally and Radu Florescu, *In Search of Dracula* (New York: Warner Paperback, 1973); Basil Cooper, *The Vampire in Legend, Fact, and Art* (Secaucus, N.J.: Citadel Press, 1974); and Christopher Frayling, "Introduction" to *The Vampyre: A Bedside Companion* (New York: Charles Scribner's Sons, 1978). Of lesser importance are a psychological study, Ornella Volta, *The Vampire*, trans. Raymond Rudoroff (London: Tandem Books, 1962); Peter Underwood, *The Vampire's Bedside Companion* (London: Leslie Frewin, 1975), chaps. 2 and 3; and an "Introduction" to *A Clutch of Vampires*, ed. Raymond T. McNally (Greenwich, Conn.: New York Graphic Society, 1974).

Emily and Charlotte Brontë, Stoker, Wilde, Poe, and Lawrence the vampire was variously used to personify the forces of maternal attraction/repulsion (Coleridge's Christabel), incest (Bryon's Manfred), oppressive paternalism (Shelley's Cenci), adolescent love (Keats's Porphyro), avaricious love (Poe's Morella and Berenice), the struggle for power (E. Brontë's Heathcliff), sexual suppression (C. Brontë's Bertha Rochester), homosexual attraction (LeFanu's Carmilla), repressed sexuality (Stoker's Dracula), female domination (D. H. Lawrence's Brangwen women), and, most Romantic of all, the artist himself exchanging energy with aspects of his art (Coleridge's Ancient Mariner, Poe's artist in *The Oval Portrait*, Wordsworth's Leech Gatherer, Wilde's Dorian Gray, and the narrator of James's *The Sacred Fount*).

As befalls any critical work that attempts to discuss English Romanticism, a major problem is organization. Chronological organization will not work, for the vampire is a mythic figure who rather than developing new sophistication and sharpness, becomes instead tedious and dull. Chronological organization thus only reverses critical expectations, for what begins in order ends in diffusion. Comparisons are also difficult because outside of the current cinema, comics, and cheap novels, the vampire myth is rarely used twice for the same pupose. Definitions are also problematic, for the artists freely altered the myth to support artistic ends. So I have organized this work first around male and female vampires in the poetry, then chronologically as the vampire figures in the novel, and finally around the various attempts to use the vampiric analogy to describe the process of artistic creation. I then conclude with a brief summary of twentieth-century adaptations of the myth, detailing its use in D. H. Lawrence's middle novels. I regret that this organization often resembles circus elephants on parade, but, alas, there is not much interconnection between the works. This in itself may tell us something important about the Romantic "movement."

I will start with the female vampire, or lamia, not out of any Victorian deference but rather because here are the least sophisticated adaptations: Coleridge's Geraldine, Keats's Lamia, and La Belle Dame sans Merci, Charlotte Brontë's Bertha Rochester, and Poe's Ligeia and Morella have all been recognized and accepted in criticism as actually or potentially destructive females who have vampiric tendencies. The adaptation is not so clear with the male vampire in poetry, however, for here Keats's Porphyro, Byron's Manfred, and Shelley's Cenci are all assertive, facinorous, and in varying degrees demonic, but are they really vampires? Their demonism is more complicated than that of their fictional sisters, and vampirism may be only one of a number of metaphors used to describe them. To make organizational matters still worse, after the first twenty years or so of the nineteenth century, the vampire rather abruptly ceased to be a subject of poetry and instead found a temporary home in the stage melodrama before finding a permanent place in the novel.[3] By the 1840s poetry had returned to more decorous subjects, allowing

3. While the vampire was a subject of Romantic poetry, it was not in the case of the Victorians. The only later nineteenth-century poems are Kipling's mediocre "The Vampire" (1897) and James Clerk Maxwell's youthful "The Vampyre" (1845). There were numerous French and English melodramas and two operas based on Polidori's *The Vampyre* (1819). *Cf.* Summers, *Vampire*, chap. 5.

the novel to absorb what was left of the gothic spirit. The first vampire stories, Byron's "Fragment" and John Polidori's *The Vampyre* (1819), introduced the demon to the worn-out Gothic novel, and in three decades the vampire had become a stock character to be exploited without mercy in Thomas Pecket Prest's *Varney the Vampyre*. Then Emily Brontë resuscitated the vampire in the poetic characterization of Heathcliff while her sister was doing the same with Bertha Rochester. For Heathcliff (at least according to Nelly Dean) acts *as if* he were a vampire, devouring both Earnshaws and Lintons for his own vivification, while Bertha has to be sequestered in the attic lest her libidinal desires destroy the men-folk. By using the vampire mythopoetically, the Brontës showed how powerful an analogy for aberrant energy transfer the vampire could be, and so set the temper for two later masterful prose treatments of the vampire: Sheridan LeFanu's *Carmilla* and Bram Stoker's *Dracula*. These two popular but critically neglected works attempted to explore the sexually explosive and ambivalent nature of the myth and are not only thrilling stories but sophisticated psychological studies as well. They also introduced what has become a dominant theme in twentieth-century vampire lore—the vampire as the "love-them-and-destroy-them" adolescent male fantasy.

This study then concludes with what I consider the most important use of the vampire legend—the adaptation of the myth to explain the process of artistic creation. Here there is no set use of the story, rather a welter of varying interpretations. In *The Rime of the Ancient Mariner* the myth is used to explain the relationship between the teller of the tale (the Ancient Mariner) and the listener (the Wedding Guest); in Wordsworth's *The Leech Gatherer* (revised and retitled *Resolution and Independence* in 1802) it explains the relationship between the "real" poet (the Leech Gatherer) and the poet manqué (the speaker); in Poe's *The Oval Portrait* it illustrates the energy transfer between the creator (the painter) and the object of art (the sitter); in Wilde's *The Picture of Dorian Gray* it is used to show the destructive nature of Realistic art; and in Henry James's *The Sacred Fount* it elucidates the interaction between artist (the narrator) and his illusionary "reality." It is in the final part of this study that we see what the other Romantic adaptations of the myth were moving toward—the coupling of human relationships, the artist himself now at the center, with the stuff of common folklore. Perhaps the best place to start, then, is with that folklore, for the Romantics did not create this beast *ab ovo*, but rather reshaped him from an already healthy body of lore.

The Vampire in Folklore

> *If ever there was in the world a warranted and proven history, it is that of vampires: nothing is lacking, official reports, testimonials of persons of standing, of surgeons, of clergymen, of judges; the judicial evidence is all-embracing.*
>
> —Jean Jacques Rousseau, "Letter to The Archbishop of Paris"

Before the nineteenth century the vampire seems to have only folkloric existence—an existence as historically old as it was culturally varied. For the vampire is truly ancient. Long before Christianity his presence was imagined among the peoples of coastal Egypt, in the Himalayan recesses of north India, and on the steppes of Russia. The proliferation of names gives some indication of mythic currency: called "Vurdalak" in Russia, "Vampyr" or "Oupir" in East Europe, "Ch'ing Shih" in China, "Lamia" in ancient Greece, the vampire was part of almost every Eurasian culture. As Bram Stoker's fictional professor Van Helsing says in broken English about Dracula:

> He is known everywhere that men have been. In old Greece, in old Rome; he flourish in Germany all over, in France, in India, even in the Chernesese; and in China, so far from us in all ways, there even he is, and the peoples fear him at this day. He have follow the wake of the berserker Icelander, the devil-begotten Hun, the Slav, the Saxon, the Magyar.[4]

And a nonfictional professor, Devendra P. Varma, has traced him into the Himalayas, where, Varma contends, the proto-vampire first proliferated through a host of different guises: the "Kali" or blood-drinking mother goddess; the "Yama" or the Tibetan lord of Death; the Mongolian God of Time afloat on an ocean of blood. From these highlands the vampire descended into the low countries, carried in the myths of the Huns and the Magyars into Eastern Europe, then into Greece, and finally into the Arabian and African cultures.[5] All these strains contributed to the legend, with each new civilization and each new generation refashioning and re-creating the vampire until he emerges as the Western monster we recognize today: a demonic spirit in a human body who nocturnally attacks the living, a destroyer of others, a preserver of himself.

From the few accounts we have it appears that blood-sucking monsters reached England relatively late, perhaps by the eighth century; the actual word "vampire" entered English writing much later, perhaps in the early eighteenth century. We know that there was a great wave of vampire mania in Central and Eastern Europe in the 1730s, and so it is probable that the word "vampire" then gained its currency.[6] The vampire that the English inherited, a mixture of Slavic, Scandinavian, and Greek stock, soon had acquired quite precise characteristics. Although the first citation (1734) carried in the *Oxford English Dictionary* describes him as "a ghost who leaves his grave at night and sucks the blood from the living," he was already a good deal more complex.[7]

Oddly enough, one can see this in a most unexpected source—the writings of

4. Bram Stoker, *Dracula* (1897; rpt. New York: Dell Publishing Co., 1978), p. 266.
5. Devendra P. Varma, "Introduction" to *Varney the Vampyre*, pp. xvii–xix.
6. The most informative books on the vampire are still those by Montague Summers, *The Vampire: His Kith and Kin*, and its sequel, *The Vampire in Europe* (1929; rpt. New Hyde Park, N.Y.: University Books, 1961).
7. Here is the *Oxford English Dictionary*'s (1961) definition: "1. A preternatural being of a malignant nature (in the original and usual form of the belief, a reanimated corpse), supposed to seek nourishment, or do harm, by sucking the blood of sleeping persons; a man or woman abnormally endowed with similar habits."

Alexander Pope. In a letter written in February 1740 to Dr. William Oliver, Pope jokes about his own ill health, which he claims will surely lead to his "death" and "burial" in the Twickenham grotto:

> Since his burial (at Twitnam) he [Pope] has been seen some times in Mines and Caverns & been very troublesome to those who dig Marbles & Minerals. If ever he has walk'd above ground, He has been (like the Vampires in Germany) such a terror to all sober & innocent people, that many wish a stake were drove thro' him to keep him quiet in his Grave.[8]

Pope's wit shows more than passing knowledge of this nocturnal fiend, for not only does he know the proper methods of vampire disposal, but he also knows this creature is not to be taken seriously, at least in England. To the sophisticated Englishman, vampires were clearly a Continental concern.[9] This was not the case for the unsophisticated Englishman, however. By the early eighteenth century the vampire had become a credible although not especially popular local fiend.

The English vampire by the end of the eighteenth century was not simply a ghost or a wraith but the devil's spirit which had possessed the body and trapped the soul of a dead sinner. In more precise terms, the vampire was an energumen—the devil's avatar, for although the human body was literally dead, the entrapped soul lived eternally under the devil's control. The vampire in English lore was therefore distinct from a ghoul, which was a living soulless body which ate corpses but did not drink blood. Also unlike the ghoul, which operated from external orders usually given by a sorcerer, the vampire obeyed internal commands.[10] The vampire's body had not always been under the control of the devil; in fact, it had once belonged to a perfectly normal human who by some sin lost the protection of Christian guardianship, thereby allowing the devil admittance. This usually happened either because the sinner refused to obey religious law or was himself the victim of a vampire's attack. Since *Dracula* (1897), possession by attack has been understandably emphasized in the popular media, but previously the vampire population was thought to be primarily augmented by sinners, especially suicides.

It seems a terrible irony that the price paid for committing suicide was to make the self indestructible, for once the devil took control, the soul could never escape to an after-life until the demon was demolished. The best the bereaved family could do was to bury the corpse at a country crossroads, hoping that the sign of the cross would deter the devil. To make matters worse for the family, it was thought that the vampire's first victims would be his closest friends and relations. It is in this context that Victor Frankenstein compares his monster to "my own vampire . . .

8. George Sherburn, ed., *The Correspondence of Alexander Pope*, 5 vols. (London: Clarendon Press, 1956), 4:227.

9. For more on Pope's knowledge of vampires, see M. R. Brownell, "Pope and Vampires in Germany," *Eighteenth Century Life* 2 (June 1976): 96–97.

10. Often the myths of vampire and ghoul are confused, as they are in India; see Garden, *Vampires*, pp. 43–46.

forced to destroy all that was dear to me" (volume 1, chapter 6). Little wonder then that when Sophia Western in *Tom Jones* (1749) claims she would rather kill herself than marry Blifil she is easily dissuaded by Mrs. Honour's recounting the folklore:

> Let me beseech your La'ship not to suffer such wicked Thoughts to come into your head. O lud, to be sure I tremble every Inch of me. Dear Ma'am, consider—that to be denied Christian burial, and to have your Corpse buried in the Highway, and a Stake drove through you, as Farmer Halfpenny was served at Ox-Cross, and, to be sure, his ghost hath walked there ever since; for several People have seen him. To be sure it can be nothing but the Devil which can put such wicked Thoughts into the Head of any body; for certainly it is less wicked to hurt all the World than one's own dear Self, and so I have heard said by more Parsons than one.[11] (book 7, chapter 7)

A hundred years later Heathcliff, for his own vampiric reasons, wants Hinley Earnshaw's body "buried at the crossroads without ceremony of any kind" (chapter 17).[12] The legal system reflected these concerns. In the early nineteenth century laws were passed in England which stated that the body of a suicide could only be interred between 9 P.M. and midnight, while a further law made it illegal to dig up the body of a suspected suicide in order to drive a stake through the heart. These laws were finally repealed in the 1880s, but they give some indication of the commonly believed link between the vampire and the suicide.[13]

An improperly buried suicide was almost a guarantee of vampiric possession, but lesser sins could also diminish the protection God afforded the true believer. Dying unbaptized, being buried in unconsecrated ground, being excommunicated, copulating with a witch or demon, being the seventh child of the same sex, being born on Christmas day (presumably for the effrontery of intercourse at the same time as the Virgin Mary—unfortunately the responsibility of the child, not the parent), being born with precocious teeth, being unruly during Lent—in fact, each culture developed a directory of such favors given the devil. The list varied with different societies, yet two classes of sins were common to all: first, sins against the church understandably carried sufficient promise of damnation to incite the devil; and second, any social peculiarity might be a sign of diabolical propensities. So in dark-eyed cultures the blue-eyed were suspect; in dark-haired societies the blond was exiled; the exception to the Procrustean norm was feared and cast out. However, persons suffering from epilepsy or anorexia were obvious choices in all societies, as well as those with cleft palates, since the deformity seems caused by the conscious drawing-up of the lip. It is almost as if the church, the state, and the community

11. For more on the treatment and burial of the bodies of suicides, with special reference to the case of "Farmer Halfpenny," see Henry Fielding, *The History of Tom Jones*, "Wesleyan Edition," ed. Fredson Bowers (London: Oxford University Press, 1975), 1:349.
12. For more detail on Heathcliff's vampirism, see chap. 4.
13. Summers, *The Vampire*, p. 151; and Masters, *Natural History of the Vampire*, pp. 180–82.

recognized, perhaps unconsciously, the terrible potency of the vampire myth and capitalized on it to enforce their own standards of conformity.

If one did not commit suicide, was publicly religious and physically conforming, there was still the possibility that the vampire might possess the body after death. This would occur in the rare case when the vampire actually attacked and successfully transformed the victim into another vampire. This doppelgänger process is surely one of the myth's most intriguing aspects, for it implies a psychic conspiracy between attacker and vampire— an interesting analogue perhaps for our current mythology in which the rapee subconsciously invites the rapist. The vampire never wantonly destroys—in fact, his initial victims are preordained; they are those whom he loved most when alive. The initial victims are friends and family who, of course, recognize the vampire as one who was loved and trusted. This recognition is important, for the vampire cannot pick and choose on his own; rather he must be picked, "invited" into the relationship. The victim, not consciously realizing that the friend or relative is the devil in disguise, understandably and ironically obliges. Usually, if the vampire is male, the first victims are female; and if the vampire is female (called "lamia," after the Greek monster), then the victim is male, but there is a distinct level of homosexuality carried in the myth that is often reflected in literary treatment.

The actual "attack" is almost always the same: it is nighttime, probably midnight, the bewitching hour. The moon should be full, for the vampire is not only revived by moonlight, he is energized by it. Assuming that the vampire is male, the female victim is preparing to sleep, in that dim world between sleeping and waking. She sees her recently deceased lover (often her late husband) standing before her, perhaps outside the window. Now the victim must make some inviting move; she must unhasp the window, open the door, do anything that shows she is acceding, even slightly. This crucial point is repeated in almost all the literary adaptations, for the vampire cannot cross a threshold without this invitation; he is bound to wait pathetically like a schoolboy until invited in. Once inside, however, his powers gradually increase. He is still not in control and so must attempt to entrance her with his hypnotic stare, for his powers are initially ocular, like those of many monsters. He need say nothing; just a look with his red, bloodshot eyes will suffice. This trance, if successful, will put the victim under his power, and she will have no memory of their encounters. He bends to kiss—the "love-bite" now quite literally the "kiss of death" or, more precisely, "kiss of deathlessness."[14] (Is the "hickey," the crimson patch on the teenager's neck, a vestige of mythic reenactment of this oral sadism?) His lips draw back, revealing his slightly extended incisors. He bows to her body; the movements are almost religious. Although he can puncture any part of her, after *Dracula* the neck became *de rigueur*. In folklore, however, he may just as

14. This kiss, the only physical action that the vampire really performs, is discussed in Masters, *Natural History of the Vampire*, chap. 3; Wolf, *A Dream of Dracula*, chap. 4; and Garden, *Vampires*, chap. 3. The best literary descriptions are in *Dracula*, chap. 3, and LeFanu's *Carmilla*, chap. 7.

easily bite the arm or the breast, or, in some cultures, even the toes! He smells putrid, for his mephitic body is in a state of arrested decay; still the victim, now finally feeling repulsion, cannot escape. He makes his puncture, sucks or laps her blood, withdraws, and then disappears. In later developments of the myth he can change shape at will, becoming as invisible as mist or assuming the more usual shapes of a wolf or a bat. (Until the middle of the seventeenth century the vampire was not associated with the bat, but after the discovery of the "Desmodus rotundus" or vampire bat, he has rarely been associated with anything else.) The victim's sensations are wildly mixed—sensual, nauseous, warm, and mystified, as she falls into a troubled, exhausted sleep.

The now pavid victim is not immediately to become a vampire. She is weakened, not possessed. She may be lucky—the vampire may be destroyed or may have a liaison elsewhere; or she may have a friend who can recognize the symptoms of her ensuing enervation and take defensive action. For by no means is all weighted on the vampire's side. Up until the very moment of possession it is a two-handed game; for instance, in Christian cultures the vampire is terrified by all icons of the church—the cross, holy water, the Bible, the rosary; even the words "God" and "Christ," when spoken by the devout, can send the vampire into a paroxysm of fear. And for some unknown reason garlic and a few other herbs are also anathema to him. Furthermore, he is photophobic; since sunlight causes him to lose strength, a bright light directly shining in his eyes will cause him to wince away in fear. Although in folklore he was not solely the "creature of the night" he has become so in the movies; he moves in sunlight with only human strength.

If the victim does not defend herself, or if she allows the vampire to return, he will eventually drain her of blood until she wastes away. Finally, she will appear to die, but in reality the husk of her body is taken over by the devil. Her soul is trapped, and now she must start an eternity of searching for new analeptic blood-energy to keep from the pains of a starvation without end, a horrible life without death. She has become a lamia.

Logically, of course, if the vampire myth were scrutinized at all, it would fold under the weight of its own contradictions. Vampires would overpopulate themselves into a Malthusian oblivion, but myths, especially this one, are wonderfully exempt from logic. So the vampire lives on, eternally gathering in new victims, yet never upsetting the population balance. Perhaps the population is controlled by the vampire's own rather pathetic susceptibility to destruction, for one God-fearing man can decimate a whole population.

This "just man," in the folk version usually a priest or a "dhampire," understands the horrid habits of the vampire, and can search out and properly destroy the beast. The priest understandably is a logical choice in any vampire hunt, as he has both the knowledge of how evil operates and access to the armory of Christian icons. But the "dhampire" is a nonreligious facet of the myth which shows how Christianity syncretically grafted itself onto the old folklore. The "dhampire" is the child of a vampire, usually a son, who intuitively understands how the parent will act.[15] His overthrow of the parent, very much in the manner postulated by Freud in his "Primal Horde" thesis, accentuates the adolescent quality of the myth.[16] This quality is reinforced in those stories where the priest or the dhampire has a young friend, a relative perhaps of the vampire's victim, who accompanies the vampire killer on the quest.

In the modern cinematic version of the story the vampire-destroyer is usually a doctor, often a hematologist, who aids the young man with his medical knowledge and paternal wisdom. Whatever the version, the posse must first locate the demon's sleeping grounds. The easiest way is to check nearby graveyards and examine all the burial plots. The vampire's grave may have tiny holes above it, through which the demon has traveled in the form of mist, for although the vampire cannot decompose, he can transpose himself into the elements as mist or storm. If these holes cannot be located, a number of alternatives are possible, the most common again involving a young boy. A male virgin must be set upon a white stallion and led around the graves, for all animals except the wolf and bat shun the vampire, and the horse will balk before crossing the vampire's turf.[17] Once the grave is located, the casket is unearthed. Understandably this disinterment should occur during the daylight, for nightfall will give the vampire his phenomenal powers. The coffin lid is swung back, and there, lying in a shallow pool of blood, is the intumescent villain, a smirk doubtless on his face and his eyes opened in a glazed and eerie stare. Utmost care must now be taken, for the vampire, seeing all, realizes who his destroyers are and knows who his next victims will be should they fail to destroy him.

Since the body of the vampire is already dead, he must be destroyed rather than killed. In old tales he could simply be burned. If he wasn't burned, it was customary to stuff his mouth with garlic after the head had been decapitated. As elaborations became standardized, staking became a more popular mode of destruction. Staking (actually called "transfixation" by the Catholic church) became something of an art, for only certain wood could be used, and the stakes had to be inserted in a prescribed manner. Aspen, thought to be the wood of the cross, was preferred, but hawthorn or whitethorn would suffice. A swift, firm thrust of the stake through the heart did not kill the demon, but forever fixed him in his coffin by impaling him to the ground. In certain cultures the vampire's body was turned face down, so that should he come loose, he would not dig to the surface, but rather deeper into the earth.[18] As he was staked, blood gushed from the wound, and, while he might

15. For more on the father-son relationship, see T. P. Vukanovic, *Gipsy Lore*, as quoted in Masters, *Natural History of the Vampire*, pp. 118–20.

16. This Freudian interpretation was first made by Maurice Richardson, "The Psychoanalysis of Ghost Stories," *The Twentieth Century* 166 (1959): 428, and reaffirmed in Royce MacGillivray, "*Dracula*: Bram Stoker's Spoiled Masterpiece," *Queen's Quarterly* 79 (Winter 1972): 523.

17. Summers, *The Vampire*, p. 200.

18. Vampire disposal is discussed in Summers, *The Vampire*, chap. 3; Garden, *Vampires*, chap. 5; Masters, *Natural History of the Vampire*, chap. 2; and Wolf, *A Dream of Dracula*, chap. 4.

well howl in agony, he was strangely relieved. For now at last he could experience what had been denied for so long—release from an eternity of half-life: the waking dead could at last sleep.

The Influence of Christianity

> *Thus properly speaking, kings are not vampires; the true vampires are the monks who eat at the expense of both kings and people.*
>
> —Voltaire, *Philosophical Dictionary*

Certain elements of the vampire myth assert themselves with such regularity in the various retellings of the story that they have become motifs anchoring each version to a central tradition. The most important of these repeated themes is of course death, or more precisely, the inability to experience death. Equally important, however, is the recurring image of blood. Blood, as both a fluid and symbol of life, seems forever imbued in man's consciousness with mystic importance.[19] Blood-drinking as a way to partake of another's energy was the logical extension of what seemed a causal nexus between blood and vigor, for as this fluid left the body, death seemed to enter. And if blood was life, then drinking blood would be absorbing that life. Understandably, the primitive warrior imbibed the blood of the enemy, for why rob him of his sword when you can have the power behind the sword? In the earliest civilizations blood was a central totem, a source of energy for man and a libation for the gods. Early literature reflects man's belief that blood was more than a metaphor or a synecdotal description of life; it was life itself. For instance, in classical lore Odysseus had to feed the shade of the seer Tiresias with animal blood before they could converse, and in Euripides' play *Hecuba* the phantom of Achilles demanded the sacrifice of a young virgin whose blood he may have drunk.[20]

If blood was important to classical myth, it was also central to early Christianity. In both the Old and New Testaments "the blood is life" motif is repeated again and again, both as objective statement and psychological truth. In fact, the sacrament of communion is based on the transfer of energy through blood. Christ himself exhorts us to drink his blood as a way of sharing his power:

> Whoso eateth my flesh, and drinketh my blood, hath eternal life; and I will raise him up at the last day. For my flesh is meat indeed, and my blood is drink indeed. He that eateth my flesh, and drinketh my blood, dwelleth in

19. For the possible sexual importance of blood in the vampire myth, see note 14 above. Blood's mythic importance is also discussed in Wolf, *A Dream of Dracula*, chap. 4; Masters, *Natural History of the Vampire*, chap. 2; and Garden, *Vampires*, chap. 3.

20. *The Odyssey*, book 2, and Euripides, *The Hecuba*, ll. 390 *ff.*

me, and I in him. As the living Father hath sent me, and I live by the Father: so he that eateth me, even he shall live by me. (John 6:53–57)

But this drinking of blood must not go unrestrained. For although we are told in Deuteronomy 12:23 that "the blood is the life," we are also warned in the same verse not to become obsessed with it. The whole scripture tells us: "Only be sure that thou eat not the blood: for the blood *is* life; and thou mayst not eat the life with the flesh." This paradox must have been a concern of early church fathers, for on one hand they wanted to assert the primordial connection between blood and life in the Eucharist, yet they recognized the need to restrain man from killing for blood. So the Bible has numerous warnings against drinking blood:

> Deuteronomy 12:16: "Only ye shall not eat the blood; ye shall pour it upon the earth as water."
> Genesis 9:4: "But flesh with the life thereof, *which is* the blood thereof, shall ye not eat."
> Leviticus 17:11: "For the life of the flesh *is* in the blood: . . . Therefore I said unto the children of Israel, no Soul of you shall eat blood, neither shall any stranger that sojourneth among you eat blood."

The strength of the early church was that it was always willing to compromise— to allow its altars to be built on the sites of earlier temples. But it was also lucky. An example of such a serendipitous syncretism is the ecclesiastical and folk concern with blood, for in the late Middle Ages the vampire story received its greatest support from the church as a way of explaining the last of the sacraments, the Eucharist. This, the most difficult of the sacraments to understand, depended on the almost inexplicable process of transubstantiation, yet it could be described in terms of the older vampire myth. For just as the devil drank the sinner's blood and partook of his spirit, so now the righteous man might drink the wine and partake of Christ's holiness. It was a simple and straightforward way to explain this complex sacrament, and, of course, it put the fear of the devil quite literally into the sinner, as it put the salvation of Christ into the righteous.[21]

The Catholic church had other than doctrinal uses for the vampire myth: it became a tool in territorial expansion and domination. By the 1600s the church had encountered its most difficult time expanding to the East, for in the Balkans it met the entrenched resistance of established religions, and here the vampire story was used as a wedge of ecclesiastical polity. The most terrible driving of this wedge was the assertion that all who were buried in unconsecrated ground would be denied eternal rest, instead becoming vampires. This assertion had a profound proselytizing effect on both Moslems and Greek Orthodox, who had relatively recently come to believe in an afterlife. Now here was the Catholic church warning that that same afterlife might be spent not just in eternal agony, but in the ceaseless

21. For more detail, see "The Vampire in Christianity" in Masters, *Natural History of The Vampire,* pp. 175–91.

ravaging of one's family and friends. In fact, the place where Christian and Eastern churches met in southeastern Europe remains to this day one of the most fertile grounds for the vampire myth. "Transylvania" became a catchword for more reasons than that Bela Lugosi could roll it off his tongue; Transylvania was the actual meeting place of Eastern and Western religions. It is no wonder, then, that the historical Dracula would live in the Balkans, caught between the Moslem and Christian empires.[22]

If the church fostered the threatening parts of the vampire superstition, it also provided solace for the true believer, for it took upon itself the defense of the local populace. It was a closed system, with the institution that was providing the monsters also providing the protection. The church's culls (excommunicants, suicides, apostates, the unbaptized) became the vampire's flock, while the vampire destroyer was the priest. The local priest, who knew the vampire's habits, had the arsenal of weapons on his side—the Bible, the cross, the rosary—and these weapons were all housed in his armory, the church. Vampire trials, especially during the Inquisition, were ecclesiastical, not secular, affairs, simply because only the church had the proof.

The process of ferreting out and punishing vampires was "done by the book," and in this case the book was one of the most extraordinary tracts ever given the papal seal. Called the *Malleus Maleficarum* or the "Witch Hammer," this *vade mecum* was commissioned to take the guesswork out of the prosecution of witches, werewolves, and vampires.[23] Set in the form of a question-and-answer catechism, examples of sinners are first proffered, and then solutions are provided. The most interesting in terms of the vampire occurs in part 1, as question 15:

> An example was brought to our notice as Inquisitors. A town once was rendered almost destitute by the death of its citizens; and there was a rumour that a certain buried woman was gradually eating the shroud in which she had been buried, and that the plague could not cease until she had eaten the whole shroud and absorbed it into her stomach. A council was held, and the Podesta with the Governor of the city dug up the grave, and found half the shroud absorbed through the mouth and throat into the stomach, and consumed. In horror at this sight, the Podesta drew his sword and cut off her head and threw it out of the grave, and at once the plague ceased. Now the sins of that old woman were, by Divine permission, visited upon the Innocent on account of the dissimulation of what had happened before. For when an Inquisition was

22. The best explanation of the historical Dracula is McNally and Florescu, *In Search of Dracula*, and Ronay, *The Truth About Dracula*.

23. The *Malleus Maleficarum*, first printed in 1486, was co-authored by two Dominicans, Jakob Sprengler and Prior Heinrich Kratmer. This book, probably the single most important work on demonology ever written, was the outgrowth of the *Papal Bull* of 1484 in which Innocent VIII called for a procedure for witchcraft trials. The accounts of demons are especially elaborate, in part because many Protestants who opposed the Inquisition accepted the *Malleus* as an authority. The Rev. Montague Summers called it "a very great and wise book," but surely he was referring to its historical impact and not its ecclesiastical worth.

held it was found that during a long time of her life she had been a Sorceress and Enchantress. [24]

The woman in question is hardly a vampire we would recognize; but this passage does establish evidence of the omophagic dead. It also prescribes the proper disposal: disinterment and decapitation. The church would live to regret this publication, as many of its more egregious statements were to be undermined by later experience, but the work undeniably sanctioned the role of the church as proper disposal agent, and more importantly, it asserted the existence not necessarily of vampires, but of vampiric monsters.

Other Influences

> There must have been a reason that these vampire stories suddenly caught the imagination of Europe. Obviously something happened, and it seems unlikely that it was pure imagination.
>
> —Colin Wilson, *The Occult*

Although the Catholic church was a major influence on the vampire myth, the superstition was given added credibility by three other events: (1) the documented evidence of aberrant persons who acted as if they were vampires; (2) the similarity between various medical symptoms and the supposed results of vampire attack; and (3) the discovery in the seventeenth century of the "Desmodus rotundus" or "vampire bat." These three unrelated phenomena probably did more to foster the belief in vampires than ecclesiastical threats or the appearance of a real vampire could have done, for they filled in all the gaps of the story with an awesome verisimilitude.

Understandably, the two most important "real life" vampires grew out of the tensions in the fifteenth century between the Eastern and Western churches. For as the vise of opposing Christian and Moslem cultures closed on central Europe, the vampire superstition became an instrument of national propaganda. In 1453 Constantinople finally fell to the Ottoman Turks, and all Christendom was fearful that, having dominated Asia Minor, these Moslem heathens would push through the Balkans. Rising to meet this challenge was an obscure Wallachian prince named Vlad Dracul. "Vlad" was his family name; "Dracul," a sobriquet earned by local membership in a Catholic paramilitary organization known as the "Order of Dragons." "Dracul" also means "devil" in Rumanian. His son was called Dracula—the "a" suffix means "son of"—hence the name that centuries later Bram Stoker would run across in the British Museum and use for his own "prince of darkness." [25]

24. Montague Summers, trans., *Malleus Maleficarum* (New York: Benjamin Blom, 1970), p. 78.
25. For more detail see "The Historical Dracula, 1430–1462" in McNally and Florescu, *In Search of*

"Dracula" has since become both a proper name and a common noun—an eponym for all vampires.

In the struggle between Christian and Moselm, Dracula, or Vlad II, was a most circumspect Machiavellian prince. In his early years he fought as often for Moslem as for Catholic, but he was finally blackmailed into casting his lot with the Christians, and central Europe and Western folklore have never been the same. It was first as a battlefield commander that he achieved prominence, for what he always seemed to lack in numerical strength he more than compensated for with tactical genius and ferocity. Leading a small band of counterinsurgents, he stopped the Turkish advance with stunning success. Dracula was a master of guerilla warfare; he would swoop down on some exposed flank of the enemy, rout them, and then, in what became his trademark, he would impale the survivors on stakes. With this grisly but effective technique he was not only to terrify the Turks, but also to gain a historical reputation that would rival Caesar Borgia's or Catherine de Medici's. This tribute to his genius for horror was carried in his other nickname, as it was in the case of, say, Jack the Ripper or Machinegun Kelly, for Vlad II became known as Vlad Tepes, or "Vlad the Impaler."

Like the Marquis de Sade, he carried his chosen form of torture almost into the realm of art. He impaled people from the front, from the back, from the side, from the stomach, feet upward, in the heart, in the navel, in the groin; he even impaled the whole population of a town (women and children included) in concentric circles leading up a hill. At the top, so that they could survey their loyal followers from their accustomed position, were the town officials—also impaled. On 2 April 1459, in his *coup de maître*, he was reputed to have impaled some twenty thousand Turks near Brasov, Rumania.[26]

As might be expected, a mythology of apocryphal tales spun out around him, thanks largely to a then-recent invention, the printing press. In fact, one of the first news stories to be carried by the nascent Western press was of the Dracula tortures. It was only to be expected that these exploits would be coupled in the European imagination with those of the legendary vampire. The fact that Vlad Tepes was trying to protect his principality from encroachment from both East and West was overlooked, and he became the personification of vampire horror. There is no proof at all that he was a blood drinker, but even before Bram Stoker recreated him as the fictional vampire, "Dracula" was commonly believed to be such by middle Europeans.[27]

Vlad Tepes had a relative, however, who really was a blood fiend. She was Eliza-

---

Dracula, pp. 31–64, and "Identifying the Historical Dracula" in Ronay, *The Truth about Dracula*, pp. 58–83.

26. Dracula's exploits, especially the impaling, are discussed in McNally and Florescu, *In Search of Dracula*, pp. 64–79, and Ronay, *The Truth about Dracula*, pp. 76–83.

27. "Dracula Horror Stories of the Fifteenth Century" in McNally and Florescu, *In Search of Dracula*, pp. 101–21, and "Renaissance Europe's Fascination with the Wallachian Warlord" in Ronay, *The Truth about Dracula*, pp. 68–76.

beth Bathory, a monied and titled Hungarian aristocrat who married at fifteen an even more monied and titled aristocrat.[28] Her husband spent much of his time out at battle, while Elizabeth spent her time at home with a demented manservant, Thorko, and a crazed old nurse, Ilona Joo. After her husband died in 1600 this threesome developed schemes of terror that would have made Rasputin blush. According to the lore, her blood lust started when a maid who was combing Elizabeth's hair hit a snarl and tried to yank it loose. Her attempts only infuriated her mistress, and Elizabeth swung around and hit the girl so hard that blood spurted from her nose. As the blood splashed onto Elizabeth's hand, she noticed her fingers felt somehow lighter and more flexible. If the hand could feel revitalized at the anointment of this fluid, why not other parts of her body? And indeed she was soon smearing parts of her body with blood. Since supplies were limited, her servants spent the next ten years canvassing the local population for young virgins who wanted what they thought would be easy work in the Bathory castle. From this stock Thorko and Ilona Joo set up a truly horrible blood bank, from which Elizabeth drew her occasional bath. Some three hundred girls were used in this fashion as donors until 20 December 1610, when officials from the Hungarian king finally came to investigate. They found one dead girl on the floor of the main hall, another writhing in pain, and yet another being forcibly bled. The pierced bodies of many others were found piled in the cellar. Ilona Joo was beheaded, while Thorko was tortured and killed, but Elizabeth, because she was of aristocratic lineage, was simply walled up in the castle to die some four years later. Like Vlad Tepes, Elizabeth Bathory became grist for the printing mills. Her story, better documented but no less horrible than his, also encouraged the blood-drinking embellishment and still to this day she is the villainess of countless vampire movies (*Countess Dracula, Daughters of Darkness, The Bloody Countess*, and others).

The vampire superstition found further reinforcements on other fronts. For if Vlad Tepes and Elizabeth Bathory lived like vampires, there were hundreds of people who died like vampires' victims. The symptoms of such an attack were well known to the folk: first the enervation and the slow wasting away, then the marked loss of blood without any visible bodily cuts or bruises, and finally a suspicious death. Once "dead," a vampire's victim could be recognized by his twisted posture in the coffin, for before he was revived to become a vampire he would writhe in pain as the devil entered his body. Although there was no indisputable evidence of actual practicing blood-drinkers in life, there did seem to be adequate proof that certain people had experienced such demonic possession in the grave.

What happened to cause people to believe in such a life after burial was this: when a vampire was rumored to be in the neighborhood, the first step after defensive maneuvers (rubbing garlic around the threshold, wearing a crucifix, going to church) was to hunt out the culprit during the day. Occasionally the suspected body

28. The Elizabeth Bathory story is recounted in McNally and Florescu, *In Search of Dracula*, pp. 148–55, and Ronay, *The Truth about Dracula*, pp. 93–101.

would be exhumed and the folk would find the burial shroud ripped, as well as other seemingly indisputable evidence of postmortem activity. Premature burial was much commoner than we imagine, primarily because death was so difficult to confirm. People were buried in comas, in catatonic fits, and in shock, especially during plague years when the hasty disposal of the body was of primary importance. Hence death would finally be caused by suffocation in the casket and the visible evidence of this last gasp of life-strength would be seen by the vampire hunters as they opened the casket. For them the contorted body was proof enough of a life beyond death; the corpse would be burned and staked.

There were other explanations for the strange positioning of an encoffined corpse. The body might be lying awkwardly because some grave robber had moved it to get whatever booty had been interred. Or worse still, there might be no body at all. With the rise of medical science, bodysnatching became a lucrative business, and the occasional lack of a body only encouraged the vampire hunters to conclude that perhaps the devil had absconded with it or that the body had become "possessed" and had moved elsewhere of its own accord.

None of the strange and horrible phenomena associated with the buried dead could compare with the strange and horrible ways in which people used to die. In the twentieth century death can still come slowly and painfully—wasting the victim away month by month. But we have elaborate explanations to protect us from the once "logical" conclusion that the body of our loved one is being consumed from the inside by evil spirits. Two centuries ago many diseases were misdiagnosed as being the result of vampire activity: pernicious anemia, a blood disorder where the victim shrivels up, needing new red blood cells to survive; porphyria, in which the photophobic patient's teeth and hair take on a fluorescent glow; tuberculosis, where the early symptoms are weight loss and the later coughing of blood; cholera, in which whole populations are slowly decimated; and, of course, the one still with us today, cancer.[29] The most horrendous of all human decimations was the plague. From the twelfth to the seventeenth century millions of people in great human waves were consumed by a silent and invisible death. Whole cities of people would be coughing blood one week, gasping on the streets the next, and dying during the third or fourth. In the first great plague of 1347–50, twenty-five million Europeans died, and although in the scourges to follow the total numbers never reached such magnitude, specific locations suffered more. As late as 1665–66 a plague swept through London, killing almost seventy thousand, and the seventeenth-century Englishman was as baffled about how it had occurred as his fourteenth-century counterpart had been. The cause was simply unknown then, and although we now know that the plague was carried to humans from rats via fleas, it was certainly more "logical" to use the time-tested explanation that had satisfied previous generations: the city was a victim of a vampire attack. For only the vampire, with his geometric population burst, could explain deaths of this magnitude.

29. The best medical explanations of vampirism are found in Garden, *Vampires*, pp. 109–23.

Like all enduring myths, the vampire legend seems marked by extraordinary propitiousness. By the eighteenth century it had received impetus from such unlikely quarters as Christianity, events in Hungary and the Balkans, premature burial, undiagnosed diseases, and the plague. Occasionally a myth seems so well fitted to its culture that it appears not just to follow events but also to predict them. The vampire myth in the West has always had animalistic overtones; in fact, in certain languages like Slavic and Greek, the word "vampire" also meant "wolf," and lycanthropy, or the human-wolf transformation, is often part of the vampire myth.[30] More startling, however, was the discovery and classification of a South American blood-sucking bat, the "Desmodus rotundus."

During the Spanish conquest of Mexico the conquistadores found a bat peculiar to Central and South America that seemed to drink blood. Aware of their own folklore, the Spanish called them "vampire bats" and, like the wolf, there were enough correspondences between the real and the mythic to allow them to mix. Vampire bats are small, not only in size (a wing span of less than fourteen inches), but also in population. They are indigenous to an area extending south from Mexico to Argentina. None has ever been located in continental Europe, and hence their extremely late introduction into vampire folklore. But what a refinement of myth, for the squealing vampire bats behave almost as if they have heard the story. They attack at night, their "bite" is actually the removal of a small plug of skin, and their subsequent "drinking" consists not of sucking but rather of lapping from the bleeding cut. Especially macabre is that they feed in groups, returning again and again until the donor is dry. Although they rarely attack man, preferring more docile hosts like cattle or horses, they do sometimes attack sleeping humans. Since they can bite the skin only in accessible areas, they usually settle on the forearm, the neck, or the foot—especially the toes (this last bodily extremity has been graciously omitted from the myth). Still, the bat has provided the most vivid and arresting visual image of the vampire in the last two centuries, and the Hollywood creature with the burning red eyes, pallid face, pointed ears and long black wing-like cape and cowl is the result of the amalgamation of this new image with the traditional vampire.[31]

William Blake was one of the first artists to recognize the visual possibilities of

30. The wolf was the preferred animal form for the vampire spirit when not in its human husk. Once again, this has a basis in reality; in fact, the etymology of the English word "berserk" means imagining oneself to be a wolf. Berserk people were thought to behave like wolves, howling, snarling, and gnashing. The overlap between the human wolf or werewolf and the vampire is much more than a linguistic one. In both cases the human victim appears normal by day but then metamorphoses at nightfall. This process, when describing the human-wolf transformation, is called "lycanthropy" and has through time been mixed with the vampire story. For instance, the human werewolf sprouts hair at nightfall and then loses it by daybreak; the vampire carries a vestige of this transformation by having hair on the palms. Also, when a werewolf is killed, he occasionally becomes a vampire, hence the preferred means of werewolf disposal is burning and/or staking. See Masters, *Natural History of the Vampire*, pp. 29–31.

31. For more on the vampire bat, see Leonard Wolf, *The Annotated Dracula* (New York: Clarkson N. Potter, 1975), p. 141, n. 7, and Volta, *The Vampire*, p. 113. It is noteworthy that one of the important facts Charles Darwin learned during his journeys about Central and South America was that the vampire bat did *not* have the face of a man.

the bat image as a means to display the power of destructive energy. In two engravings that accompany *Jerusalem* he used the vampire bat to symbolize the Spectre. The Spectre in Blake's mythology represented the annihilating, divisive, constricting energies in man's psyche that, when externalized, become doubt, compulsion, rage, insanity, and tyranny. What better image of cannibalistic force than the Spectre-bat. In plate 6 the vampire bat's page-wide wings separate Los, the prophetic artist, from higher realms.[32] And in plate 33 the Spectre-bat not only separates Jerusalem from Albion above, but also seems ready to devour her. In the upper picture of the expiring Albion in the arms of Los/Jesus, Blake seems almost to have engraved a vampiric pose—Los at the neck of Albion drawing off his strength.[33]

The image of the demon attacking the innocent was elsewhere present in the iconography of English art, seen for instance in such central paintings as Henry Fuseli's "The Nightmare." Fuseli's painting is intriguing, not only for its arresting imagery, but also for its profound influence on Neoclassic art. It is often cited as a "precocious example of nineteenth-century Romanticism," and with good reason; it returned the externalizing of psychological states to its proper place as just matter for artistic examination.[34] "The Nightmare" did not achieve this distinction without some critical rancor, however; for, like most artistic turns in taste, it was initially considered dreadful. When it was exhibited in 1782 at the Royal Academy in London, Horace Walpole summed up popular opinion in the single word "shocking."[35] And he was right; it was and is still shocking. It makes no immediate sense (who is that crouching demon? why the bug-eyed horse? the assaulted lady?), yet it makes

32. David V. Erdman in his notes to *The Illuminated Blake* (New York: Doubleday, 1974) comments: "The Spectre interposes his canopy of bat wings and distracts Los with arguments of despair. . . . The Spectre ought to stop his howling and get to work pumping the bellows" (p. 285).

33. James Brogan, "Vampire Bats and Blake's Spectre," *Blake Newsletter* 37 (Summer 1976): 32–33, believes that Blake found the image of this winged cannibal while helping Joseph Johnson with the engravings to John Stedman's *Narrative of a five year's expedition against the Revolted Negroes of Surinam*, for Stedman not only mentions the vampire bat but refers to it as "Spectre." In his *Narrative*, as quoted by Brogan, pp. 32–33, Stedman relates how he has been bitten by

the *vampire* or *spectre* of Guiana, which is also called the *flying-dog* of New Spain. . . . This is no other than a bat of monstrous size, that sucks blood from men and cattle when they are fast asleep, even sometimes till they die; and as the manner in which they proceed is truly wonderful, I shall endeavour to give a distinct account of it. —Knowing by instinct that the person they intend to attack is in a sound slumber, they generally light near the feet, where, while the creature continues fanning with his enormous wings, which keeps one cool, he bites a piece out of the tip of the great toe, so very small indeed that the head of a pin could scarcely be received into the wound, which is consequently not painful; yet through this orifice he continues to suck that blood, until he is obliged to disgorge. He then begins again, and thus continues sucking and disgorging till he is scarcely able to fly, and the sufferer has often been known to sleep from time into eternity. . . . Having applied tobacco-ashes as the best remedy, and washed the gore from myself and from my hammock, I observed several small heaps of congealed blood all round the place when I had lain, upon the ground: upon examining which, the surgeon judged that I had lost at least twelve or fourteen ounces during the night. . . .

34. *Exhibition Catalogue for the Romantic Era* (Indianapolis, Ind.: Herron Museum of Art, 1965), no. 22.

35. As quoted in Algernon Graves, *The Royal Academy of Arts . . . A Complete Dictionary* (London: Henry Graves & Co., 1905), 3:184.

His Spectre driv'n by the Starry Wheels of Albions sons. black and
Opake divided from his back; he labours and he mourns.'

For as his Emanation divided, his Spectre also divided
In terror of those starry wheels: and the Spectre stood over Los
Howling in pain: a blackning Shadow. blackning dark & opake
Cursing the terrible Los: bitterly cursing him for his friendship
To Albion. suggesting murderous thoughts against Albion.

Los rag'd and stamp'd the earth in his might & terrible wrath!
He stood and stamp'd the earth: then he threw down his hammer in rage &
In fury: then he sat down and wept. terrified! Then arose
And chaunted his song. labouring with the tongs and hammer:
But still the Spectre divided, and still his pain increas'd!

In pain the Spectre divided: in pain of hunger and thirst:
To devour Los's Human Perfection, but when he saw that Los

1. William Blake, *Jerusalem*, plate 6, copy "D" (The Houghton Library, Harvard University).

And One stood forth from the Divine Family & said

I feel my Spectre rising upon me! Albion, arouze thyself!
Why dost thou thunder with frozen Spectrous wrath against us?
The Spectre is, in Giant Man; insane, and most deformd
Thou wilt certainly provoke my Spectre against thine in fury:
He has a Sepulcher hewn out at a Rock ready for thee:
And a Death of Eight thousand years forgd by thyself, upon
The point of his Spear! if thou persistest to forbid with Laws
Our Emanations, and to attack our secret supreme delights

So Los spoke: But when he saw blue death in Albions feet
Again he joind the Divine Body, following merciful;
While Albion fled more indignant; revengeful covering

His

2. William Blake, *Jerusalem*, plate 33, copy "D" (The Houghton Library, Harvard University).

3. Henry Fuseli, *The Nightmare*, 1781 (The Detroit Institute of Arts, gift of Mr. and Mrs. Bert L. Smokler and Mr. and Mrs. Lawrence A. Fleishman).

4. G. Kininger, *The Dream of Eleanor*, c. 1795 (Albertina Museum, Vienna).

Toni Johannot.   Lith. de V. Ratier

JOHANNOT   ANDREW

7. *Smarra*, 1845, after Tony Johannot (Bibliothèque Nationale, Paris).

5. Tony Johannot, *Rêve*, c. 1830 (Bibliothèque Nationale, Paris).

6. *Cauchemar*, 1830, after Tony Johannot (Francis Haskell Collection, Oxford).

8. Francisco Goya, *The Sleep of Reason Produces Monsters*, 1796–98, plate 43 (Museum of Fine Arts, Boston).

instantaneous psychological sense. It is about something we have all felt. It is the nightmare of suffocation, the oppressive feelings of nocturnal violation, the fear of the demonic in the one place we cannot control—our subconscious world of sleep. (Little wonder then that Freud hung a print of "The Nightmare" in his Vienna apartment.)

I would not contend that the demon here is in any way an actual vampire, although it is tempting to speculate: the woman seems sexually assaulted, the fiend is certainly an incubus type, and the mirror on the dressing table, which should hold a reflection of this entire scene, is surprisingly blank. Still what is more striking is not the demon but the context. For it is into just this setting that the Romantic vampire will be fit. It comes as no surprise then that as the vampire gains mythic currency around the turn of the century, he gradually displaces Fuseli's amorphous demon from this very scene. We see this transformation first in Georg Kininger's "The Dream of Eleanor" (1795), where the demon (on the left) is now equipped with extended incisors and batlike wings.

The vampire's displacement of Fuseli's vague incubus can be seen even more clearly by the 1830s. For by this time the vampire had achieved considerable popularity, thanks in large part to the popular misconception that a tale called "The Vampyre" (1819) had been written by Lord Byron. The French book illustrator, Tony Johannot, thrice adopted Fuseli's composition, each time leaving the maiden in a position of sexual violation but varying the violator. We see this first in a print entitled "Rêve," then more clearly in an illustration called "Cauchemar" for a novel by "Michel Raymond," and finally in 1845 as the frontispiece for an edition of Charles Nodier's *Smarra ou les démons de la nuit,* which, incidentally, details a vampiric nightmare based on Fuseli's painting. The witches and goblins of "Rêve" become the cadaverous vampire of "Cauchemar," which is finally stylized into the griffinlike fiend of *Smarra.*[36] With pictorial concision we have here the sharpening of the vampire image—all occurring within the first fifty years of the nineteenth century.

A decade after Fuseli's "Nightmare" Goya also painted a series of vampiritic figures who were devouring with surrealistic hideousness the unfortunate dreamers who had created them. The most famous of these *Los Caprichos* is "The Sleep of Reason Produces Monsters" (plate 43), which has a sky full of batlike creatures. These blood-sucking bats also populate the skies of other plates as well. In "There Is Plenty to Suck" (plate 45) the bats hover behind three paedophagic elders who are preparing to dine on a basketful of babies; as Goya's gloss explains: "Those who reach eighty suck little children; those under eighteen suck grown-ups. It seems that man is born and lives to have the substance sucked out of him."[37] As arresting as the visual images of the vampire by Blake, Fuseli, and Goya may be, however, their literary counterparts are equally intriguing and far more complex.

36. I am indebted to Nicolas Powell for pointing out this imagistic progression; *Fuseli: "The Nightmare"* (New York: The Viking Press, 1973), pp. 91–93.

37. See also plates 8, 46, 64, and 72 of Goya's *Los Caprichos* for possible repetition of the vampire motif.

The Vampire in Pre-Romantic English Literature

*Until we come to Polidori's novel [The Vampyre, 1819] nowhere, so far
as I am aware, do we meet with the Vampire in the realm of Gothic
fancy. So vast, however, is this fascinating library and so difficult to
procure are these novels of a century and a quarter ago that I hesitate
sweepingly to assert that this theme was entirely unexploited. There
may be some romance which I have not had the good fortune to find
where a hideous vampire swoops down upon his victims, but if such be
the case I am at least prepared to say that the Vampire was not generally
known to Gothic lore, and had his presence made itself felt in the
sombre chapters of one votary of this school I think he would have reappeared on many occasions, for the writers were as accustomed to convey from one another with an easy assurance, as they were wont deftly
to plunder the foreign mines.*

—Montague Summers, *The Vampire:
His Kith and Kin*

The vampire, or for that matter any bloodsucking monster, never had the success
in Northern Europe that he had in the Mediterranean and Balkan countries. While
other monsters fared well in English and Germanic literature, the blood-drinkers
were neglected, only occasionally being referred to in such early ballads as "Margaret's Ghost," "Sweet William's Ghost," "Fair Margaret and Sweet William's
Grave," and then only in the most elliptical terms.[38] Oddly enough, however, the
motif of a superhuman demon who steals about at night sucking the blood of the
living may play an important role in the first of all English masterpieces, Beowulf.
For here the monster Grendel, with its "horrible fierce eyes" and blood lust, seems
to derive in part from some folk belief that perhaps sprouted from the vampire story.
But even Grendel has undergone the syncretic layering with Christian mythology
that was so often the case with the vampire superstition. For Grendel's mother, we
are told, is a descendant of the race of Cain, and thus is presumably still possessed
by the devil. Like the vampire, this monster works only at night, does not like the
grisly life it leads, and can only be destroyed by decapitation. It may even be that
when the Beowulf poet refers to Grendel's mother as a "she-wolf," he is depending
on his audience's understanding of lycanthropy; but the term may be nothing more
than an epithet of derision, for wolves were uncommon in England, although
populous in the Scandinavian countries where the *Beowulf* saga was first told.

The best argument tying Grendel into the vampire tradition has recently been

38. A survey of pre-Romantic vampire ballads is in Margaret L. Carter, *Shadow of a Shade: A Survey
of Vampirism in Literature*, pp. 6–13.

made by Nicolas Kiessling in "Grendel: A New Aspect" in *Modern Philology*.[39] Kiessling contends that when the monster is referred to as a "mære mearcstapa" (l. 103 of the Klaeber edition) and again as "se mæra" (l. 762), "mæra" does not mean "notorious" or "infamous" but rather "night monster." This confusion may have been caused by a scribe's mistaking "mære" (monster) for "m$\bar{æ}$re" (notorious), a plausible enough mistake since early copyists were not at all consistent with diacritical marks. From this mistaking of seeming homographs and from other semantic and linguistic evidence, Kiessling concludes:

> The author of the *Beowulf* story, in giving Grendel the ancestry of Cain, and also in giving him "Eotenas ond ylfe ond orcneas/Swylce gigantas . . . " (112–13) as siblings or close relatives, might very well have been familiar with the *incubus* and *lamia* of Judeo-Christian tradition, for, by A.D. 500–600, the *lamiae* were fairly well known in Germanic countries. . . . These witches could consume the insides of men and so kill them, or they could act as vampires (Grendel himself sucked out the blood of Hondscioh). Whether these continental witches engaged in illicit love affairs is not known, but from the Leiden gloss entry to *lamia* we might assume as much.[40]

If this is so, it certainly reinforces the diabolical nature of Grendel, for indeed "mære" would have been a most appropriate name for this night ravager.

From the eighth to the twelfth centuries, there was little interest in describing the vampire in any imaginary literature. In the twelfth century Walter Map, a clerk to Henry II and later archbishop of Oxford, collected superstitions and gossip for his *De nugis curialium distinctiones quinque*. One story he recalls tells of a nobleman whose children have been bled by a demon nurse. The nurse's identity is discovered by a passing stranger, who catches her at midnight attempting to bleed the child. The mysterious stranger "pressed a key to a nearby church against her face, branding her with its holy impression." Later it is learned that she has disguised herself as the real nurse in order to conduct her nefarious deeds undetected.[41] These motifs could have come from any number of folk stories and are hardly images of vampirism. Also in the twelfth century William of Newbury chronicled the history of the Sanguisugae, or human bloodsuckers, in his *Historia Rerum Anglicarum*. William tells of the "extraordinary" tale of a man who died and was thought by all to be safely interred. But he soon returned at night to molest first his wife, then his family, then his animals, then his comrades, each time becoming more audacious and bold, until finally he was raiding during the daylight. The townsfolk went to the church for aid. The learned priests suggested burning, but the archdeacon demurred, knowing a simpler way. The "dead" body was exhumed, and indeed, true to form, it was plump with blood and "uncorrupt." The archdeacon laid the "Charter of Episcopal Absolution" on the body, resealed

39. Nicolas K. Kiessling, "Grendel: A New Aspect," *Modern Philology* 65 (Feb. 1968): 191–201.
40. Ibid., p. 196.
41. A translation of Map's tale is included in Raymond McNally, *A Clutch of Vampires*, pp. 35–38.

the tomb, and the dead man was finally at peace.[42] Certainly there is much more vampire material here but, alas, it is never really exploited.

Why the vampire had such a long period of stony sleep from the twelfth to the eighteenth century is a perplexing question, made more baffling because the vampire's mythic cousins, the incubus and succubus, were certainly healthy. The incubus does almost everything the vampire does except take on bodily form, sleep in coffins, and suck blood. He is a dreamlike night molester who sexually assaults and enervates young women, and although he is noncorporeal, he can be destroyed by Christian ritual. He has, in short, much the same mythic structure and derivation as the vampire.[43] Furthermore, the incubus/succubus was as common in Renaissance literature as the vampire/lamia was to become in the Romantic: Marlowe's Faustus is bewitched by the lamiaesque succubus, Helen of Troy: "Her lips suck forth my soul: see where it flies" (V, i, 101); in *The Witch* Middleton cast Heccat and Firestone from the incubus/succubus mold; and Shakespeare explained Caliban's foulness as a result of his parentage—Sycorax and an incubus (*The Tempest*, I, ii, 321). But here in Elizabethan drama where one would expect every other demon to be a bloodsucking vampire, there is nothing.

It is no surprise, however, that the vampire should come slouching into the literature of the late eighteenth century, for the English common reader had come out of the counting houses of pedantic literature to wander the graveyard of sentimental stories. Although it may at first seem paradoxical that the Age of Enlightenment and Reason should end in the Age of Darkness and Unreason, it is no stranger than the fact that Tennyson should follow Shelley or that Wordsworth at fifty should try to rewrite the poems of Wordsworth at twenty-five. The other side of Pope, Dr. Johnson, and Cowper *should be* Warton, Collins, and Gray, for what one generation considered spurious the next was all too eager to make serious; the "silly" became the sophisticated.[44] In fact, when Thomas Pecket Prest set the action of *Varney the Vampyre* (1847) in the reign of Queen Anne, he wonderfully underscored the ironic improbability of his story. In 1736 George I deemed all witchcraft foolish and imaginary, so by 1780 ghosts and goblins were cavorting in poetry and the novel. In fact, Horace Walpole even claimed to Lady Ossory that George II, "though not apt to believe more than his neighbours, had no doubt of the existence of vampires and their banquets on the dead."[45] Much of the macabre eighteenth-century literature is absolutely dreadful in both the modern and eighteenth-century sense; it is Burkean "sublimity" run amok. But in retrospect it did the English

42. A translation of William of Newburg's account is included in McNally, *A Clutch of Vampires*, pp. 40–41, along with a second tale about the "Berwick Vampire," which also describes how a human bloodsucker is destroyed, pp. 41–42.

43. For more on the link between the vampire and the incubus/succubus, see Nicolas K. Kiessling, "Demonic Dread: The Incubus Figure in British Literature," in *The Gothic Imagination*, ed. G. R. Thompson (Pullman: Washington State University Press, 1974), pp. 22–41.

44. This thesis is promulgated in Patricia Meyer Spacks, *The Insistence of Horror: Aspects of the Supernatural in Eighteenth Century Poetry* (Cambridge, Mass.: Harvard University Press, 1962).

45. "Letter to Lady Ossory, 16 Jan. 1786, *The Yale Edition of Horace Walpole's "Correspondence*," ed. W. S. Lewis (New Haven, Conn.: Yale University Press), 33:508.

Romantics a favor, for it made folk superstitions a legitimate subject of literature; it gave them a context. Within fifty years English "sobriety" with all its concern for monkish darkness, mesmerism, satanism, and deviancy of all sorts, had not only revived the vampire but made him an artistic figure of some complexity.

The immediate predecessors of the English literary vampire were German. In the early eighteenth century as a result of the "vampire epidemics" in the Balkans, the vampire had become a serious subject of study on the Continent. Treatise after treatise was written, not necessarily affirming the vampire's existence (that was already generally accepted), but rather explaining the vampire as a personification of demonic energies on earth.[46] The most important of these works, both because it was based on actual occurrences and because it was written by a Benedictine abbot, was Dom Augustin Calmet's *Traité sur les Apparitions des Esprits, et sur les Vampires . . .* (Paris, 1746). Calmet was possibly the greatest Catholic Biblical scholar in the eighteenth century (certainly the greatest in France) and his work, really an anthology of folk horror stories, was quickly translated into English. Although Calmet's reputation suffered as a result of this—at least according to Voltaire—it did kindle considerable scholarly interest which, in turn, was soon exploited by the German poets, who recognized the artistic potential of this "pariah among demons." First Ossenfelder wrote "The Vampire" (1748), Bürger wrote "Lenore" (1773), then Goethe wrote "The Bride of Corinth" (1797), and for the next century the Western world would know no respite from this monster. Since these Germans gave the vampire his first literary form, it may be useful to sketch him in his Teutonic setting, for the English did not really change him until midcentury.

Of all the German efforts, "Lenore" was certainly the most influential for the English poets. Three years after its German publication in the *Göttinger Musenalmanach*, "Lenore" had been translated almost into tatters. All the English Romantics were familiar with it, thanks first to William Taylor's translation, and then to Sir Walter Scott's adaptation.[47] In fact, in the closing decade of the eighteenth century, translations and parodies were liberally sprinkled through both German and English periodicals. Part of the popularity of "Lenore" was its stark simplicity, which made it not only wonderfully scary but eminently translatable. Here is the story: a young bride-to-be, Lenore, has waited for her lover, Wilhelm, to return from the Crusades. When the other warriors return without him, a Job-like Lenore

46. Gabriel Ronay, *The Truth about Dracula*, p. 19, has catalogued vampire studies for 1728–34:

Karl Ferdinard Schertz's *Magia Posthuma*, printed in Olmutz in 1706, was the forerunner of a host of eighteenth-century studies of vampirism in Central Europe. It was followed by Michael Ranftius's *De masticatione mortuorum in tumulis liber*, Leipzig, 1728; John Christopher Rohlius's *Dissertatio de hominibus post mortem sanguisugis, uolgo dictis Uampyrea*, Leipzig, 1732; Johann Christian Stock's 1732 Jena edition of *Dissertatio de cadaueribus sanguisugis*; and two more German-language treatises published in Leipzig in 1732. In 1733 Johannes Heinrich Zopfius had his *Dissertatio de Uampyris Serviensibus* printed in Duisburg. Ranftius also published an enlarged version of his work in Leipzig in 1734, in German, under the title *Tractatus von dem Kauen und Schmatzen der Todten in Grabern, worin die wahre Beschaffenheit der Hungarischen Vampyrs oder Blutsauger gezeiget.*

47. For more on the importance of "Lenore," see Summers, *The Vampire*, pp. 275–77.

rants against God's unfairness. Late one night, after she has been especially bitter, Wilhelm appears on a prancing black steed outside her window. Come away, he says; it is time for us to be married. Lenore, happy at last, rushes to join him, and they thunder off into the night.

> See here! See here! the moon shines clear
>   We and the dead ride fast;
> I promise thee to bridal bed
>   To bring ere night hath past . . .
> Six boards and two short planks our bed,
>   Far, far still, cool, and small . . .
> Dost fear, sweet love? the moon shines clear,
>   The dead they ride in full career.

The reader realizes now what Lenore is soon to discover: Wilhelm is a revenant come back from the dead to gather up his bride. At the cemetery his grave mysteriously opens to receive the pair as ghosts and goblins chant a devil's epithalamion. For now on her wedding night she is finally to sleep with her love, the demon death. The sparse story, clearly derived from folklore, is embedded in ballad form, which gives it an especially eerie surface effect while underneath it plumbs the depths of terror. The incremental repetition of the refrain line adds to this terror as it first reads: "We and the dead ride fast," then changes to "Hurrah; the dead ride fast," and finally becomes, as Lenore is initiated into the cold fraternity of the dead, "for the dead ride fast."

"Lenore" is a compelling poem in terms of suspense and reversal, but characterization is negligible, for Wilhelm is hardly a Count Dracula. He hungers for love, not blood. The English ballad has already developed this theme of the dead love returning; in fact the art ballad was already imitating it. As early as the 1720s William Hamilton in "The Braes of Yarrow" told of a star-crossed lover, killed by the family of his bride-to-be, who returned from the dead:

> Ah me! what ghastly Spectre's son
> Comes, in his pale Shroud, bleeding after?
> Pale as he is, here lay him, lay him down,
> O lay his cold Head on my Pillow . . .
> Pale tho' thou art, yet best, yet best belov'd,
> O could my Warmth to Life restore thee;
> Yet lie all Night between my Breasts,
> No Youth lay ever there before thee.

Alas, for literary vampire hunters, he has come only to sleep with her, not to drink her blood. A more famous bit of macabre sublimity was David Mallet's "William and Margaret." Here it is the female who returns from the dead to send her lover to the grave, but again the motivation is unconsummated love, not blood lust. This motif of lover returning from the dead is repeated through the century in such poems as John Aikin's "Arthur and Matilda," where the dead bride-to-be coaxes her unwary lover to share her charms, which, by the way, include the grave. The variations on the William and Margaret theme multiply in number but not in quality; they remain singularly true to the traditional version. The names could be changed, the locale could vary, but the paradigm of dead lover returning to gather in the living counterpart continues. Then near the end of the century, perhaps under the influence of German Gothic and nascent English Satanism, the tenor changes. The dead lover turns sadistic. He now wants more than a consummation of love in death; he wants life, the life of his lover. And he will have this life at the expense of love.

It is Robert Southey more than anyone else who starts linking the vampire with the revenant lover of the folk ballad. In 1798 he wrote of a lamiaesque witch, the "Old Woman of Berkeley," who herself relates:

> I have 'nointed myself with infant's fat,
> The fiends have been my slaves,
> From sleeping babes I have suck'd the breath,
> And breaking by charms the sleep of death,
> I have call'd the dead from their graves.
> And the Devil will fetch me now in fire,
> My witchcrafts to atone;
> And I who have troubled the dead man's grave
> Shall never have rest in my own.

A year earlier Southey had written *Thalaba the Destroyer*, a high Gothic art ballad that simply could not stop until all superstitions had been exploited, until all ghouls were accounted for. Midway through this fustian prose romance the protagonist, Thalaba, must undergo a number of horrible experiences, not the least of which is the realization that his true love is demonically possessed. Accompanied by his sage father-in-law-to-be (shades of the young male/older advisor combination that will later become important) he descends into the vault of his beloved Oneiza, who died on their wedding day. They weave through darkness until they finally reach the innermost chamber, and there

> In silence on Oneiza's grave
> Her father and her husband sate.
> The Cryer from the minaret
> Proclaim'd the midnight hour.
>
> 'Now, now!' cried Thalaba;
> And o'er the chamber of the tomb
> There spread a lurid gleam.
>
> Like the reflection of a sulphur fire;
> and in that hideous light

Oneiza stood before them. It was She . . .
Her very lineaments . . . and such as death
Had changed them, livid cheeks and lips of blue;

But in her eye there dwelt
Brightness more terrible
Than all the loathsomeness of death.
'Still art thou living, wretch?'

In hollow tones she cried to Thalaba;
'And must I nightly leave my grave
To tell thee, still in vain,
God hath abandoned thee?'
'This is not she!' the Old Man exclaim'd;
'A Fiend; a manifest Fiend!'
And to the youth he held his lance;
'Strike and deliver thyself!'
'Strike HER!' cried Thalaba,
And palsied of all power,
Gazed fixedly upon the dreadful form.

'Yea, strike her!' cried a voice, whose tones
Flow'd with such a sudden healing through his soul,
As when the desert shower
From death deliver'd him;
But obedient to that well-known voice,
His eye was seeking it,
When Moath, firm of heart,
Perform'd the bidding: through the vampire corpse
He thrust his lance; it fell,
And howling with the wound,
Its fiendish tenant fled.
A sapphire light fell on them,
And garmented with glory, in their sight
Oneiza's spirit stood.   (book 8, stanzas 8–11)

Not only is this a most spirited entrance of the vampire into English literature, but Southey also went to considerable pains to authenticate it. For he wrote an elaborate explanation assuring his readers of the reliability of his description. His copious gloss covers vampire practices in Hungary, Greece, and Turkey, and is the most encyclopedic prose description before John Stagg's "Argument" preceding his poem "The Vampire" and John Polidori's 1820 "Introduction" to *The Vampyre*.[48]

48. Southey's gloss, which gives a description and short history of the vampire, can be found in *Poetical Works* (London: Longman, Orme, Brown, Green and Longmans, 1838), 4:297–305.

The vampire resurfaces almost two decades later in John Stagg's ballad "The Vampire." This rather pedestrian poem, like Southey's *Thalaba*, is interesting more for its prose gloss than for its poetic content. The "Argument" is bloated with wondrous scholarship (the vampire "phelbotomises" the victim by "suckosity") and pedantic posturing ("I do not imagine that a thousandth part of the world are acquainted with the reason why the segundine, immediately after the nativity of the foetus, is so carefully deflagrated by the obstetric and others who preside at the accouchement"), but the text itself is only occasionally lively. A virtuous wife complains of her husband's lethargy, until finally the husband (Herman) confesses that a recently deceased male friend (Sigismund) has been returning from the grave to "suck from my veins the streaming life,/ And drain the fountain of my heart." The faithful wife is persuaded to guard the husband while he sleeps and flash a light in the face of Sigismund should he appear. Lo and behold, the horrible specter of his once-best friend appears. The wife flashes the light which makes the demon both visible and terrified:

> Indignant rolled his ireful eyes,
>> That gleam'd with wild horrific stare;
> And fixed a moment with surprise
>> Beheld a ghost with the enlightening glare.
> His jaws cadaverous were besmear'd
>> With clotted carnage o'er and o'er,
> And all his horrid whole appear'd
>> Distant, and fill'd with human gore!
> With hideous scowl the spectre fled;
>> She shriek'd aloud;—then swoon'd away!
> The helpless Herman in his bed,
>> All pale, a lifeless body lay.

The husband is dead, and the good wife, almost as if she has read Stagg's "Argument," knows what to do. The coffin of the "friend" is unearthed,

> The choir then burst the funeral dome
>> Where Sigismund was lately laid,
> And found him, tho' within the tomb,
>> Still warm as life, and undecay'd.
> With blood his visage was distain'd,
>> Ensanguin'd were his frightful eyes,
> Each sign of former life remain'd,
>> Save that all motionless he lies.[49]

Both bodies are staked, and we are left with the comforting assurance that if the dead are properly disposed of, we need fear no harm.

49. John Stagg, *The Minstrel of the North, or Cambrian Legends* (Manchester, Eng.: Mark Wardle, 1816), pp. 228–35.

For insight into the possibilities of vampire myth one must go from Southey and Stagg to the works of the major Romantics. For these poets were not only the first to have the myth and the corresponding literary forms; they were the first to have suitable subject matter. Their overriding concern was psychological: how do people interact or how is it that lovers, or artists, or parents, or the insane, or just ordinary people trade energy with those they contact? The Romantics really did not care about vampires; in fact, they rarely if ever wrote about vampires *as* vampires; instead the vampire was the means to achieve various ends. For an explanation of these various ends we need to examine the works themselves.

2. The Female Vampire

[The "Mona Lisa"] is expressive of what in the ways of a thousand years men had come to desire. Hers is the head upon which all "the ends of the world are come," and the eyelids are a little weary. It is a beauty wrought out from within upon the flesh, the deposit, little cell by cell, of strange thoughts and fantastic reveries and exquisite passions. Set it for one moment beside one of those Greek goddesses or beautiful women of antiquity, and how would they be troubled by this beauty, into which the soul with all its maladies has passed. All the thoughts and experience of the world have etched and molded there, in that which they have of power to refine and make expressive the outward form, the animalism of Greece, the lust of Rome, the mysticism of the Middle Age with its spiritual ambition and imaginative loves, the return of the Pagan world, the sins of the Borgias. She is older than the rocks among which she sits; like the vampire, she has been dead many times, and learned the secrets of the grave.

—Walter Pater, *The Renaissance*

Pater is here discussing Leonardo da Vinci's *Mona Lisa* from a peculiarly Romantic point of view. The lady is almost phantasmagoric, drawn not from life but from dreams. Her appeal is aesthetic, to be sure, but it is also psychological, for she is the grand seductress, the object of adolescent desire, the image of a special kind of forbidden love. She is dangerous but not cruel, passionate but not loving, delicate but not feeling. She is eternal, having been given perpetual life by all who have seen her, by all who have dreamed of her. She is the destroyer and preserver, the femme fatale or, in Pater's word, the vampire. And her story is one the young Romantics never tired of telling.

While the male vampire story was a tale of domination, the female version was one of seduction. In the usual scenario a young man has to deal with an older supernatural temptress who somehow drains his energy, leaving him weak and desperate. It appears as a simple story because the complicated part, namely the seduction, has been excised. Exactly how she drains the young man's energy is for the reader to imagine, for, like the cinematic fade-out, the Romantic poet takes us up to, and then abruptly around, this explosive scene. What does Geraldine do with Christabel between part 1 and part 2 of the poem? What happens to the knight in La Belle Dame's grotto? What has occurred that makes Lycius so eager to be married to Lamia or what exactly has happened that the narrator cannot remember in *Berenice* or *Morella* or *Ligeia*? We are never told.

I believe that in each of these works a young man (even in *Christabel*) has been seduced by an older woman, that in each instance the sexual action has been censored or sublimated and that, as a result of this action, the young man is introduced to the perplexities of manhood. I would further contend that when we consider all these stories together we find a "text," so to speak, of a Romantic rite of initiation, a text that depends in part on our understanding of the legend of the lamia.

This reading is reinforced when we see what happens when a female writer creates a female vampire, as with Charolotte Brontë's Bertha Rochester. For Bertha is libidinal, not at all seductive, not at all sympathetic. She is instead the wretched impediment to the heroine's happiness. For the male artist, the older female seductress is paradoxical, confusing and alluring, but to the female artist this same figure is unalloyed, hateful and repulsive.

The figure of the destructive woman is by no means solely a Romantic one—she is one of the oldest figures in classic and Christian lore. But as Mario Praz has contended, she was revived in the nineteenth century and made specifically vampiric; she became the literal femme fatale.[1] There was a mythic precedent: Lilith was the Hebraic temptress who supposedly turned to blood-sucking after being spurned by Adam, and Lamia was her classical counterpart, who, when found by Hera to be Zeus's lover, was transformed into a child-eater.[2] It is this Lamia who became the prototype of the Romantic seductress, acquiring, as the myth developed, an appetite for young men whom she would lure into her cave with promises of love. What happened to her victims we are never told, for, unlike the male vampire story, in which the female victim is eternally enthralled, in the female version the male victim is simply used and presumably forgotten.

The myth had gained sufficient currency by the eighteenth century for the word "lamia" to have become a generic term for all female vampires. And just as her male counterpart had characteristics of the wolf, the lamia retained certain serpentine qualities. For instance at the moment of attack her skin became moist and scaly, her breath became hot, her eyes contracted, and she would emit a soft hissing sound.[3] Other than this, she performs like the male: attacking at night, alone with her victim, first mesmerizing and then enervating him.

In *Christabel*, Geraldine is a lamia, as asserted by A. H. Nethercot in *The Road*

1. Mario Praz, *The Romantic Agony* (1933; rpt. London: Oxford University Press, 1970), chap. 4.

2. For an account of the lamia myth in classical lore, see A. H. Nethercot, *The Road to Tryermaine* (1939; rpt. New York: Russell & Russell, 1962), pp. 84–85.

3. This hissing sound is called "poppysma," a word coined by an early vampirologist Peter Thyraeus de Neuss, as reported in Ornella Volta, *The Vampire* (New York: Tandem Books, 1962), p. 140. Although in the classical myth she made this sound only while sucking, Coleridge has his lamia hiss whenever she is starting to attack.

to Tryermaine and reinforced later by Elisabeth Schneider.[4] There is simply too much vampire evidence to ignore: the midnight hour, the full moon, the spectral appearance of Geraldine, the importance of Christabel's touch, Christabel's invitation to the castle, Geraldine's fainting at the threshold, her refusal to pray, the old mastiff's growling acknowledgment of an evil presence, the blazing-up of the embers as Geraldine passes, Geraldine's weakness when she sees the carved cherub (a Christian icon of sorts) on the ceiling of Christabel's bed chamber—all these are indications, part mythic, part Coleridgean, not only of Geraldine's demonic character but also of her specifically vampiric nature.

Through the first two hundred lines or so of the poem there can be little doubt who Geraldine is; the question is, who is Christabel? I believe that to best understand the poem Christabel must be considered masculine, or at least bisexual. There are hints of this androgyny in the poem, hints that Nethercot was unconcerned with because he accepted the Geraldine/Christabel relationship at face value as homosexual. He understood the external contours but not the psychological content of the lamia myth. Even Elisabeth Schneider, who attempted a psychological interpretation, tried to work only within the context of the poem, neglecting the wider import of the myth. However, an understanding of the vampire myth as a rite of initiation, and an awareness that Coleridge is consciously using it not only to shock, but also to explore states of sexual awareness, may prove helpful for a deeper appreciation of the poem.

The crux of the poem concerns what occurs in Christabel's bedroom, for here Coleridge makes his own variation in the myth. Christabel decants a bottle of wildflower wine that her dying mother had set aside for her, having made Christabel promise to save it for the midnight hour of her nuptial night. We know from the first lines of the poem that it was twelve o'clock when Christabel met Geraldine, and so since she is now decanting that wine, she may realize that her wedding is soon to occur. This point is reemphasized when the spirit of her mother appears, seemingly to protect Christabel from the demonic marriage. But too late, for Gerladine casts the spirits of the good mother away, claiming that "this hour is mine" (l. 211).

Here, midway through part 1, the central mix-up of characters occurs. Geraldine is older than Christabel; she seems to "mother" her; she also seems to have a pact with Christabel's real mother that allows her to violate Christabel's virginity. This peculiar overlapping of mother figures will be redoubled in part 2, for as Geraldine becomes companion/lover to Christabel's father, she becomes a surrogate or "stepmother" to Christabel. Psychologically and mythically this relationship makes sense only if we suppose that Christabel is a displacement or substitution of male consciousness, perhaps even a projection of the poet himself.

4. Coleridge's use of vampire lore is substantiated in Nethercot, *Road to Tryermaine*, pp. 59–106; Elisabeth Schneider, "Notes on *Christabel*," *Philological Quarterly* 32 (1953): 197–206; and my gloss to l. 21 of *Christabel* in *The Explicator* 35 (Winter 1976): 28–29 (which explains why Coleridge is setting the time of his poem near the Walpurgisnacht).

This relationship is made clearer as the seduction scene continues. Geraldine's eyes dilate and contract, Christabel sinks to the bed and watches, trance-like, as Geraldine disrobes. Then as Christabel sees Geraldine's naked breast, she is startled by "a sight to dream of, not to tell," for there is some horrible deformity in Geraldine's body. The breast that once could have carried life to the nursing child is now withered and decayed. Christabel is literally dumbstruck by what she sees, and here Geraldine, half-undressed, hesitates. For the Hollywood version notwithstanding, no vampire relishes the task of destroying a loved one, and Geraldine is no exception. She "seeks delay" (l. 259) and "with a doleful look" asks Christabel to reaffirm the demonic process by touching her again, this time on the breast. This is the touch that will finally transfix Christabel, for as Geraldine says, "In the touch of this bosom there worketh a spell,/Which is lord of thy utterance, Christabel" (ll. 267–68). Knowing this, Christabel does touch, and in so doing, seals her fate.

Again this whole scene may be better understood if we treat Christabel as a masculine figure.[5] For just as there is ambivalence between Geraldine and the "real" mother, there is also ambivalence between Christabel and Coleridge. This perhaps explains the strange breast imagery, for the very "object" that the child has been forbidden to touch or nurse from is now his if he is willing to be punished, to be possessed for touching it. That Geraldine's breast is shriveled up and decayed is significant, for what was once full and life-giving for the baby has become forbidden as well as infecund for the adolescent.

I would not be willing to offer such a Freudian interpretation of the confused sex roles and of the breast imagery if the poem were not set in such a dreamscape and if the imagery had not been so clearly vampiric. The atmosphere of the poem, its eerie half-light and strange incompleteness creates a sense of subsconscious or even hypnagogic states. To understand the import of this dreaminess it may be helpful to look at a poem Coleridge wrote a few years later. In *The Pains of Sleep* he tells of a dream he has had that makes him feel "a desire with loathing strangely mix'd." Coleridge reports that since dreaming this oxymoronic fantasy he has been in "anguish and in agony" because each time he closes his eyes, "a fiendish crowd / Of shapes and thoughts" comes out of his subconsciousness to torture him with a "sense of intolerable wrong." We are never told what the dream is about but the yells of an obsessed man come screaming off the page:

> Fantastic passion! maddening brawl!
> And shame and terror over all!
> Deeds to be hid which were not hid,
> Which all confused I could not know
> Whether I suffered, or I did:
> For all seemed guilt, remorse or woe,

5. I made this argument in more detail before I realized its importance to the vampire myth in "'Desire with Loathing Strangely Mix'd': The Dreamwork of *Christabel*," *The Psychoanalytic Review* 61 (1974): 33–44

My own or others still the same
Life-stifling fear, soul-stifling shame.   (ll. 25–32)

So horrendous was this dream-act that on the third night he is awakened by his "own loud scream" and

I wept as I had been a child;
And having thus my tears subdued
My anguish to a milder mood,
Such punishments, I said, were due
To natures deepliest stained with sin,—
For aye entempesting anew
The unfathomable hell within,
The horror of their deeds to view,
To know and loathe, yet wish and do!   (ll. 40–48)

What the act in this dream is we do not know, but this is certain: it was something dreadful for it has made him howl like a child. Yet in spite of all its horror, it is still something the dreamer wishes "to know and loathe, yet wish and do!" Although we don't know what its antecedents are, the theme of "desire with loathing strangely mix'd" pervades each stanza. This is the same response Christabel has; she somehow wants to do what she must not do.

It is interesting to see that in Coleridge's notebooks during the time of the writing of the poem, he himself was experiencing these disturbing dreams. For instance, an entry for "Friday Night, November 28, 1800, or rather Saturday morning" reads:

—most frightful Dream of a Woman whose features were blended with darkness catching hold of my right eye and attempting to pull it out—I caught hold of her arm fast—a horrid feel—Wordsworth cried out aloud to me hearing my scream—heard his cry and thought it cruel he did not come but did not wake till his cry was repeated a third time when I awoke, my right eyelid swelled.

And nearly three years later he has another dream to this effect:

My dreams uncommonly illustrative of the non-existence of Surprize in sleep. . . . I was followed up and down by a frightful pale woman who, I thought, wanted to kiss me, and had the property of giving a shameful Disease by breathing in the face, and again I dreamed that a figure of a woman of gigantic Height, dim and indefinite and smokelike appeared—and that I was forced to run up toward it and then it changed to a stool—and then appeared again in another place—and again I went up in great fright—and changed to some other common thing—Yet I felt no surprise.[6]

6. *Notebook* 4, f. 34, and 3 Oct. 1803, *Notebook* 21, f. 41, in *The Notebooks of Samuel Taylor Coleridge*, ed. Kathleen Coburn (New York: Pantheon, 1957–62).

There is much in *Christabel* to suggest that Coleridge was working out in poetry such a dream of ambivalent effect, using the lamia myth as organizing metaphor. There is the eerie, surrealistic, and "dreamy" moonscape of the woods into which Christabel ventures, reminiscent of a child's nightmare. Additionally Christabel is out in these woods because "she had dreams all yesternight / Of her own betrothed knight" (ll. 27–28). Just before publication Coleridge deleted the next two lines which described Christabel's reactions to these dreams: "Dreams, that made her moan and leap,/As on her bed she lay in sleep." (First edition, between ll. 28–29). When Geraldine disrobes and shows Christabel her fetid and decaying bosom, the narrator, a kind of displaced Coleridge, blurts out: "Behold! her bosom and half her side—/A sight to *dream of*, not to tell!/O shield her! shield sweet Christabel!" (italics mine, ll. 252–54). Knowing how Coleridge felt about these dreams, it must have been a dreadful sight indeed. Also the morning after their night together, Christabel seems to be in a hypnagogic state:

> With open eyes (ah woe is me!)
> Asleep, and dreaming fearfully,
> Fearfully dreaming, yet, I wis,
> Dreaming that alone, which is—
> O sorrow and shame!   (ll. 292–96)

Christabel's subsequent panic when she realizes that she has been between these two "realities" of sleeping and waking points out that, if nothing else, she is profoundly disturbed about not knowing whether she has dreamed or experienced the act of shame. And finally, as if to reemphasize the importance of dream life, a fully conscious Coleridge has Bard Bracy retell a dream that *is* blatantly prophetic. In his dream Bracy saw a snake (Geraldine) throttling a dove (Christabel), and this dream took place at exactly the same time that Geraldine was seducing Christabel. There can be no doubt that Coleridge intended *this* dream to be symbolic.[7]

Based on the relationship between the major characters and the dream imagery, I believe that *Christabel* is in part, at least, an enactment of a sexual desire of the son for his mother. Christabel, the focal point of the poem, is the poet himself, displaced in dream life across sexual lines, to make representable a tabooed act.[8] It

7. For more on this dream within the dream, see Edgar Jones, "A New Reading of *Christabel*," *The Cambridge Journal* 5 (Nov. 1951): 106. Jones disagrees with Nethercot, *The Road to Tryermaine*, who believes that the snake is just a snake, nothing more. Most critics agree with Jones in believing that the snake in Bracy's dream is none other than a symbolic Christabel.

8. In some ways it is easier to interpret the dreamwork of a poem if little is known about the early life of the poet because the "biographical fallacy," which is inevitable with a psychological interpretation, is kept from overwhelming the work of art. This is conveniently the case with Coleridge, for little is known about his early life. In fact, all that is really known aside from the usual persons-places-events information is that he was remarkably ambivalent about his mother and fond of his father. His father was his best friend—this in spite of having fourteen other siblings, but Coleridge was the last child, the baby boy, and so perhaps this special relationship was natural. His relationship with his mother was different. For example, DeQuincey tells us that Coleridge was "almost an object of persecution to his mother," and Coleridge himself explains, "I was hardly used from infancy to boyhood, and from boyhood

is this act, or rather the feeling about this act, that makes Christabel/Coleridge feel not simply shame but rather this pervasive "desire with loathing strangely mix'd." Coleridge is not, however, going to explain this act; he lets the lamia myth do it for him.

The lamia myth takes on special importance in the scene where Geraldine and Christabel spend the night together. For although there is no mention of any sexual act or bloodletting, we do see the results of some energy flow between them. Not only are we told that they sleep "like a mother and child" (l. 301), but also that Christabel fitfully grows weaker as Geraldine calmly strengthens. The paradigm of parasite and host, vampire and vamped, is expressed here not in sanguine but in psychological terms: the mother is "living off" of the child. Once the energy transfer is completed, Christabel

> Gathers herself from out of her trance:
> Her limbs relax, her countenance
> Grows sad and soft; the smooth thin lids
> Close o'er her eyes; and tears she sheds—
> Large tears that leave the lashes bright!   (ll. 312–16)

Day breaks in the beginning of part 2, and Geraldine rises refreshed: "Yet more fair! For she belike had drunken deep/ Of all the blessedness of sleep!" (ll. 374–76). She has drunken more than sleep, for Christabel rises enervated—she has been "bled." They dress, and then, like the lamb leading the wolf home to the sheepfold, Christabel obediently conducts Geraldine to her father, Sir Leoline. If ever there was a man whose moral myopia blinded him to the evil at the end of his nose, it is Leoline. For hearing that Geraldine's father was once a childhood friend, he instantly demands that he become her guardian and protector. He needs no priming; he hurriedly embraces her, and as he does Christabel sees across her inner eye the horror of Geraldine's body. The enthrallment grows still more complete: "Again she saw that bosom old,/ Again she felt that bosom cold,/ And drew in her breath with a hissing sound" (ll. 456–59).

Christabel herself has now started a lamia metamorphosis. Geraldine has her literally spellbound and continues to strengthen at Christabel's expense. With Christabel knowing but powerless to act, and Leoline powerful but lacking knowledge, Geraldine's only possible antagonist is the poet, Bard Bracy. For Bracy, as the bard, as the artist, as Coleridge's "other half," if you will, can see reality through

---

to youth most, MOST cruelly." But this is controvertible, for Coleridge had a flair for the hyperbolic, especially in his letters. He would just as easily say the same thing with a different meaning: "My father was very fond of me, and I was my mother's darling: in consequence I was very miserable," or "I was petted and fondled excessively almost from my nativity."

So we know very little for certain about how Coleridge felt toward his parents. Certain events do stand out: he was the last child, his father died when he was eight; a year later (1781) he was sent away by his mother to Christ's Hospital, and the rest is history. I suspect we may learn more of Coleridge's formative years from carefully reading *Christabel* than we will ever learn from the scanty and contradictory biographical material we have.

the correcting prism of the imagination. He has had a dream the night before, he tells Leoline, in which he has seen the dove known as "Christabel" being throttled by a snake in the high grass near an old tree. The bard does not know what to make of the dream other than that he must remain at the castle to destroy the evil snake. In terms of the vampire myth perhaps he is the priest or dhampire who must be trusted to destroy the vampire; in terms of the psychodrama he is the superego. But Leoline remains dull to the very end, concluding that Geraldine must be the dove and that he and her father will later have time to crush the snake.

Geraldine, almost safe at last,

> . . . again turned round,
> And like a thing, that sought relief,
> Full of wonder and full of grief,
> She rolled her large bright eyes divine
> Wildly on Sir Leoline.   (ll. 580–84)

Soon both Leoline and Christabel are thoroughly bewitched. Christabel continues to assume the serpentine character of her persecutor, "so deeply had she drunken in" the spell of Geraldine. Both father and daughter, the former by overbearing ignorance and the latter by overbearing innocence, have been unable to deal with this demonic force. At least innocence has the potential to resist, and Christabel now makes a valiant effort. Falling at her father's feet she blurts out: "By my mother's soul do I entreat/ That thou this woman send away!" (ll. 615–16). But too late: innocence can be educated, but ignorance is steadfastly recalcitrant. The baron turns on his daughter, claiming she has dishonored him with this untimely outburst, and exits to his doom with Geraldine on his arm.

As Geraldine's relationship with Leoline has developed, as Geraldine has become in a sense "lover" to Leoline, she has become by extension surrogate "mother" to Christabel. At first it may seem ironic that Christabel should invoke her real mother's name to cast the substitute mother out, but in terms of the psychodynamics of the situation, it makes sense. Christabel/Coleridge is upset over having to share the mother's affections. We know Coleridge had a difficult time finishing *Christabel*, and even though he repeatedly claimed that he "always had the entire plan from beginning to end in my mind," the fact remains that even after twenty years of friendly prodding, he could never get it done.[9] This is partly because of his own pathological uneasiness with finishing projects, but also because he had tied a mythic knot he could not finally untangle. For to remain true to the vampire motif he would now either have to introduce a third party to destroy the lamia or resuscitate Bard Bracy to set things right. We know from what Coleridge later said that he may have intended to introduce Lord Roland de Vaux of Tryermaine and somehow to show Geraldine's reformation, but given the analogical matrix he had already developed, this deus ex machina ending would have been almost impos-

9. *Table Talk* (London: Oxford University Press, 1917), 6 July 1833.

sible.[10] Geraldine as lamia can be destroyed but not rehabilitated. In any case, Coleridge seems more interested in the process of psychic energy transfer, dark eroticism, and the infection of evil than with the process of redemption.

So if the conclusion to part 2 is confusing it is in part because the mythic roles have become so mixed up and Coleridge does not seem to want to straighten them out. Leoline is Christabel's father, but he seems to be enthralled by Geraldine, who, as she becomes his "lover," becomes by extension "mother" to Christabel. Christabel has behaved with Geraldine like a "lover" and she has also slept with her "like a child." This ambiguity about roles is not ours alone, however, for if there is one quality of mind shared by both Leoline and Christabel toward their new wife/ mother, it is utter discomposure. Leoline's own obsessive devotion to his dead wife (he had Bard Bracy ring the vesper bells each morning to her memory) seems to be an attempt on the dreamer's part to distance the "real mother" so that her surrogate may be experienced, just as earlier Christabel had told Geraldine that her real mother—although dead—still cares for her and will protect her from harm. Yet Leoline and Christabel proceed to react to Geraldine as if she were exactly what we have been assured she is not: Christabel's mother and Leoline's wife. No wonder Christabel's mind is falling apart (ll. 240, 385 ff.), or that Leoline is losing control (ll. 638, conclusion to part 2). By the end things are so topsy-turvy that Christabel calls on the good mother to redress the wrongs committed by the evil mother: "By my mother's soul do I entreat/ That thou this woman send away!" (ll. 616–17). But it is clearly too late.

Christabel is in a sense having it both ways, and so is Coleridge. We will see this same situation reenacted later in the century in LeFanu's *Carmilla*, which is in fact an intriguing gloss on *Christabel*. In both works the female protagonist is having a sexual encounter with a she-vampire, an encounter that makes her feel "desire with loathing strangely mix'd." The vampire myth with the reversal of sex roles has provided a safe psychological distance even though the artist/dreamer has had to pay the artistic price of incompleteness and confusion.

If *Christabel* is incomplete and confusing, the imagery is not: it is consistent and self-contained. For instance, the breast image, the most important in the poem, is finally resolved. At first Geraldine's breast is withered; when Christabel first sees it, it is "a sight to dream of, not to tell" (l. 253), for it is "lean and old and foul of hue." Geraldine even warns Christabel that "In the touch of this bosom there work-eth a spell,/ Which is lord of thy utterance . . . " (ll. 367–68), but Christabel by her own accord touches it and is entranced. However, after Geraldine and Chris-tabel have slept together, the breast becomes full almost as if the mammary gland had been stimulated. We are told that as Geraldine dressed in the morning " . . . her girded vests/ Grew tight beneath her heaving breasts" (ll. 379–80). It is also noteworthy that when Christabel sees Geraldine embrace his/her father, a "vision

10. See, for instance, B. R. McElderry, "Coleridge's Plan for Completing *Christabel*," *Studies in Philology* 29 (1936): 437–55.

falls upon her soul," a vision of the breast. So although the poem may not be artistically complete, the energy transfer (if we can trust the imagery, and in *Christabel* this is really all we can trust) is achieved. The mother has nursed the child and now the child must be separated. It is with this separation trauma that the poem "ends."

If this reading is valid, or even if it is only partly valid, we can understand why Coleridge was unable to continue. He had moved the poem up so close to himself that he would never be able to find the "proper" distance again. He had given poetic expression to urges that are tabooed, urges that can only end in feelings of "desire with loathing strangely mix'd." It is crucial to remember that all along Christabel knows what she is doing is potentially explosive, but she does it. She does not have to invite Geraldine back to the castle, but she does. She does not have to share her bed with her, but she does. She knows that "the saints will aid men if they call" (l. 330), but she does not call. She knows the "touch" of Geraldine's bosom will be traumatic, but she still touches. And by giving in to what she knows is forbidden, she almost destroys herself.

Historically, this kind of interpretation is by no means sanctioned; critics have usually followed either a psychosexual or a historical frame of reference.[11] The former is frankly autobiographical—the poem is seen as an expression of Coleridge's own anxiety, fright, loneliness, and motherlessness—while the second is literary, appealing to the conventions of genre, especially the medieval romance and the tale of terror.[12] An interpretation of the poem in terms of the psychology of the lamia myth has the advantage of combining both approaches, for embedded within the myth is the psychological significance. As Charles Tomlinson has written, *Christabel* ends "as a tragedy in which neurosis, not death, strikes the final blow."[13] I think even Coleridge did not completely understand when he reportedly said a year before his death as an explanation of why *Christabel* was still unfinished, that ". . . I could not carry on with equal success the execution of the idea, an extremely subtle and difficult one."[14] For if such an Oedipal reading of the lamia myth in *Christabel* is even partially acceptable, then it was a far more subtle and difficult theme than Coleridge knew how to explore safely.

If Coleridge's use of lamia lore is the best documented in Romantic literary criticism, certainly the most blatant use of the she-vampire would seem to be in Keats's *Lamia*. After all Keats does call his major character by the very name of the mythic demon and he does endow her with all the serpentine characteristics. Her

11. These two views in Coleridge criticism have been summed up in Virginia R. Radley, "*Christabel*: Directions Old and New," *Studies in English Literature* 4 (1964): 531–42.

12. The best example of the psychosexual approach is in Roy P. Basler, "*Christabel*," in *Sex, Symbolism and Psychology in Literature* (New Brunswick, N.J.: Rutgers University Press, 1948), pp. 25–52, and the best genre interpretation is Nethercot's *Road to Tryermaine, passim*, and R. H. Fogle's chapter on "*Christabel*" in *The Idea of Coleridge's Criticism* (Berkeley: University of California Press, 1962), pp. 130–61.

13. Charles Tomlinson, "Coleridge's *Christabel*" in *Interpretations: Essays in Twelve English Poems*, ed. John Wain (London: Routledge and Kegan Paul, 1955), p. 105.

14. *Table Talk*, 6 July 1833.

mythic personality is so obvious that Oliver Wendell Holmes had a not-very-bright character in his novel *Elsie Venner* compare *Christabel* with *Lamia* in ophidian terms.[15] Modern criticism, however, has not extended the comparison beyond the physiological, in part because, although she is called "Lamia," Keats's character does not seem all that evil. In fact, his lamia has been so defanged and is so polite and courteous that one may well wonder if Keats did not change his mind halfway through the poem. Keats may even be using the myth against itself to show how he could take a received story and tell it for the opposite effect. For Lamia, although she may be a she-vampire, is by no means a Geraldine; in fact, she may even be the heroine of the piece.

Lamia is indeed, as Robert Gittings has observed, a "critic's puzzle."[16] There is no character in the poem who has not been championed by some critic at one time or another. Witness what has been the fate of poor Apollonius: in the nineteenth century he was the Newtonian sorcerer, the archetypal uninvited guest come to ruin a good time; then a generation later he was reversed to become the hero, arriving like St. George to rescue not the damsel but the young dandy in distress. Keats has set such a moiré pattern into the fabric of *Lamia* that each time the poem has been turned in the critic's hands, it reflects different colors. There is little one can say dogmatically other than this: the poem seems to have two almost independent themes, one dealing with art and reality that is developed as a colloquy between the Neoclassical Apollonius and the Romantic Lycius, and a second theme exploring the dynamics of human interaction. These themes are by no means mutually exclusive; in fact the vampire analogy in part links them. For the vampire motif in the poem helps explain not just how friends and lovers "get along" but also how poets may be tempted to make too much of illusion.

Keats's source is significant, for his Lamia is not a demon from folklore; rather she is from Burton's *Anatomy of Melancholy*, which in turn was derived from Philostratus' *Life of Apollonius*. It is important to realize, however, that Burton did not summarize Philostratus but rather, as was his wont, Burtonized it considerably. So the early critics who insisted on seeing Keats's Lamia as a she-vampire and hence evil to the core assumed that since the poem was called *Lamia* and since the source was in a sense Philostratus, and since Philostratus *was* writing about vampires that Keats, too, must have intended his Lamia to be evil. Instead it may be an indication of how popular Keats believed the lamia myth to be that he probably intended nothing of the kind. For the "mature" Keats was nothing if not a playful ironist as eager to turn this myth back on itself as he had been to creatively retell Boccaccio in *Isabella* or Shakespeare in *The Eve of St. Agnes*.

Since the matter of sources may hold a key to what Keats intended Lamia to be, it may be useful to look there first. In his *Life of Apollonius*, Philostratus tells of a young man, Menippus, who was enthralled with a foreign woman and had been

---

15. For more on this comparison, see Kathleen Gallagher, "The Art of Snake Handling: *Lamia, Elsie Venner* and *Rappaccini's Daughter,*" *Studies in American Fiction* 3 (1975): 50–64.

16. Robert Gittings, *John Keats* (Boston: Little Brown, 1968), p. 337.

captivated by her wine, song, and magical powers. Although Menippus did not realize that she was in truth only an apparition, the young scholar's tutor Apollonius did. Apollonius warned his charge not to become involved, but too late, for Menippus had decided to wed this temptress and indeed would have, had Apollonius not appeared during the ceremony. This ravishing bride-to-be was a demon, a she-vampire, a lamia, Apollonius explained to the wedding guests, and was planning to devour Menippus. Lamia rebutted but it was in vain, for her gold, silver, and ceremonial paraphernalia all disappeared, along with the wine bearers and servants, leaving her alone to confront her accuser. She pretended to weep, but Apollonius doggedly pursued his examination. Finally—and this is crucial, but Burton neglected to translate it—"she admitted she was a vampire and was fattening up Menippus with pleasure before devouring his body, for it was her habit to feed upon young and beautiful bodies because their blood is pure and strong."[17] So she is indeed nasty and rightfully destroyed; Menippus is saved, and Apollonius is the hero. In terms of the vampire myth, all important parties are present: the vampire, the victim, and the "dhampire" or vampire destroyer.

When Burton gave his account it was somewhat different:

> Philostratus, in his fourth book *de Vita Apollonii*, hath a memorable instance in this kind, which I may not omit, of one Menippus Lycius, a young man twenty-five years of age, that going betwixt Cenchreas and Corinth, met such a phantasm in the habit of a fair gentlewoman, which, taking him by the hand, carried him home to her house, in the suburbs of Corinth, and told him she was a Phoenician by birth, and if he would tarry with her, he should hear her sing and play, and drink such wine as never any drank, and no man should molest him; but she, being fair and lovely, would live and die with him, that was fair and lovely to behold. The young man, a philosopher, otherwise staid and discreet, able to moderate his passions, though not this of love, tarried with her a while to his great content, and at last married her, to whose wedding, amongst other guests, came Apollinius [*sic*]; who, by some probable conjectures, found her out to be a serpent, a lamia; and that all her furniture was, like Tantalus' gold, described by Homer, no substance but mere illusions. When she saw herself descried, she wept, and desired Apollonius to be silent, but he would not be moved, and thereupon she, plate, house, and all that was in it, vanished in an instant: many thousands took notice of this fact, for it was done in the midst of Greece.[18]

In Burton's version, there is no confession, no admission of evil intent, nothing but the hint that Apollonius' invective was sufficient to cause the lamia to vanish. We are not told that she "pretended to weep," as Philostratus said, but just the opposite—in Burton she did indeed weep. More importantly, we are not told of her self-

17. Philostratus, *Life of Apollonius*, book 4, sec. 25.
18. Robert Burton, *Anatomy of Melancholy*, part 3, sec. 2, memb. 1, subs. 1.

incriminating admission that yes, she was fattening up Menippus and that yes, she intended to devour him. Rather in Burton's version she begs Apollonius to be quiet, and when he won't be silenced, she simply disappears.

Burton's humanizing of the she-vampire is crucial for Keats's poem because in *Lamia* Keats is setting up a very delicate ménage à trois in which simple jealousies can set things askew. In a sense this is the rationale for part 1, where Lamia reverses the process Coleridge described in *Christabel* by transforming herself from snake to human. Her metamorphosis is of course nowhere to be found either in Burton or Philostratus; and it shows how insistent Keats is in accepting the myth but at the same time redirecting its consequences. Keats knew enough about the lamia to realize that she must have a serpentine form, but he added the tortuous transformation to assert the genuineness of her commitment to Lycius. She lives for love, not blood.

> Left to herself, the serpent now began
> To change; her elfin blood in madness ran,
> Her mouth foam'd, and the grass, therewith besprent,
> Wither'd at dew so sweet and virulent;
> Her eyes in torture fix'd, and anguish drear,
> Hot, glaz'd, and wide, with lid-lashes all sear,
> Flash'd phosphor and sharp sparks, without one cooling tear.
> The colours all inflam'd throughout her train,
> She writh'd about, convuls'd with scarlet pain:
> A deep volcanian yellow took the place
> Of all her milder-mooned body's grace;
> And, as the lava ravishes the mead,
> Spoilt all her silver mail, and golden brede;
> Made gloom of all her frecklings, streaks and bars,
> Eclips'd her crescents, and lick'd up her stars:
> So that, in moments few, she was undrest
> Of all her sapphire, greens, and amethyst,
> And rubious-argent: of all these bereft,
> Nothing but pain and ugliness were left.   (ll. 146–64)

This is no simple shedding of the scales; it is agony and it begins a theme of sacrificial love that continues to the end. Lamia is always willing to do more for Lycius than he is ever willing to do for her. That is not to deny that Lamia is tainted with evil, for Keats will not have her unalloyed; he keeps just enough of her mythic background to have us forever wondering. She is vampiric; that cannot be denied. For instance, in part 1, like the vampire of folklore, she is able to send herself into the dream world of her lover (ll. 208–14); she can cast a spell with her eyes (ll. 258, 291–93) and she can entrance her victim with a kiss (l. 295), but Keats defuses the myth by having her, not Lycius, initiate the affair (l. 345), having her able to see her reflection in a mirror of water (ll. 182–84), and having her able to cross a threshold ("They pass'd the city gates, he knew not how" [l. 348]). Keats knew what he was doing; knew he was simultaneously mythologizing and demythologizing, trying, like Coleridge, to have his Geraldine/Lamia both human—victim of emotion—and supernatural—victim of immortality. She cannot help how she feels and she cannot deny what she needs. She literally and figuratively hungers for love, yet she realizes that if pressed too far, she may destroy the very love that gives her life.

Once Keats has established Lamia as being human enough or foolish enough to destroy the object of desire, he proceeds to do the same thing in reverse to Lycius. For if Lamia is a powerful spirit made human by love, Lycius is a human who wishes love to make him spiritual. In terms of the vampire analogy, what happens as part 2 begins is that Lycius, having been "vamped" by Lamia, now turns into the vampire—not an actual but a metaphorical vampire. He now wants the power to control her; he wants the same power Lamia gave up when she became human. Now "possessed,"

> Against his better self, he took delight
> Luxurious in her sorrows, soft and new.
> His passion, cruel grown, took on a hue
> Fierce and sanguineous as 'twas possible
> In one whose brow had no dark veins to swell.
> Fine was the mitigated fury, like
> Apollo's present when in act to strike
> The serpent—Ha, the serpent! certes, she
> Was none.   (ll. 73–81)

She is no longer the serpent; he is. She has "Put her new lips to his, and [given] afresh/ The life she had so tangled in her mesh" and eagerly he has "drunk her beauty up." Lamia only wants their love to survive, to provide her strength, but Lycius wants more. He wants recognition, acclaim, and power. It is he who forces her from their shielded world of mutual energy exchange by demanding that they be married, ironically demanding the social exposure that Lamia cannot withstand. But her love is so complete and his fury so forceful that she accedes. She accedes on one condition—that the learned philosopher, the priest, the "dhampire" Apollonius, not be invited.

The wedding day arrives, as it had in Philostratus and Burton, and arriving with it is the thirteenth guest, Apollonius. It is a wondrous affair, as richly laden as Porphyro's tray for Madeline, as splendid as the banquets of Hyperion. Apollonius enters, spots his opponent, recognizes her as a lamia (l. 269), and cries out, "Begone, foul dream!" (l. 271). She blanches, figuratively losing blood (l. 273), and attempts to counter his assertion, but it is in vain. With the same power of the eye that Lamia had used to entrance Lycius, Apollonius now stares her into submission. Lycius, at last realizing that his precious bauble may be shattered, lashes out at his mentor:

Corinthians! look upon that grey-beard wretch!
Mark now, possess'd, his lashless eyelids stretch
Around his demon eyes! Corinthians, see!
My sweet bride withers at their potency.   (ll. 286–90)

Apollonius, with his lidless eyes and serpentine character, is just as "lethal" as
Lamia. He is a vampire of another sort; his means of destruction are not sensual
but scientific; he "murders to dissect." The balance has been tipped; it is he who is
now in control. Lamia quite literally withers as "the sophist's eyes,/ Like a sharp
spear, went through her utterly,/ Keen, cruel, perceant, stinging" (ll. 299–301). She
is vanquished, metaphorically staked, if you will, and with a frightful scream disappears. Lycius, symbiotically dependent on her love, dies soon after.

But what does this all mean? Why has Keats made these characters so paradoxical? If Apollonius is the force for good, then he has won at best a Pyrrhic victory,
for he has destroyed both Lamia and Lycius. If Lamia is a force for good, she has
allowed herself to become intimidated by Lycius into a compromise (the public
marriage) that has led to her destruction. And if Lycius is a force for good, he has
so belligerently tried to force his photophobic love into the light she cannot long
endure that he is hardly to be commended. The poem ends in a Hobson's choice:
if one chooses the life of the dissecting intellect, "reality" will be ruined (see the
notorious lines attacking Newton, ll. 229–30), but if one chooses the life of the
imagination, one will never be able to reconcile it with "truth." There is no way
out. Each member of the threesome is described as vamping at least one other.
Lamia draws energy from Lycius, and he reciprocates by draining her; Apollonius
drains energy from Lamia, who in turn depletes the dependent Lycius. When one
member is removed from this ménage à trois, the energy flow ceases.

By the end of the poem there is no resolution, only bafflement. Simply by making Lamia human, as he does in part 1, Keats lessened our concern for her victim;
then by making the "victim" vamp the vampire in part 2 he has even made her
sympathetic. Although we know Apollonius is right—Lamia is an illusion, she is
ethereal—we also know she is "a thing of beauty and a joy forever," or almost
forever. She is so fragile that relationships with her cannot be too demanding. She
can live off our imaginative energies, but we will destroy her (and ourselves as well)
if we attempt to make her "real."

An understanding of the vampire analogy may well lead to the conclusion that
Lamia personifies part of the artistic experience. She is, in a sense, the muse. Or
in terms of Keats's other poetry she is the nightingale's song or the figures on the
Grecian urn; she has momentary vitality that can only "come alive" when she has
a human partner. Art for Keats is such a reciprocal process—an interaction between
artifact and perceiver, between imagination and man, muse and poet. It is in the
figurative "marriage" of subject and object that aesthetic bliss is achieved, yet this
bliss is by its very nature short-lived. Lycius' sin, if it can be considered so, is to be
pathetically human. Lycius wishes to make that marriage real and permanent. He

attempts to circumvent the mediating influence of the art and exist directly and solely with inspiration. He is thwarted, for the ideal, the infinite, the dream, can only vamp and enervate the artist whose being is not firmly settled in the "real world."

This interpretation of Keats's poetry is by no means new, although it is a view not usually taken of Lamia.[19] In 1819 the vampire analogy was a new (Polidori's/Byron's story *The Vampyre* had been published in April) and startling means for Keats to explore a favorite theme, and it is curious that such an interpretation has not been proferred before. Vampirism is predictably a part of the Gothic strain in Keats's work, a strain that appears early and continues through the *Odes*. So, for instance, in *The Living Hand* Keats implicitly uses the analogy to explain the revivifying effects of love:

> The living hand, now warm and capable
> Of earnest grasping, would, if it were cold
> And in the icy silence of the tomb,
> So haunt thy days and chill thy dreaming nights
> That thou wouldst wish thine own heart dry of blood
> So in my veins red life might stream again,
> And thou be conscience-calmed—see here it is.
> I hold it towards you.

Here, however, the blood-flow describes only the process of energy exchange between lovers, and is used more as a Gothic conceit than as a means to convey insight. When Keats combined the psychology of the lamia myth with the macabre, he created a delightfully perplexing poem, *La Belle Dame sans Merci*.

La Belle Dame sans Merci was written as a folk ballad and, like many ballads, constructed around a number of seemingly rhetorical questions. Often the ballad will riddle the reader by having an internal questioner ask the central questions such as "Where are you going, Lord Randall?" or "Why are you looking so sad, Lady Marjory?" Earl Wasserman, the most influential critic of the poem, believed Keats may well have had a specific ballad in mind, and for Wasserman this ballad was "Thomas Rymer."[20] But I suspect Keats might also be remembering the early revenant ballads such as "Margaret's Ghost," "Sweet William's Grave," or "Fair Margaret and Sweet William." For these ballads have much in common with *La Belle Dame*, not only superficially in stanza pattern but internally with the asking of the riddle. Although the central riddle that the questioner asks in Keats's ballad is "Why are you looking so woebegone, knight-at-arms?" there are other puzzles as

19. Although this view is a commonplace since Earl Wasserman's *The Finer Tone: Keats' Major Poems* (Baltimore: Johns Hopkins University Press, 1953), it is best put forward in Jack Stillinger, "Imagination and Reality in the Odes," Introduction to *Twentieth Century Interpretations of Keats' Odes* (Englewood Cliffs, N.J.: Prentice Hall, 1968) and C. I. Patterson, *The Daemonic in the Poetry of John Keats* (Urbana: University of Illinois Press, 1970).

20. Wasserman, *Finer Tone*, pp. 68–83.

well. For instance, what has long hair and wild eyes, speaks a strange language, forages for unusual foods, and causes grown men to grow pale? In other words, who is this woman? This, the unstated riddle of Keats's *La Belle Dame sans Merci*, has raised a goodly number of answers, none of them entirely satisfactory and many of them contradictory.

First to answer were those who said that La Belle Dame is none other than the playful coquette Fanny Brawne, and that the poem expressed the bitterness Keats felt over her various deceptions.[21] Then came those critics who said such biographical explanations are too reductive and that the place to start is with the study of nonbiographical sources. These critics usually claimed that La Belle Dame was lifted from *Palmerin of England* or *The Faerie Queene*.[22] A source study does not really answer the riddle of who she is, however; at best it tells where she came from. Then a decade or so ago Wasserman tied source study to allegorical interpretation. For Wasserman the most important source is the English folk ballad, and he interpreted the poem as a metaphorical rendition of Keats's own *Pleasure Thermometer*.[23] In other words, the knight, through the agency of La Belle Dame, ascends into the ethereal world beyond the "enchanted bourne," but then has a vision of pale kings which reminds him of his mortality, and he returns to the mutable world. The knight's spiritual quest is heroic to Wasserman, whose reading was considered standard a generation ago. Recently, however, there have been other interpretations that reverse Wasserman's by seeing the knight as an Innocent duped by La Belle Dame, "a fairy mistress from Hell."[24] All that remained was for someone to say that she is not Fanny Brawne and that she is neither a saint nor a Circe and indeed, this too has been said. For these critics, she represents an amoral level of consciousness, a state of awareness that is neither good nor bad.[25] So, in short, critics have answered the riddle of who La Belle Dame is by saying either she is good or bad or beyond judgment. What more could be said?

In this context of confusion I would like to reintroduce an answer first put forward twenty-five years ago by Edwin Clapp but never developed: that La Belle is a vamp—a female vampire, a lamia.[26] Two external facts are important to Clapp's argument. First, in the three months after *La Belle Dame* appeared, Keats wrote *Lamia*. Lamia's physical description is strikingly similar to La Belle Dame's: Lamia

21. Edward Bostetter, *The Romantic Ventriloquists: Wordsworth, Keats, Shelley, Byron* (Seattle: University of Washington Press, 1963), p. 160; Claude Finney, *The Evolution of Keats' Poetry* (Cambridge, Mass.: Harvard University Press, 1936), 2:593; John Middleton Murry, *Keats and Shakespeare: A Study of Keats' Poetical Life from 1816–1820* (London: Oxford University Press, 1926), p. 124.

22. See such interpretations as Amy Lowell, *John Keats* (Boston: Houghton Mifflin, 1925), 2: 220–24.

23. Wasserman, *Finer Tone*, p. 69.

24. Francis Utley, "The Infernos of Lucretius and Keats' *La Belle Dame sans Merci*," *ELH* 25 (1958): 121.

25. See Bernard Breyer, "*La Belle Dame sans Merci*," *Explicator* 6 (Dec. 1947), art. 18; and Charles I. Patterson, *The Daemonic in the Poetry of John Keats*, pp. 125–51.

26. Edwin R. Clapp, "*La Belle Dame as Vampire*," *Philological Quarterly* 28 (1948): 89–92. Clapp's note is primarily concerned with establishing possible sources for Keats's vampire knowledge, not with showing the vampiric interaction between La Belle Dame, the knight, the narrator, and the reader.

is a temptress (l. 15) with a "mournful voice" (l. 35) who "haunts" the "meads" (l. 17) looking for human spoils. She is the literal and figurative "snake in the grass." This is not to say that La Belle Dame is the prototype of Lamia, or that La Belle Dame is the "trying out" of Lamia, only that Keats seems interested in the subject of female vampires. Second, Keats was not alone in his interest. Vampires were becoming a popular subject by 1819. Although Coleridge, Scott, Southey, and Stagg had already experimented with poetic adaptations of the myth, it may be that Keats had read John Polidori's novella *The Vampyre*. For this work, the first use of the vampire in prose, appeared under Byron's name in the *New Monthly Magazine* in early April 1819. It caused an immediate sensation, was dramatized several times in England and on the Continent, and was soon published in book form.[27] We know the exact date of *La Belle Dame*: it was written without preface in a long journal letter to George Keats on 21 April 1819, so there may be a connection between Keats's poem and current literary fashions.

Here is the story told in *La Belle Dame sans Merci*. The narrator meets a knight-at-arms (a man presumably of vigor and action) who is now "palely loitering" in the meads. Since the weather is nippy, one might expect the knight to have a wind-burned complexion, but instead, as the narrator reports:

> I see a lily on thy brow,
>> With anguish moist and fever dew
> And on thy cheeks a fading rose
>> Fast withereth too.   (ll. 9–12)

The knight is right now in the process of growing pale, and presumably as he tells his part of the story he grows paler still. The knight proceeds to tell his story within the narrator's frame: a while ago he met a wild-eyed lady in the meads, who was like (but was *not*) a "faery's child." He was entranced by her and she seemed to (but did *not*) return his affection, for he says, "She look'd at me *as* she did love,/ And made sweet moan" (italics mine). Perhaps this is a Petrarchan lover's moan, but maybe she is moaning about something she does not want to do, yet is somehow forced to. The knight puts her on his steed and is quite literally overcome by love; he sees nothing but her. If she had wanted only his body in love surely she could have had it, but she seems to want more. For soon she sings him a "faery's song," feeds him exotic and intoxicating foods ("honey wild and manna dew"), and then *seems* to tell him that she loves him. I think that the ambiguity here is important, for the knight says, "And sure in language strange she said,/ I love thee true." Does she tell him she loves him, or does he so badly want to believe it that he tries to convince himself that what she said was "I love you"? If the former is the case, Keats might simply have written something like, "And sure in language soft she said . . . ," but instead he calls it "language strange." Perhaps she is a native of some foreign land; perhaps her true tongue is some satanic dialect.

27. For more on the publishing history of *The Vampyre*, see Henry R. Viets, "The London Editions of Polidori's *The Vampyre*," *The Papers of the Bibliographical Society of America* 63 (1969): 83–103.

Could her music, exotic food, and strange words be charms to lure the knight into her power? Next she takes him into her grotto, where instead of joyfully consummating their love, she "wept and sigh'd full sore." Why should she be so unhappy? The knight now enters her demonic world by an act of his own volition; perhaps drugged and charmed, he leans over and shuts her wild eyes with "kisses four." A minor characteristic of vampires is that they sleep with their eyes gazing open and thus his closing them with kisses may imply collusion.[28] Also in folklore numerology, if things were above-board, we would certainly expect the number three, not the evil number four. Keats playfully explained this away by saying that three would have made the kisses asymmetrical, whereas four would mean two kisses for each eye, but surely he knew enough about the ballad content to recognize the implications of the number four.[29]

The knight then falls asleep and has a dream. In terms of the meeting of the narrator and the knight, this dream has just occurred, for it is his "latest" or most recent dream. So the adventure with La Belle Dame has also recently occurred. The knight is fresh from the experience, as the changing of his facial color implies, and this impression of immediacy is reinforced with the last two lines of the penultimate stanza: "And I awoke, and found me here/ On the cold hill side." In this context the dream he has had is particularly interesting, for it is what he has most recently seen: "I saw *pale* kings, and princes too,/ *Pale* warriors, death-*pale* were they all" (italics mine). The knight, we remember, is also turning pale: "palely loitering . . . a lily on [his] brow." Could the loss of blood have caused this pallor? Additionally in his dream these once-noble men announce to the knight that he is soon to join their ranks. He has become one of them, enthralled to La Belle Dame. It is important to see what they look like, for they represent what he is becoming. Along with their pallor they share one strange characteristic—not long hair, or wild eyes, or fiery nostrils—rather, the knight sees their "starved lips in the gloam/ With horrid warning gap'd wide." They are obviously thirsty. The narrator does not know what they may be thirsty for and perhaps even the knight does not yet know, but there are hints he will soon find out.

The dream is over. In a typically balladic touch the first stanza is reworded and spoken, not by the narrator as it originally was, but by the knight. It is as if the knight has taken control of the narrator's world. We don't know what happens next (Keats is depending on our completing the poem) but if La Belle Dame is a lamia, and if the knight is turning pale because she has vamped him, is the narrator about to be the next victim?

The ending of the poem is a macabre tour de force as art and reality, dream and waking, meet and merge within the poem itself. And we, who in a sense have stood behind the narrator prodding him to ask more questions, narrowly escape his fate.

28. Montague Summers, *The Vampire: His Kith and Kin* (1928; rpt. New Hyde Park, N.Y.: University Books, 1960), pp. 179–81.

29. Keats playfully explains away the four kisses in his "Letter to George Keats, 21 April 1819," *Letters of John Keats, 1814–1821,* ed. Hyder Rollins (Cambridge, Mass.: Harvard University Press, 1958), 2: 95–96.

That Keats has been so daring with the lamia myth here in *La Belle Dame* and so subtle with it in *Lamia* attests not just to the superstition's popularity but to its wonderfully flexible nature as well; it can be both risible and horrible, profound and silly.

What Coleridge and Keats did to the vampire myth was to liberate it from the past. If *Christabel, Lamia,* and *La Belle Dame* are really the results of the poets' serious analysis of the lamia myth, then they are important not for providing Romantic consensus but rather just the opposite. In each case the femme fatale is profoundly different: Geraldine is maternal, Lamia a self-sacrificing goddess, while La Belle Dame sans Merci is exactly that—a beautiful woman without pity. Whereas the female may change in the various retellings, it is noteworthy that the male protagonist (accepting now, if only for argument's sake, my hypothesis about *Christabel*) stays remarkably consistent. The victim of the lamia attack is docile, a willing co-conspirator. The female seductress has all the power. Ernest Jones's conjectures about the adolescent nature of the myth itself may in part explain the docility of the male in these poems. Discussing the vampire seduction from the victim's point of view, he contends:

> The explanation of these phantasies is surely not hard. A nightly visit from a beautiful or frightful being, who first exhausts the sleeper with passionate embraces and then withdraws from him a vital fluid; all this can point only to a natural and common process, namely to nocturnal emissions accompanied with dreams of a more or less erotic nature. In the unconscious mind blood is commonly an equivalent for semen.[30]

If this is the case (and we shall see this masturbatory fantasy played out again in Jonathan Harker's dream adventures in Dracula's castle), then it is crucial that the male not be the aggressor. For he is being initiated into sexuality with all of its frenetic energy and bizarre confusions.

No one has ever been better qualified to explain this oxymoronic nature of the vampire attack than Edgar Allen Poe. Poe wrote a number of variations on the lover-as-vampire theme, but the best examples of his female vampire are to be found in *Morella* and *Ligeia*. For these two stories, ambiguous and perplexing in the extreme, explore the dynamics of human relationships using the vampire metaphor. The critic who saw this first was D. H. Lawrence, who wrote not just of Poe's lovers, but of his own as well:

> . . . the secondary law of all organic life is that each organism only lives through contact with other matter, assimilation, and contact with other life, which means assimilation of new vibrations, non-material. Each individual organism is vivified by intimate contact with fellow organisms. . . . In spiritual love, the contact is purely nervous. The nerves in the lovers are set vibrating in unison like two instruments. The pitch can rise higher and higher.

30. Ernest Jones, *On the Nightmare* (1931; rpt. New York: Liveright, 1971), p. 19.

But carry this too far, and the nerves begin to break, to bleed, as it were, and a form of death sets in. . . . It is easy to see why each man kills the things he loves. To *know* a living thing is to kill it. You have to kill a thing to know it satisfactorily. For this reason, the desirous consciousness, the SPIRIT, is a vampire.[31]

But Lawrence, concerned with the later stories, did not realize how long Poe had experimented with his analogy to explain an aberrant state of lover's consciousness. For the development of the vampire analogy was one of Poe's central artistic concerns.

Berenice (March 1835) is Poe's first and, in retrospect, rather clumsy attempt to incorporate the myth into a tale. It seems obvious that here his initial concern is to exploit current events and that the vampire material is only added along the way. For *Berenice* is partly based on newspaper reports of grave robbers who were seeking teeth for either Baltimore or New York dentists.[32] Such stories both in fiction and in the press were only too common by the 1830s, pandering as they did to an audience made eager for scandal and shock by the sensational Salisbury Street novels and tabloid journalism. For here in the 1830s was the first generation to find in its newspapers that life indeed did imitate art, and so when Poe made premature burial and grave robbing central, he was not doing anything new but rather carrying "imitation" to a new level of Gothic sublimity.

Berenice is important for more than historical reasons; here begins a series of Poe lamias that will include Morella, Ligeia, and maybe even Madeline Usher. Admittedly *Berenice* shows Poe at his most derivative, but he is also experimenting with material he will master some eight years later in *The Oval Portrait*.

If he experiments with the female protagonist, he does not experiment with the narrator. As with the later variations of the vampire lover, *Berenice* is told by a highly questionable source; in fact it may be told by the vampire himself. In each of the early stories the teller of the tale is explaining his relationship with a woman who is now dead, a woman who, according to him, is responsible not only for her demise, but for his present debilitation as well. In each of these stories we play detective, attempting to trap the now-frantic narrator in his own story. That we never entirely succeed in assessing blame is partly what makes these tales so annoyingly enjoyable.

This is the narrator's story in *Berenice*. Once he was sickly and ill, while his cousin Berenice was robust and healthy. Soon, however, "a fatal disease—fell like a simoon upon her frame," and she weakened. As she weakens, he mysteriously gains strength, strength he uses not to pursue his normal activities, but rather in his

---

31. D. H. Lawrence, *Selected Literary Criticism*, ed. Anthony Beal (1932; rpt. New York: Viking Press, 1966), pp. 331–35. This aspect of Poe's interest in the Gothic is also discussed briefly in Allen Tate, *The Forlorn Demon* (Chicago: Regnery, 1953), pp. 79–95.

32. Poe's main concern in *Berenice* seems to be exploiting then-recent occurrences of grave robbing; see Killis Campbell, *The Mind of Poe and Other Studies* (Cambridge, Mass.: Harvard University Press, 1933), p. 167; and Roger Forclaz's elaboration, "A Source of *Berenice* and a Note on Poe's Reading," *Poe Newsletter* 1 (1968): 25–27.

own words, to follow his "monomania." The ebb and flow of their mutual energies cause first one, then the other, to enter uncontrollable trancelike states. Just what these trances entail he is unable to recall, but their effects on her are obvious. Berenice becomes physically distorted and then literally wastes away. However, the narrator, sensing our suspicions, claims he never laid a hand on her—"My passions *always were* of the mind"—but later she regains strength and proceeds to do to him exactly what he has done to her. He now grows pale at her approach, shudders in her company, and is enervated by her mere presence. Finally, in an attempt to force this energy flux into equilibrium, he proposes marriage. But too late, she refuses. The narrator has somehow vamped Berenice, deprived her of her vitality, and now she, desperate to regenerate energy, prepares revenge. She does not want marriage—a union of equals—she wants control. Here she is in all her lamialike horror:

> The forehead was high, and very pale, and singularly placid; and the once jetty hair fell partially over it, and overshadowed the hollow temples with innumerable ringlets now of a vivid yellow, and jarring discordantly, in their fantastic character, with the reigning melancholy of the countenance. The eyes were lifeless, and lustreless, and seemingly pupil-less, and I shrank involuntarily from their glassy stare to the contemplation of the thin and shrunken lips. They parted; and in a smile of peculiar meaning, the teeth of the changed Berenice disclosed themselves slowly to my view. Would to God that I had never beheld them, or that, having done so, I had died.[33]

The pallor, the bewitching eyes, the thin lips curling back to reveal the teeth, here are all the lamia traits in cinemagraphic array. Like Frankenstein's monster, which Poe may have had in mind, the product of evil genius returns to haunt the maker. The vampire's victim now victimizes the vampire.

In desperation the narrator focuses on those instruments of vengeance—the teeth. He must defang her before she can attack. Exactly how this dedentation occurs we are never told, for the narrator has selectively forgotten the most important parts of his own tale. Instead we learn from a servant that Berenice has died of "epilepsy," which, as Poe knew, was a common cause of premature burial. The "stunned" narrator waits until midnight and even then is only able to recall "the shrill and piercing shriek of a female voice . . . ringing in my ears." A servant enters to tell him that the diagnosis of Berenice's death was hasty, that she is still alive, and as he says this he notices that the narrator's clothes are all "clotted with gore." Only now do we (the servant, the narrator, and the reader) realize what has happened. The narrator rushes across the room, grabs a small box from the table, and empties it of the fruit of his gruesome labor—the means of her vengeance—Berenice's teeth.

In *Berenice* the vampire motif is unattached to any theme, and is included more

33. *Poe: Selected Poetry and Prose* (New York: Modern Library, 1951), p. 88. Hereafter page numbers will appear parenthetically in the text.

for gothic stuffing than for sense. Poe's interest is clearly in capitalizing on then-current stories of premature burial and grave robbing, but he does a number of things in *Berenice* that will affect vampire stories to come. Most importantly is that he makes the narrator sympathetic. He is making us party to recklessness. For the narrator takes us into his confidence; he trusts us. He is out of control and worse than that, he knows it. But he is not a conniving master of subterfuge; he is no blackguard and scoundrel; rather he is sick. He even diagnoses his own sickness as "monomania," which is exactly the plight of the vampire. He needs what he should not have, yet he must have it. In the other stories as well Poe made this monomania the psychological explanation of the vampirism, and in so doing emphasized that aspect of the myth which is most perplexing, namely how the vampire becomes his own victim.

In doing this Poe knew he was describing the human condition as well, and a month after the publication of *Berenice* he attempted to retell the story without all the gothic silliness in *Morella*. However, he retained the same unstrung and suspect narrator, the same concern with describing the lovers' loss of emotional equilibrium, and the same driving for "a certain single effect." First the narrator: again he is writing after the fact, and again his faculties have been grossly diminished after contact with a strange and mysterious woman. He lacks all conviction, almost as if he had been "bled" of willpower, which is exactly what has occurred. Yet he intends to tell us a story he himself cannot remember. "In all *this, if I err not*, my reason had little to do. My convictions, *or I forget myself*, were in no manner acted upon by the ideal, nor was any tincture of the mysticism which I read, to be discovered, *unless I am greatly mistaken*, either in my deed or in my thoughts" (p. 91). (Italics mine.) He has become a cipher, a milquetoast, a bloodless nonentity, while Morella, his inamorata, has energized herself to live beyond death.

Morella is initially described with all the lamia accoutrements: cold hands, strange, almost cabalistic language, a crimson spot (a witch's mark?) on her blood-less face, and hypnotic eyes. In fact, the narrator's hints become, though unknown to him, more and more important for us. Morella, he says, "attached herself" to him; her glance could send him into a trance ("my soul sickened and became giddy with the giddiness of one who gazes downward into some dreary and unfathomable abyss"), and at the sound of her voice, he "grew pale and shuddered inwardly at those two unearthly notes" (p. 92).

Like her fictive sister Berenice, Morella soon weakens. So woefully out of touch is the narrator that although he perceives her weakening, he attributes this debilitation to the fact that she is a woman, with weakness a natural condition. In truth it is he who is being drained so that she might later be fortified. She says as much on her deathbed: "I am dying, yet I shall live" (p. 93), but he is too far gone to understand. With no previous mention of her being pregnant, we are now told that she miraculously delivers forth a posthumous female child. Here Freudians should have a field day, for if blood is metaphorical semen, and if the narrator's relationship has been vampiric, then the displaced result of their union should be the same as if they had had a sexual relationship. It is. Curiously, the narrator, who had been unable to love the demonic Morella in life, soon dotes on the child, this weird issue of their mysterious conjunction. As strange as the child's birth may be, it is nothing compared to her phenomenal growth, for she grows almost overnight from infant to grown child; finally the narrator realizes that he must have this superannuated baby baptized before it is too late. He takes his nameless daughter to church and there at the baptismal font hesitates, realizing he has thought of no name.

> What prompted me, then to disturb the memory of the buried dead? What demon urged me to breathe that sound, which, in its very recollection was wont to make ebb the purple blood in torrents from the temples to the heart? What fiend spoke from the recesses of my soul, when, amid whose dim aisles, and in the silence of the night, I whispered within the ears of the holy man the syllables—Morella? What more than fiend convulsed the features of my child, and overspread them with hues of death, as starting at that scarcely audible sound, she turned her glassy eyes from the earth to heaven, and, falling prostrate on the black slabs of our ancestral vault, responded—"I am here!" (p. 95)

When he later takes the body of his daughter, who has presumably died of shock, to be interred in her mother's tomb, he finds there are no traces of his late wife. Presumably she has left her body to successfully reincarnate herself into the child's form, but we are never assured that this is so. We are left here, as elsewhere, unsure of resolution, wondering if indeed a page has been left out.

Lee J. Richmond correctly calls Morella a "vampire of volition," for she does indeed "live off" the narrator's energy like a parasite.[34] But what Professor Richmond does not comment on is that as with *Berenice* a month earlier and with *Ligeia* a few years later, Poe is using the vampire metaphor to describe an aspect of human interaction. The story is about the disintegration of consciousness as one partner attempts to consume and control the other. What happens in *Morella* parodies Christian transubstantiation, for Morella transubstantiates herself by consuming the will or metaphorical blood or metaphorical semen of her devotee. The narrator is, as he says, her "pupil," and she does indeed introduce him to "worlds unknown" but in the process she uses him most dreadfully. He is an addictive drug to her, and she will never be satisfied until she uses him up. It is by the loss of his spirit that her spirit prevails, almost but not quite until the end. Then somehow the mention of the name both revives and destroys her, and Poe's interest wanes. He is unconcerned with detailing the narrator's fate. The story is done. Morella has achieved a life-in-death while forcing the narrator into a death-in-life. Like Keats's knight in *La Belle Dame sans Merci*, we see him at the beginning of the story as he really is at the end, barely able to endure, all but destroyed. Poe, like Coleridge

34. Lee J. Richmond, "Edgar Allan Poe's *Morella*: Vampire of Volition," *Studies in Short Fiction* 9 (1972): 93–94.

and Keats, has used the lamia myth to make his *effect*, and is seemingly unconcerned with describing consequences.

The last of Poe's lamia lovers is the Cinderella sister for which the first two have
been preparing us. Ligeia combines the eerie horror of a toothless, mouldering
Berenice, slowly writhing in the grave, with a more sophisticated demonic Morella
gloating in a life beyond the grave. Once again Poe returns to his trusted form of
untrustworthy narrator and once again the narrator's job is to explain away a strange
energy transfer. This time, however, Poe increases the dramatic tension by having
the narrator become addicted to, or at least claim to be addicted to, opium. It is
only a guise, for, like the narrator in Poe's most complex vampire story, *The Oval
Portrait*, the "drugged" narrator here in *Ligeia* cannot acknowledge his own participation in the gruesome ceremonies of blood.

Ligeia, like her sisters, has by now (September 1838) all the lamia characteristics:
no family, shadowlike moves, marble cold hands, pallid complexion, bewitching
voice, and, before the terrible rapprochement, an emanciated body. In fact, she
even has Berenice's mouth, which the narrator ironically describes:

> I regarded the sweet mouth. Here was indeed the triumph of all things heav-
> enly—the magnificent turn of the short upper lip—the soft, voluptuous slum-
> ber of the under—the dimples which sported, and the color which spoke—the
> teeth glancing back, with a brilliancy almost startling, every ray of the holy
> light which fell upon them in her serene and placid, yet most exultingly ra-
> diant of all smiles. (p. 103)

What the narrator focuses on more than anything else is her overlarge, transfixing
eyes: "Those eyes! those large, those shining, those divine orbs! they become to me
twin stars of Leda, and I to them devoutest of astrologers" (p. 104). All these physical attributes are passed off by the narrator in a good Romantic fashion as the
"addition of strangeness to beauty," but in truth they are precisely the attributes that
should have alerted him, and do alert us, to impending danger. He almost knows
this, but at the instant of enlightenment he is stymied. It is with the eyes that the
lamia entrances the victim, and the narrator, now writing in retrospect, almost
understands their import:

> . . . we often find ourselves *upon the very verge* of remembrance, without
> being able, in the end, to remember. And thus how frequently, in my intense
> scrutiny of Ligeia's eyes, have I felt approaching the full knowledge of their
> expression—felt it approaching—yet not quite be mine—and to at length en-
> tirely depart! (p. 104)

The lovers' battle commences: she first attempts to dominate him; he struggles to
protect himself and then to control her. In this seesawing of internal energies she
occasionally explodes:

> . . . the ever-placid Ligeia, was the most violently a prey to the tumultuous

vultures of stern passion. And of such passion I could form no estimate, save by the miraculous expansion of those eyes which at once so delighted and appalled me—by the almost magical melody, modulation, distinctness and placidity of her very low voice—and by the fierce energy (rendered doubly effective by contrast with her manner of utterance) of the wild words which she habitually uttered. (p. 105)

The dilating eyes, the hypnotizing voice, the strange language, but most importantly, these bursts of energy, all reinforce Poe's recurring metaphor of the lovers as vampires. First one lover is passive while the other attacks, then when the attacker finally thinks the day is won, thinks control and domination is his, the victim regenerates and becomes an attacker—Poe's "Orc cycle" for lovers.

As in *Morella*, the narrator, once he believes he is in control, wishes to consolidate his gains. Ligeia grows ill, and though her eyes still blaze, she is too far gone to revive the struggle. At midnight on her deathbed she asks that her verses be read. As in *The Fall of the House of Usher*, the poem plays a central role in alerting the reader to the real state of affairs, a state of affairs the narrator cannot be trusted to explain, let alone to understand. Her poem describes a heavenly drama with mimes acting out some form of creation story until

> Amid the mimic rout,
> A crawling shape intrude!
> A blood-red thing that writhes from out
> The scenic solitude!
> It writhes!—it writhes!—with mortal pangs
> The mimes become its food,
> And the seraphs sob at vermin fangs
> In human gore imbued.

Ligeia's poem is ostensibly about the "tragedy of man," but it is also her own psychodrama, her realization that she is to be consumed by the bloodsucking love of her husband, yet she is victim of her own awful desires; she has vamped her lover only to have him return to her for sustenance. Their symbiosis has gone awry; the nerves have, in D. H. Lawrence's terms, "vibrated at too high a pitch," and now the shattering is inevitable.

The narrator survives the shattering but enters a state of shock that he never, according to him, completely overcomes. He claims that it is the opium, but by now we know better. Instead he has become addicted to a new state of consciousness, a lust for awful knowledge, a desire not simply to control, but to forever dominate. He has, in a sense, become a sexual being. As is the historical case of the vampire in Romantic literature, the narrator leaves Germany and goes to England where he takes up with a new victim, Lady Rowena Trevanion of Tremaine. Poe, as if he had not given us enough hints, adds this last one, a master stroke, for Coleridge's Geraldine, the first English lamia, was the daughter of Lord Roland de

Vaux of Tryermaine, and lived in the wilds of the Lake District. Here we have Poe's narrator leaving Germany for "an abbey I shall not name, in one of the wildest and least frequented portions of England," quite possibly the Lake District. If so, he has now at last come to the Valhalla of English lamias.

At the abbey in the pentagonal (a favorite shape of sorcerers) bridal chambers, the narrator stalks his new prey. He succeeds, as Lady Rowena, like Ligeia, Morella, and Berenice before her, soon becomes ill and takes to bed. He "nurses" her through uneasy nights until one September she wakes at midnight, and he, to calm her spirits, offers her wine.

> But, as I stepped beneath the light of the censer, two circumstances of a startling nature attracted my attention. I had felt that some palpable although invisible object had passed lightly by my person; and I saw that there lay upon the golden carpet, in the very middle of the rich lustre thrown from the censer, a shadow—a faint, indefinite shadow of angelic aspect—such as might be fancied for the shadow of a shade. But I was wild with the excitement of an immoderate dose of opium, and heeded these things but little, nor spoke of them to Rowena. (p. 111)

The second event is indeed interesting, as the whole scene is so reminiscent of Christabel's "wedding" night. Like Geraldine in Christabel's bedchamber where she spies the carved figure of an angel, the narrator is weakened by seeing shadows of some angelic sculpture cast on the floor. For both these vampires cannot endure the sight of Christian symbols and visibly weaken. The narrator revives, takes the wine to his Rowena, and there, by her side, sees or as he says, "dreams" that he saw, drops of a blood-like liquid fall into the glass. Rowena drinks, and a few days later, exhausted, she dies—or rather she seems to die. Actually, like Morella being reanimated through the body of her child, it is Ligeia who now forces her way through the dying body of Rowena. The narrator rushes to the metamorphosing Rowena just in time to see Ligeia's large black eyes open where Rowena's smaller ones had been. Ligeia has returned from the dead; the lovers' game is almost over.

Once again Poe, having exploited the moment of utmost effect, is content to leave us stranded before resolution. How has Ligeia performed this feat? What will she do now? How has the narrator escaped her vengeance to tell her story? Did these events actually occur or are they all parts of his drugged imagination? These questions are simply left unanswered, for Poe wants to explain the dynamics of personal relationships, not to describe ultimate consequences. Like a magician he pulls the rabbit out of the hat, but what happens to the rabbit after the trick is anyone's guess. To get the rabbit out, or in this case to show Ligeia's ability to escape death, Poe has first to get us to accept the validity of the lamia myth, if only as supposition. He is not saying people really act this way; rather, he is saying that their actions may be understood through this analogy. It is not that Ligeia is a vampire any more than Morella was a vampire; rather it is that she acts *as if* she were such a blood-sucking fiend who could, if only *we* would suspend our disbelief, perform such a metempsychosis. Again like Coleridge and Keats, Poe is primarily interested in explaining how people act, and the vampirism is only a metaphor, albeit an incredibly bold one, to explain an aspect of this process. Poe's lamias, Berenice, Morella, and Ligeia, join the Romantic sorority that already includes Coleridge's Geraldine and Keats's La Belle Dame and Lamia, prefiguring the later lamias of LeFanu, Stoker, and D. H. Lawrence. Poe used the vampire myth later in *The Fall of the House of Usher* and *The Oval Portrait*, but the emphasis changed from describing lovers at war to explaining the relationship between siblings or between art and life. But before discussing them, we must turn first to the only lamia created by a female artist, for it shows among other things how malleable this creature could be, depending on conscious artistic concerns as well as subconscious psychological ones. When the lamia is created by a female artist, she is still dramatically sexual, not as the seductress who takes the young male protagonist into unknown worlds, but rather as the demonic "other woman" who deprives the young woman of her man. She is a hazard, an impediment that must be removed, before the heroine can find happiness.

As one might imagine, this kind of woman in literature has recently become a subject of considerable interest. In essence the problem to be addressed is this: could the myth of the femme fatale represent a sublimated male desire to deprive the woman of her sexuality and thus make her subservient to his will? For the femme fatale is wonderfully attractive, to be sure, but she is not the kind to be taken home, and not the type to be entertained for long. She can castrate as well as seduce. She is no "lady," not because she is immoral, but because she is too powerful, too threatening to the male ego. Hence she can only be an "object" of male fantasy, not of reality. When she is presented by the female, however, she becomes an object of jealousy, of spite and scorn, for she epitomizes the fears of displacement.

In this context Bertha Rochester, the crazed and sequestered wife who is the legal impediment to the marriage (and hence Victorian happiness) of Mr. Rochester and Miss Eyre, has of late been treated by many feminist critics as the personification of "animal aspects of womanhood," "Jane's secret self," "the suppressed id," "a dark double," "the unsocialized female," "a pariah among the sisterhood," in short a social and psychological stigmata.[35] The gist of many of these modern arguments is

35. Although I realize it may be unfair to link all these recent critical interpretations under the shibboleth of "feminist criticism," they do share a view of Charlotte Brontë as a social critic, more specifically as an interpreter of class and sex oppression. With regard to Bertha Rochester, see Adrienne Rich, "Jane Eyre: The Temptations of a Motherless Woman," *Ms.* 2 (Oct. 1973): 68–72, 98, 106–7, who argues that Bertha is locked up for the very sins that Rochester himself prates, namely his sexuality; Judith Weissman, "Women and Vampires: *Dracula* as a Victorian Novel," *The Midwest Quarterly: A Journal of Contemporary Thought* 18 (July 1977): 392–405, who claims that Bertha is the only violently sexual woman in Victorian literature, and that "her sexuality has cost her her humanity in Rochester's eyes." She continues by arguing that Bertha deserves pity, not scorn, and that Jane should have spurned Rochester for the way he treated another woman. Other interpretations of Bertha, less "feminist" but still concerned with her social or metaphorical role, can be found in Richard Chase, "The Brontës or Myth Domesticated," *Forms of Modern Fiction*, ed. William Van O'Connor (Minneapolis: University of Min-

that Bertha represents those female traits that can be accepted in fantasy but not in a male-dominated society; hence she must be "tamed," controlled, incarcerated, considered mad, anything to remove her from infecting others in the sorority. And of course those traits that made her so "dangerous" to Jane Eyre and to Victorian society are predominantly sexual. For here is a woman who cannot sublimate her wild desires; here is a woman who gives play to her bestial lusts; here is a woman who can make men afraid. So like the host of other "bad" women in nineteenth-century literature such as Anna Karenina, Madame Bovary, Sister Carrie, Hetty Sorrell, and Tess of the D'Urbervilles she must be "sent to her room" by the man until she can learn to "suffer and be still," or at least control her lusts. More important to the feminine consciousness, however, is not that she is a carnal woman, but that her mere presence prohibits other females access to the male. Bertha may be a beast to Rochester but she is a demon to Jane. She never attacks Jane, but it is clear that Jane also suffers by Bertha's existence.

To Jane Eyre, Bertha Rochester is a vampire—well, almost a vampire. This is astonishing because although we might accept that her personality is vampiric, that is to say she is a psychosexual cannibal living off the energies of others, it violates our expectations of verisimilitude to contend that Bertha Rochester is not meta-phorically, but almost actually, a vampire. If we don't believe Bertha is such (at least to Jane), we have only to listen to Jane herself. Two nights before her wedding day Jane has two understandable anxiety dreams as well as an experience that seemed dreamlike but which actually happened. She later explains to Rochester that as she woke from her uneasy dreams, she heard a rustling in the closet, looked up to see a phantasmic creature handling her wedding veil, the symbol of Jane's conjugal future. Rochester asks for a description of this dreamlike visitor and Jane obliges:

> "O, sir, I never saw a face like it! It was a savage face. I wish I could forget the roll of the red eyes and the fearful blackened inflation of the lineaments!"
> "Ghosts are usually pale, Jane."
> "This, sir, was purple: the lips were swelled and dark; the brow furrowed;

nesota Press, 1948), pp. 102–19, where she is considered as the "woman who has given herself blindly and uncompromisingly to the principle of sex"; Peter Grudin, "Jane and the Other Mrs. Rochester: Excess and Restraint in *Jane Eyre*," *Novel: A Forum on Fiction* 10 (Winter 1977): 145–57, sees Bertha as representing what happens "when a woman moves beyond the parameters society has established for sexual behavior"; Helen Moglen, *Charlotte Brontë: The Self Conceived* (New York: W. W. Norton, 1976), pp. 124–30, considers her "the monstrous embodiment of psychosexual conflicts which are in-trinsic to the romantic predicament"; Barbara Hill Rigney, *Madness and Sexual Politics in the Feminist Novel* (Madison, Wisc.: The University of Wisconsin Press, 1978), believes Bertha represents "a distorted mirror image of Jane's own dangerous propensities toward 'passion'"; Sandra M. Gilbert, "Plain Jane's Progress," *Signs: Journal of Women in Culture and Society* 2 (Summer 1977): 779–804, sees her as "Jane's dark double . . . an agent of Jane's desire" as well as a "monitory image" and Elaine Showalter, *A Literature of Their Own* (Princeton, N.J.: Princeton University Press, 1977), pp. 118–21, claims Bertha is "the incarnation of the flesh, of female sexuality in its most irredeemably bestial and terrifying form." If you go back twenty years or so in criticism you will find Bertha treated as a projection of Rochester, not Jane. Times change.

the black eye-brows wildly raised over the bloodshot eyes. Shall I tell you of what it reminded me?"

"You may."

"Of the foul German spectre—the Vampyre."[36]

Note that Jane does not say that the creature was a vampire; that would have made the novel startlingly Gothic, and in doing so make the plight of the protagonist far less credible and sympathetic. Note also that this fiend is like "the foul German spectre—the Vampyre," almost as if to say that such a thing may menace the Continent but surely never appears on English soil. So the upstairs monster is not, at least not yet in the story, an actual practicing vampire, but already she comes close. As the novel settles in the reader's mind, however, the difference between actual and analogous becomes less and less distinct, as it does to Jane herself.

Bertha Rochester comes so close to being purely mythic (a projection, if you will, of the protagonist's own sublimated sexuality) because Jane Eyre herself is someone who is very alert and susceptible to the Gothic ethos. Jane, who is after all telling us the story, is acutely aware of the demons of folklore and is not entirely sure that such creatures do not actually exist. As a young girl locked up in the red-room of Gateshead Hall she has had a wondrously macabre night fantasy full of revenants, ghosts, and demons (chapter 13) that prefigures this very experience before her wedding. She even says as much to Rochester, in explaining her reaction to this night visitant: "I lost consciousness: for the second time in my life—only the second time—I became insensible from terror" (p. 359). Still the "frantic anguish and wild sobs" (p. 16) of the first experience of losing consciousness at Gateshead Hall are nothing compared to this encounter with the specter lady of Thornfield Hall.

We are not at all unprepared for this night marauder because between the seams of the first-person narration we have already garnered considerable information. We know, for instance, that there is a strange creature with a "preternatural laugh" (pp. 130, 133), living in the "leads" or under the roof of the old hall, and although Mrs. Fairfax may pass her off as Grace Poole, it is a deception that does not fool us for long.[37] For soon the same creature with the "goblin-laughter" (p. 182) has attacked Mr. Rochester and attempted to set him aflame. Even at this point Jane Eyre somewhat naïvely still believes that Grace Poole is responsible, which may be understandable because the man she loves is telling her so. But our credulity has been overstrained. Admittedly this is the expected result of the first-person narra-

36. Charlotte Brontë, *Jane Eyre, An Autobiography*, ed. Jane Jack and Margaret Smith (Oxford: Clarendon, 1969), p. 358. All subsequent references to the novel are to this edition and will appear in parentheses within the text. References to chapters follow the three-volume format of this (and the first) edition.

37. I'm not sure what to make of this, but I think it is interesting that in our culture vampires are creatures of the cellar; they inhabit the lowest level of the haunted world, while ghosts inhabit the attics. This was not always so; for instance, the 1847 *Varney the Vampyre* is often an attic demon. Perhaps it is the considerable influence of Bram Stoker's *Dracula*, or just that the vampire sleeps in the earth that has made him happiest when he is "downstairs."

tion: there should be dramatic irony generated by the narrator's seeming naïveté, but Jane's gullibility seems a little excessive.

The tension between what we know and what Jane does not know reaches an almost unsupportable climax by the middle of the Thornfield Hall section of the book, for in chapter 5 of book 2 (chapter 20 in modern versions) Bertha Rochester makes her vampiric attack not by returning to her husband but by attacking her nearest blood kin, Mr. Richard Mason. Jane tells us all from her limited point of view. One night (a full moon, incidentally) Jane is awakened by the same scream she had earlier heard, except that this time it clearly comes from above. The house-guests all flutter into the halls and are soon calmed by Rochester, who asks Jane if she will accompany him up the stairs. "You don't turn sick at the sight of blood?" he asks (p. 261), and when she says no she is taken upstairs into the heart of dark-ness. Like the uninitiated virgin, she is led into experience, into the windowless room in which unimaginable and unspeakable acts have occurred. There in the shadows she sees Mr. Mason nursing his mangled neck and shoulder, while nearby the hideous form of a snarling beast cringes in the corner (p. 264). As the local doctor reports, these flesh wounds Mason has suffered were not inflicted with a knife but rather with teeth, the teeth of this hideous wolf-woman. Jane may have been psychologically prepared to accept earlier gothic incongruities, but this is a most shocking and surreal scene. She is literally dumbfounded by it, and we are too. The boundary between Realism and Gothicism has been crossed; the world of "polite" fiction is irretrievably over.

As if to make sure we do not pass by the vampire nature of this she-beast, Char-lotte Brontë has Rochester warn the doctor to make sure Mason is soon spirited out of the county before another full-mooned night has passed. "Hurry! hurry! The sun will soon rise, and I must have him off," and Mason, also dumbstruck, can only mutter, "She sucked my blood: she said she'd drain my heart" (p. 267). Rochester gives Mason a phial of some mysterious potion (that makes no sense in terms of the vampire myth) and sends him off into the rising sun and safety. Jane is still under-standably confused as to the nature of this attic beast, and when again queried, Rochester responds in the best tradition of the schauerroman that there is no reason for a young girl to fret, all danger is past. When she next asks if she may be of future service to him, Rochester answers only that she will be able to aid him the night before his marriage; for on that night, he darkly implies, this kind of trouble may recur. Such foreshadowing may be missed by the naïve Jane, but not by us. For it is during the night before his wedding that the upstairs demon again returns downstairs.

Two nights before Jane's wedding to Rochester she is understandably nervous and restless. Wandering through the orchard, she comes upon the cloven trunk of a chestnut tree. Standing before this wonderfully apt image of blasted unity, she sees suddenly "the moon appear momentarily in that part of the sky which filled their fissure; her disk was blood-red and half overcast: she seemed to throw on me one bewildered, dreary glance, and buried herself again instantly in the deep drift of cloud" (p. 349). Although Jane tries to cast aside this "evil presentiment" (p. 350), it is nonetheless there and is indeed an accurate foreboding of what is to come. For the next night, that very night Jane had promised that she would sit up with Rochester to protect him from the menace upstairs, she slackens in her task, falls asleep, and dreams again of being abandoned by her future husband and of the demise of Thornfield Hall.

These dreams are only a calm prelude to the central terror of the book, a terror that so much of the previous action from the red-room at Gateshead Hall onward has been preparing us for. No longer are diabolical forces directed at others; now they converge on our heroine. In what seems a waking dream Jane is visited by the horrible woman, "a woman, tall and large, with thick and dark hair hanging long down her back. I know not what dress she had on; it was white and straight; but whether gown, sheet, or shroud, I cannot tell" (p. 350). This woman does not attack Jane as she had attacked Rochester and Mason, but rather only rends the wedding veil, the "princely extravagance" that Jane had specifically ordered from London. The metaphorical significance of this act is clear enough, but the reappearance of this night-monster is not. Jane tells all to Rochester, and then understandably asks for an explanation. He answers, again in the best tradition of Mrs. Radcliffe, and others, that the vision that has so terrified Jane is nothing more than the creation of her "overstimulated brain" (p. 359). Although this answer might well have satisfied an eighteenth-century ingenue, it simply will not do for this "modern" woman. Jane forces him: explain that "awful visitant," she demands, but still he hedges: "Jane, it must have been unreal" (p. 359). Finally, and this is only after Jane has produced the corpus delicti, the torn veil, does Rochester become specific. The woman was Grace Poole, he says, and Jane simply made up all the goblin nonsense, the disheveled hair and fiery eyes. He concludes: "I see you would ask why I keep such a woman in my house: when we have been married a year and a day, I will tell you; but not now. Are you satisfied, Jane? Do you accept my solution of the mystery?" (p. 360). This solution satisfies no one, neither Jane nor us.

Thankfully, however, we will not have to wait out the entire year and a day for "curiosity," as Rochester calls it, to be allayed—we need only wait a few hours. For Rochester, in order to explain the extenuating circumstances of what would legally be bigamy, leads the procession of invited and uninvited wedding guests upstairs. Once again Jane also goes. There in a windowless room behind the tapestries we see how correct Jane's earlier assessment of the upstairs horror was.

In the deep shade, at the further end of the room, a figure ran backwards and forwards. What *it* was, whether beast or human being, one could not, at first sight, tell: *it* grovelled, seemingly, on all fours; *it* snatched and growled like some strange wild animal: but *it* was covered with clothing; and a quantity of dark, grizzled hair, wild as a mane, hid *its* head and face. (Italics mine) (p. 370)

At last we learn that this wolf-woman is not, as Jane has earlier said, "like" the "foul German spectre—the Vampyre"; to Jane, at least, this beast *is* a vampire, an "*it*." We need wait only a minute to see this:

> The maniac bellowed: she parted her shaggy locks from her visage, and gazed wildly at her visitors. I recognised well that purple face,—those bloated features. Mrs. Poole advanced.
>
> "Keep out of the way," said Mr. Rochester, thrusting her aside: "she has no knife now, I suppose? and I'm on my guard."
>
> "One never knows what she has, sir; she is so cunning: it is not in mortal discretion to fathom her craft."
>
> "We had better leave her," whispered Mason.
>
> "Go to the devil!" was his brother-in-law's recommendation.
>
> "'Ware!" cried Grace. The three gentlemen retreated simultaneously. Mr. Rochester flung me behind him; the lunatic sprang and grappled his throat viciously, and laid her teeth to his cheek: they struggled. . . . At last he mastered her arms; Grace Poole gave him a cord, and he pinioned them behind her: with more rope, which was at hand, he bound her to a chair. The operation was performed amidst the fiercest yells, and the most convulsive plunges. Mr. Rochester then turned to the spectators: he looked at them with a smile both acrid and desolate.
>
> "That is *my wife*," said he. "Such is the sole conjugal embrace I am ever to know—such are the endearments which are to solace my leisure hours!" (pp. 370–71)

This is an incredible scene, for it is the only place in an otherwise believable tale in which the context of verisimilitude is completely wrenched apart. Admittedly we have been prepared, prepared by the narrator's earlier acknowledgment in the red-room of a darker side of reality, prepared by the foreshadowing symbols of the dream, by the blasted tree, by the eerie night storm, as well as by the previous nocturnal attacks in Thornfield Hall. But still here we have been moved completely through the aesthetic tangle from Realism into the Gothic, and we are shocked. No matter how quickly we may retrace our steps back to the relative safety of Romance, we will never be quite the same. Wisely Bertha Rochester is quickly removed from our closer consideration; she is resequestered, safely packed away and distanced from the reader. Not only must we get on with the heroine's story, we must also regain our aesthetic balance. We will not see Bertha again; we will only hear about her fiery demise from the safely removed vantage point of an addle-pated innkeeper. Still there is no doubt we are fascinated by her, and not a little disappointed not to learn more.

Why is Bertha there? What is this weird woman doing in a serious novel? Does Bertha simply play a cameo role, passing by only to tantalize us, or does she have some more dynamic purpose in the rhetorical pattern? Is she the dea ex machina who prohibits Jane and Rochester from union, thereby necessitating the otherwise flaccid Moor House episodes, or is her role more central to Jane's maturation? To understand possible answers to these questions we need to first set the vampire back into its mid-nineteenth-century context, especially as he must have been perceived by the Brontë sisters at Haworth Parsonage.

Near the end of *Wuthering Heights* (a work that shares with *Jane Eyre* not just the same publication date, but such similar characters, themes, and images that they are often treated together), Nelly Dean muses about Heathcliff. She remembers his seemingly demonic powers, the strange facts of his arrival at Wuthering Heights, his occasionally fiendish behavior, and most of all the rare intensity of his love for Catherine. We too may recall how their love energized both of them to such an extent that without Catherine, Heathcliff seems to deteriorate, how he twice digs down to be with her corpse and how towards the end he almost starves himself to death. All this and more—his glistening teeth, his nocturnal wanderings, his capacity to enervate both Lintons and Earnshaws—conspire to have Nelly, at least, ask the question, "Is he a ghoul or a vampire?"[38]

Of course Heathcliff was no vampire, and if anything this conjecture tells us more about Nelly than about anyone else. Still Heathcliff does have certain indisputable vampiric or simply gothic, if you will, characteristics, and these characteristics reaffirm and inform the central event in the novel, the supernatural quality of his misguided and misunderstood love for Catherine.

If Heathcliff acts *as if* he were a vampire it is because his behavior could not be explained in any other way—at least not to Nelly Dean. Could the same be true of Bertha Rochester, except that with Bertha the vampiric outline is clearer than the human one? She is more monster than mortal: she is almost pure gothic. She is a vampire to Jane. Her characterization poses one of the major technical problems in the book because once introduced, Bertha cannot easily be spirited away like a Blanche Ingram. A novel is not a poem; plots cannot be left incomplete. It is clear that Charlotte Brontë does not know what to do with Bertha. A century ago Leslie Stephen precisely isolated this dilemma: "What would Jane Eyre have done, and what would our sympathies have been, had she found that Mrs. Rochester had not been burnt in the fire at Thornfield? This is a rather awkward question."[39] Awkward indeed, and a central one for both the critic and the reader. Charlotte Brontë is clearly in a bind about how to dispatch Bertha. On one hand, Bertha stands between Jane and happiness, between Jane and the man she loves, between Jane and the future. As long as Bertha is, Jane cannot be.

We must remember that to all the other characters Bertha is simply a crazy woman to be restrained: to Grace Poole, to Rochester, to the doctor, even to her brother, Bertha is berserk. But to Jane Eyre, Bertha is surreal—a force, a powerful, libidinal, uncensored, maniacal, unpredictable passion—a vampire. Jane intui-

38. Emily Brontë, *Wuthering Heights* (1847; rpt. Boston: Houghton Mifflin, 1956), p. 280. I will discuss Heathcliff in chap. 4.

39. Leslie Stephen, "On Charlotte Brontë," *The Cornhill Magazine* (Dec. 1977): 723–29; rpt. in *The Brontës: The Critical Heritage*, ed. Miriam Allot (London: Routledge and Kegan Paul, 1974), pp. 413–23, 421.

tively understands that Bertha's real victim is not the menfolk, but Jane herself. Bertha does not have to attack Jane; all she has to do is continue snarling about in the attic. In the short run Bertha is victorious; Jane has to leave.

The friction generated between the oppositions of actual and symbolic, real and surreal, leads Charlotte Brontë into writing what Robert E. Heilman has called the "new Gothic."[40] Instilling terror is not enough; there must be insight into character. Charlotte Brontë generates this tension by consciously building the myth, then undermining it. So she provides Bertha with a Creole ancestry, a keeper in the personage of Grace Poole, even a knife, all things that work against the mythic stereotype and make Bertha human, while at the same time she has this same character perform the requisite acts of vampiric possession, at least as perceived by Jane.

How to destroy this character must have been perplexing because Bertha cannot be plotted out of the novel in any usual way. This is very much the same problem her sister was facing in *Wuthering Heights*. Bertha (or Heathcliff for that matter) cannot voluntarily withdraw; that would be counter to the demands of both character and vampire myth. Bertha cannot conveniently die; the myth precludes this escape. She must therefore be destroyed by authorial fiat. And indeed she is. Charlotte Brontë performs this coup de grâce by having Bertha consumed in the acceptable vampire manner, by a fiery leap.[41] It is an action sufficiently removed from the story line for us to let it pass by unexamined: two years after Bertha's self-destruction Jane hears third-hand of what happened two months after her departure from Thornfield Hall. (Has there ever been any other central event in fiction more coddled in narrative and temporal distance?) In any case Jane intuitively recognizes that the way to Rochester is clear, and so with Bertha conveniently removed the story can now continue.

This characterization by Charlotte Brontë of Bertha Rochester is indeed masterful—almost as inimitable as her sister's Heathcliff. She has made a character both literal and figurative, actual and symbolic, and in so doing has introduced poetic dimension into the supposedly "real" world of prose fiction. For indeed Bertha is more like her vampiric predecessors in Romantic poetry (Coleridge's Geraldine and Keats's Lamia) than her descendants in Victorian prose (LeFanu's Carmilla and Stoker's Dracula women)—an extraordinary hybrid of poetic symbolism and human character. If we ever wonder about the potency of the female vampire to the adolescent male consciousness, we need only be reminded how the same character is cast by the female. To the male she may well be a masturbatory fantasy—voluptuous, enthralling, dangerous, enervating; but to the female she is cruel, demonic, selfish, and hideous.

40. Robert B. Heilman, "Charlotte Brontë's 'New' Gothic," *From Jane Austen to Joseph Conrad*, ed. Robert C. Rathburn and Martin Steinman, Jr. (Minneapolis: University of Minnesota Press, 1958), pp. 118–32.

41. Staking (actually called "transfixation" by the Catholic church) is a relatively recent method of vampire killing and currently the most popular, at least in the cinema. The more usual method of vampire disposal was decapitation and then burning. Charlotte Brontë has thankfully spared us the former, but the death by fire is maintained as well as the addition of the suicidal jump.

3. The Male Vampire in Poetry

To me, who with eternal famine pine,
Alike is Hell, or Paradise, or Heaven,
There best where most with ravin I may meet:
Which here, though plenteous, all too little seems
To stuff this maw, this vast unhidebound corpse.

—*Paradise Lost*, X, 597–601

One of the unusual aspects of English Romanticism is that so many of its artistic achievements resulted not from an individual artist's careful deliberations, but rather from a series of partially planned encounters between the major figures. The most famous of these meetings was of course when in 1796 Wordsworth moved to Alfoxden to work with Coleridge in "find[ing] religious forms in nature." The fruitful cross-pollination of these fertile minds led to the germination of the *Lyrical Ballads*. But if this lucky happenstance was a turning point for the first generation of English Romantics, then rivaling it in interest, though of less literary importance, was an equally fateful meeting in June 1816. For in that year Byron, Shelley, Mary Shelley, Claire Clairmont, and John Polidori (Byron's personal physician) all decided to write Gothic tales, and their results produced the two Romantic monsters that still haunt our popular culture, the Frankenstein monster and the vampire.

Although I will discuss the events of that productive summer at the beginning of the next chapter, we should realize that the first really distinguishable male vampire appeared in John Polidori's *The Vampyre* (1819) and was the indirect result of Byron's attempt to write a horror story. I mention this now because the works I'm about to discuss all occurred within a few years of one another—*Manfred* in 1817, *The Cenci* between 1818 and 1819, *The Eve of St. Agnes* in 1819—and although none of the protagonists in these works is a vampire, each has traits that suggest a growing artistic concern with the demonic and perhaps vampiric. In the characterizations of Manfred, Cenci, and Porphyro we may find insights into one of the major changes within Romanticism itself—the growing disillusionment with earlier ideals of heroic manhood and the growth of negative Romanticism that presaged so much of what would make up the divided character of the Victorian temper.[1]

---

1. Morse Peckham, "Toward a Theory of Romanticism," *PMLA* 66 (1951): 5–23, has detailed this kind of negative Romantic protagonist "who is filled with guilt, despair, and cosmic and social alienation.

The male vampire certainly should have been a most attractive demon to the second generation of Romantics, for here was the personification of a most peculiar kind of exiled man, eternally outcast yet dependent on others, a lover yet incapable of loving, a superman yet a pathetic weakling, a Napoleon among men. Here was the gothic Don Juan, Milton's Satan reborn, the Romantic artist himself. Here was, in fact, the psychic vampire, whose needs of self-perpetuation depended on the destruction of others. True, Southey had used the vampire myth in *Thalaba the Destroyer*; Coleridge had used the lamia in *Christabel*; and perhaps even Wordsworth had implied vampirism in *The Leech Gatherer*; but it was really Lord Byron (admittedly via Polidori) who first emphasized the masculine and demonic side of the myth—the metamorphosis of Faust, the solipsist gone awry. To a considerable extent the myth's currency is a tribute to this one man, for not only was Byron one of the first to think seriously about telling a vampire story, he also constructed the skeleton that would support the vampire in its many reincarnations. By the early nineteenth century the Byronic Hero already had many of the mythic qualities of the vampire: here was the melancholy libertine in the open shirt, the nocturnal lover and destroyer, the maudlin, self-pitying, and moody titan, only a few years away from Nietzsche's Superman.

Although Mario Praz was the first to contend that without the Byronic Hero the vampire might never have become elevated into a serious subject, his next assertion, that the Byronic Hero led to the proliferation of vampiric demons in nineteenth-century literature, is by no means unchallenged.[2] The most knowledgeable rebuttal has come from Peter Thorslev:

> Finally, Praz maintains that for the fashion of vampirism, too, "Byron was largely responsible," and, sure enough, a few pages later the Byronic Hero has an added attribute, and we read of "the vampire loves of the Byronic Fatal Man." This attribute Praz bases on a passing reference in one poem and on the fragment of a ghost story written as a joke. The passing reference to vampirism in *The Giaour* (755 ff) is part of a Mohammedan curse on the hero, complete with references to his wife and daughter (when so far as the poem shows, he has neither); Byron obviously intended the curse as a bit of "local color," and there is no evidence whatsoever that the passage became at all notorious in Byron's time. . . . For the most part the Byronic Hero was a typical romantic lover, and nowhere in all of the poems is he referred to either literally or figuratively as a vampire-lover.[3]

Not only has Thorslev misread Byron's *Giaour* and his "Fragment of a Novel," but he has also overlooked Byron's use of vampirism in the characterization of some of his major protagonists. Although Praz points to the Giaour, the Corsair, Conrad,

---

They are often presented as having committed some horrible and unmentionable and unmentioned crime in the past. They are often outcasts from men and God, and they are almost always wanderers over the face of the earth." It is from this stock that the vampire descends.

2. Mario Praz, *The Romantic Agony* (1933 rpt; London: Oxford University Press, 1970), chap. 2.

3. Peter L. Thorslev, *The Byronic Hero* (Minneapolis: University of Minnesota Press, 1962), p. 9.

and Lara as being Byronic Heroes who share with the vampire a love of darkness, hypnotic eyes, an obsession with the destructive side of love, sneering smiles, and quivering lips, I should like to concentrate on the figure Thorslev himself considers the most Byronic, Count Manfred.

The first three acts of *Manfred* we know were written at the Villa Diodati during the summer of 1816 just after the famous pact to produce a horror story. In no way do I wish to imply that *Manfred* was Byron's attempt at such a horror story, only that he was discussing vampires with Shelley and presumably also with Polidori. Much of the vampirism in the drama dovetails with the more sensational motif of incest. Yet these hints of incest have understandably been emphasized in the numerous biographically based interpretations of the poem as Byron's sordid confessions. Admittedly with Byron the biographical fallacy is an occupational hazard, but *Manfred* also can be understood simply as a Gothic drama, a melodrama in which a pathetically strong man is doomed *not* to die, but rather, like the vampire, to live.

Manfred is the Byronic Hero par excellence. He is alone in exile, more powerful than other men, yet blighted by that power. He has done some terrible nameless deed, and now wishes only forgetfulness, release, escape, death. The drama depicts a number of attempts by both the protagonist and others to find this release. First, he calls on the spirits of nature, but they can provide no palliative: in fact, the seventh spirit appears as an apparition of his beloved, asserting that he will find no release, rather that he will continue to live on, becoming "his own proper hell" (I, i, 252). Next he plans suicide by leaping from the mountaintop, but is foiled by the Chamois Hunter, the first of a number of characters whose role in the drama is to counterpoint Manfred. The Chamois Hunter leads Manfred back from the precipice to his home, where he offers him a draught of red wine. It is here that we first get some indication of Manfred's sin, for as the Chamois Hunter offers his guest the glass of wine, Manfred reacts:

> *Manfred.* Away, away! there's blood upon the brim!
> Will it then never—never sink in the earth?
>   *Chamois Hunter.* What dost thou mean? thy senses wander from thee.
>   *Man.* I say 'tis blood—my blood! the pure warm stream
> Which ran in the veins of my fathers, and in ours
> When we were in our youth, and had one heart,
> And loved each other as we should not love,
> And this was shed: but still it rises up,
> Coloring the clouds, that shut me out from heaven,
> Where thou art not—and I shall never be.   (II, i, 21–30)

Biographical critics, especially in the nineteenth century, have no trouble with these lines. They are Byron's thinly disguised references to his famous assertions that he had had incestuous relations with his half-sister Augusta Leigh. The blood here must refer to the hymeneal blood, and so the sin that Manfred is unable to forget is this defilement, this incest. But why have him drinking the blood? Couldn't Byron also be experimenting with the superstition that the vampire not only drinks blood, but also that his first victims are those he has most dearly loved, in this case his half-sister? And so the drinking of blood here metaphorically repeats what was once actual. The incest and vampire motifs are not mutually exclusive; rather, they seem complementary.

Act II continues with Manfred's pursuit of release, of forgetfulness. Like a good Romantic poet he goes to the forces of Nature for help, here personified in the form of the Witch of the Alps. But Byron, the Neoclassicist, is not about to have his Romantic hero so easily relieved. When the Witch of the Alps asks the same questions that we, the readers, are also eager to ask—namely "What's really the matter with you, Manfred?"—he replies only by defining himself once again:

> From my youth upwards
> My spirit walked not with the souls of men,
> Nor looked upon the earth with human eyes;
> The thirst of their ambition was not mine,
> The aim of their existence was not mine;
> The joys, my griefs, my passions, and my powers,
> Made me a stranger; though I wore the form
> I had no sympathy with breathing flesh,
> Nor midst the creatures of clay that girded me
> Was there but one who—but of her anon.   (II, ii, 50–59)

We needn't wait long to find out more about "her." For fifty lines later we are told that "she" was just like Manfred in thought, appearance, and deed, but Manfred destroyed her. "How have you destroyed her?" queries the witch, "With your hand?" Manfred replies:

> *Man.* Not with my hand, but heart—which broke her heart;
> It gazed on mine, and withered. I have shed
> Blood, but not hers—and yet her blood was shed;
> I saw—and could not stanch it.   (II, ii, 118–22)

Once again, biographical critics would assert that this blood must be a metaphor for Augusta Leigh's maidenhead, neglecting to note, it should be added, that at the time any sexual relations with Byron could have occurred Augusta was no longer a virgin. But no matter; once again, I would not deny this interpretation's validity, but I would like to suggest that Byron may also be discussing the relationship between Manfred and his ill-starred love in psychological terms, using the image of blood as a metaphor of energy. Blood defilement is the central term coupling incest and vampirism. Manfred is a superhuman man, a man who has been unaccustomed to dealing with mere mortals, yet he has fallen in love with a woman who, although she resembles him, still cannot absorb his terrific power. He has been so intense that he has, as he himself implies, drained her of vitality so that she could live no longer. Incest has become vampiric; he has destroyed what he loves best.

When Manfred finally does see her, when he has Astarte summoned from the dead, he must first go into the very center of evil, the court of Arimanes. But Manfred, unlike the traditional vampire, is not a tool of the devil; he is possessed, but not with Satan so much as with knowledge. He is a most Faustian of vampires. Arimanes first demands that Manfred pledge himself to evil before the uncharnel-ing of Astarte, but Manfred refuses, and Arimanes gives in. When his henchman Nemesis asks, "Who would you uncharnel?" Manfred replies, "One without a tomb—call up Astarte" (III, iv, 85–86). Immediately Astarte, a spirit who has never been completely able to leave her body since being "loved" by Manfred, appears. Manfred begs forgiveness, but she will not speak. He asks again, but she only says "Farewell" and disappears. All we ever know about their strange relationship is that he has done something terrible to her that has made her unable to die completely and for which she is unwilling to forgive him.

It seems only fair that since the Chamois Hunter (representing society) and the Witch of the Alps (representing nature) have tried to convert Manfred, the abbot (representing the church) be given a chance. After all, the church historically was the institution that knew best how to give all sinners, even vampires, final peace and release. But even though the abbot of St. Maurice attempts to reconcile Manfred with the church, Manfred will have none of it. He is not, and Byron stresses this repeatedly as if he knew how his hero would be interpreted, demoni-cally possessed. He is a superhuman man whose powers may cause him to act *like* a vampire, draining the vitality of Astarte and those around him, but he is em-phatically not Satanic. So when the abbot repeatedly pesters him with plans of penitence and pardon, Manfred replies that he belongs only to a special order of mortals who are exempt from the ordinary concerns of mutability. He will die, true, but not from old age; rather, he will burn himself out, exhausting his energy.

This subject of Manfred's death is, of course, central to Byron's handling of the gothic. In the beginning of the play Manfred is denied death; his hope for release is refused by the curse of the Seventh Spirit, and his actual attempt at suicide is thwarted by the Chamois Hunter. But Manfred, like most Byronic Heroes, must finally die, not the victim, but the master of mortality. By the end of Act III he is running out of life and visibly weakening. The abbot, tenacious to the end, is still hoping for a deathbed conversion. Finally the end seems near: there from his mountaintop aerie Manfred looks down to see an awful figure ascending in hell-fire. The abbot assumes, as we do, that this is the Devil come for his due. But again Manfred makes clear that such is not the case. He defies demonic possession here, as he had earlier with Astarte, declaring nobly, "I'll die as I have lived—alone" (III, iv, 90). Still the Spirit persists, sure that anyone who has lived like Manfred must ultimately be demonic. Manfred is obstinate:

> Back to thy hell!
> Thou hast no power upon me, *that* I feel;
> Thou never shalt possess me, *that* I know;
> What I have done is done; I bear within
> A torture which could nothing gain from thine:
> The mind which is immortal makes itself
> Requital for its good or evil thoughts,—
> Is its own origin of ill and end
> And its own place and time. . . .   (III, iv, 124–32)

Here, in this heroic burst, Manfred repels the forces of evil to face death in solitude. At the very end, as death is almost upon him, he whispers to the abbot, "Old man! 'tis not so difficult to die," and then "expires." Byron was justifiably furious when his publisher cut Manfred's last line, for it is central to the way the Byronic Hero must be that he should on one hand suffer the terrible "fatality to live," while on the other be able to accept death unflinchingly.

The vampire myth in *Manfred* is admittedly only a small part of the characterization, and Byron is careful to use it only as an analogy to explain how his hero is simultaneously victimizer and victim. Manfred is so powerful that he acts with ordinary people *as if* he were a vampire, destroying all who come within his orbit, especially women. As Mario Praz pointed out, here we have l'homme fatal, cultural brother to *la belle dame sans merci*, who will reappear again and again in Romantic literature.[4] We needn't look far to find his reappearance, for soon after *Manfred* Shelley wrote his less subtle although psychologically profound variation on the theme, the poetic drama *The Cenci*. Where Byron implies that Manfred's appetites for life are more than ordinary, Shelley makes it clear that Cenci's desires are voracious and brutal. Vampirism that is at most metaphoric and tangential in *Manfred* becomes actual and central in *The Cenci*, and once again it is tied to the more specific theme of incestuous blood defilement.

Shelley was, of course, present in 1816 at the Villa Diodati when the famous bargain was struck to write the horror stories. He doubtless was kept up to date with Byron's progress with his vampire "fragment," but Shelley did not need Byron to introduce him to vampire lore. In fact, of all the poets, Shelley was probably the most knowledgeable about vampire superstitions and stories. We are told by Medwin that as a young man Shelley translated Bürger's "Lenore," which he (as Dowden continues the story) often enjoyed reciting, "working up the horror to such a height of fearful interest" that often his listeners "fully expected to be visited by the Prussian vampire."[5] A later biographer, Charles Middleton, even went so far as to assert that Bürger's poem first kindled the Gothic flame that flared up in Shelley's early

---

4. Praz, *Romantic Agony*, p. 75.

5. Thomas Medwin, *The Life of Percy Bysshe Shelley* (1847; rev. ed., London: Oxford University Press, 1913), 1: 62; and Edward Dowden, *The Life of Percy Bysshe Shelley* (1886; 7th impression, London: Routledge and Kegan Paul, 1954), 2: 123.

poems and adolescent novels.[6] But there was enough general interest in translating the vampire-horror from German literature to English that Shelley was probably reacting more to literary fashion than to any specific work. Oddly enough, although Shelley's original contact with the literary vampire may have been through the German poets, the most important influence in *The Cenci* seems to be Coleridge's *Christabel*. For Coleridge was first to use the myth without all of its popular trappings of blood and horror as a metaphor for interpersonal dynamics, a discussion of human interactions. Coleridge had shown how certain people, especially people in a family unit, gain energy and power by enervating and preying on one another. Shelley was clearly fascinated with this psychological aspect of the myth as he may have been with Byron's development of its more physical aspects in a work such as *Lara* or perhaps even *Manfred*. But to understand Shelley's continuing interest in Coleridge's *Christabel*, we need to recall the events of the summer of 1816.

A month after the fateful June evening when Byron, John Polidori, and Percy and Mary Shelley pledged to write ghost stories there was a soirée in which Byron delighted the same group (now including "Monk" Lewis) by reading the yet-unpublished *Christabel*. They all knew that Geraldine was a female vampire, a lamia: Shelley knew this from his readings of Bürger and Goethe; Byron was certainly aware of it, for he had already incorporated the vampire myth into his incredibly popular *Giaour* (first edition 1813; fourteenth edition 1815!); and the others were probably aware not only of Southey's use of the vampire superstition in *Thalaba the Destroyer*, but more importantly of his elaborate explanatory notes.[7] Polidori relates what happened, taking artistic license to link the July event with the earlier June meeting:

> It appears that one evening Lord B., Mr. P. B. Shelly [*sic*], two ladies and the gentleman before alluded to, after having perused a German work, entitled *Phantasmagoriana*, began relating ghost stories; when his lordship having recited the beginning of "Christabel," then unpublished, the whole took so strong a hold of Mr. Shelly's mind, that he suddenly started up and ran out of the room. The physician and Lord Byron followed, and discovered him leaning against a mantle-piece, with cold drops of perspiration trickling down his face. After having given him something to refresh him, upon enquiring into the cause of his alarm, they found that his wild imagination having pictured to him the bosom of one of the ladies with eyes (which was reported of a lady in the neighbourhood where he lived) he was obliged to leave the room in order to destroy the impression. It was afterwards proposed, in the course of

6. Charles Middleton, *Shelley and His Writings* (London: T. C. Newby, 1858), I, 47. Anthony Masters, in *The Natural History of the Vampire* (London: Mayflower Books, 1972), pp. 198–99, claims that Shelley used to tell a story of how a Turkish Janisary berated a vampire back into his grave, but unfortunately Masters does not document his source. This story is the same one mentioned by Southey in his notes to stanzas 8–10, book 8 of *Thalaba the Destroyer*.

7. Stanzas 8–10, book 8. Southey quotes at considerable length from a number of vampire stories in his notes. *The Poetical Works of Robert Southey* (London: Longman, Orme, Browne, Greene, and Longmans, 1838), 4: 297–305.

conversation, that each of the company present should write a tale depending upon some supernatural agency, which was undertaken by Lord B., the physician, and one of the ladies before mentioned.[8]

This was not quite the story Mary Shelley told later, but no matter. The salient point is Shelley's awareness of *Christabel* (a month later he will read it out loud to Mary) and the group's continuing interest in creating artistic effects that would make the flesh shiver, the schauerroman.[9]

Terry Otten, in "Christabel, Beatrice and the Encounter with Evil," has already made the case for an important similarity between *Christabel* and *The Cenci* that transcends the fact that they are both genre pieces, both Gothic romances.[10] Otten argues that the poets shared a common view of evil as an external infection easily contracted by the unwary person. As a result, both created works in which evil was developed not in collision with good, but rather in a dialectic encounter. The all-too-innocent heroine meets the all-too-evil antagonist not head-on but tangentially. Clearly both works employ similar Gothic trappings—the morbid, oppressive atmosphere, victimized virgins, sexual violations, actual or displaced father figures— but the one similarity Otten does not discuss is that both antagonists, Geraldine and Count Cenci, are drawn from the same mythic stock—the vampire. In fact, he even goes out of his way not to discuss it: "I have chosen to avoid the complex question of whether Geraldine is a vampire or a lamia figure."[11] This is unfortunate, for the theme Shelley is most concerned with in *The Cenci* is the way evil infects his unsuspecting and hence morally careless heroine. As Shelley had seen in *Christabel*, this process could be accomplished in psychological terms by employing the analogy of the evil vampire who drains the strength of the good, thereby forcing the heroine to rely on desperate means to rectify the situation. Obviously Christabel (at least in the unfinished version that we are left with) never goes as far as Beatrice, but we are given inklings of what is to come. For at the end of part 2 Christabel is starting to metamorphose into a snake (ll. 451, 591), and—at least according to Leoline—her behavior is becoming uncharacteristically assertive and impolite. Her encounter with evil ironically has contaminated her, but it has also initiated her into the actual world where evil must be recognized.

In a sense this is precisely the same problem Shelley was attempting to describe the *The Cenci*. In 1819 he had written *Prometheus Unbound* up through Act III, leaving a regenerated man "pinnacled dim in the intense inane." But was that really man's cosmic position? Was Shelley honestly portraying the battle between good

8. John Polidori, "Extracts of a Letter to the Editor from Geneva," preceding *The Vampyre* as quoted in *Three Gothic Novels*, ed. E. F. Bleiler (New York: Dover, 1966), p. 260. This letter may not have been written by Polidori, but by his publisher Henry Colburn. See Christopher Frayling, "Introduction" to *The Vampyre: A Bedside Companion* (New York: Charles Scribner's Sons, 1978), p. 17.

9. On 26 August 1816 Shelley read the whole of *Christabel* aloud to Mary. F. L. Jones, ed., *Mary Shelley's Journal* (Norman: University of Oklahoma Press, 1947), p. 61.

10. Terry Otten, "Christabel, Beatrice and the Encounter with Evil," *Bucknell Review* 17 (1969): 19–31.

11. Ibid., p. 22, n. 5.

and evil, or was he forcing evil out by fiat at the ultimate expense of good? Exactly how did evil work? It was here that he decided to rework the historical Cenci story, not into a parable of a good-versus-evil dichotomy, but rather as a good-versus-evil dialectic. And to do this he had to add a number of different levels to the inherited Cenci story: the incest, or actual union of good and evil; the ardent Catholicism on the parts of both the Cenci and of Beatrice, to show how the church can be no standard for judgment; and Orsino, the only genuinely conscious evil character, who is too subtle to be destroyed and yet too evil to be overlooked. However, to show the process of evil in operation, to show evil as a communicable disease, as it were, he would need new poetic imagery.

Shelley must have realized the need for new language when he set *Prometheus Unbound* down at the end of Act III, for he wrote in "The Preface" to *The Cenci*:

> I have avoided with great care in writing this play the introduction of what is commonly called mere poetry, and I imagine there will scarcely be found a detached simile or a single isolated description, unless Beatrice's description of the chasm appointed for her father's murder should be judged to be of that nature.
>
> In a dramatic composition the imagery and the passion should interpenetrate one another, the former being reserved simply for the full development and illustration of the latter. Imagination is as the immortal God which should assume flesh for the redemption of mortal passion. It is thus that the most remote and the most familiar imagery may alike be fit for dramatic purposes when employed in the illustration of strong feeling, which raises what is low, and levels to the apprehension that which is lofty, casting over all the shadow of its own greatness. [12]

He continues, asserting that in such a drama "we must use the familiar language of men" so that the widest possible audience will be reached. In this he succeeds; imagery and passion do indeed "interpenetrate one another" in *The Cenci* through the specific image of the vampire.

Stuart Curran, in *Shelley's "Cenci": Scorpions Ringed with Fire*, has already discussed how specific clusters of images reveal a depth of meaning barely suggested by the surface plot. Curran contends that this figurative language is

> an essential organizing principle of drama by which the poet is able to disclose the subtlest nuances of thought. And given the nature of *The Cenci*, where moral ambiguity constantly attends upon the destruction of conventional values and one character after another is compelled toward solipsism, the structural demands on this essential organizing principle are extraordinary, necessitating the creation of intricate metaphorical patterns. [13]

12. "Preface to *The Cenci*," *The Complete Works of Shelley* (Julian edition), ed. Roger Ingpen and Walter E. Peck (New York: Scribner's, 1965), 2: 72.
13. Stuart Curran, *Shelley's "Cenci": Scorpions Ringed with Fire* (Princeton, N.J.: Princeton University Press, 1970), p. 100.

And Curran points to aggregations of images around such subjects as commerce, hunting, darkness, bestiality, and imprisonment to show how this organizing principle operates. But he overlooks an important image cluster that I believe more than any other illustrates his point that when the movement of the work is not toward resolution but ambiguity, there is a special need for intricate metaphorical patterns. The major theme of the play is the dynamics of evil, and the vampire as both solipsist and casuist is a ghoulishly apt mythologem of the centripetal and centrifugal forces of disorder. For the vampire is both a festering center of evil and a contaminating carrier, an ambiguous destroyer of others and preserver of himself.

Finding an image of evil as a human process seems to have been in Shelley's mind at the end of Act III of *Prometheus Unbound*. For some sixty lines before he leaves man "pinnacled dim in the intense inane," Shelley has the Spirit of the Hour explain to Asia what the world looks like devoid of evil. The Spirit reports that everything looks the same except the thrones are kingless, prisons are empty, and altars are unattended. There is no more "hate, disdain, or fear"; evil, "the wretch [who] crept a vampire among man,/ Infecting all with his own hideous ill" (III, iv, 147–48), has been cast out. Shelley's use of the image of the vampire serves here, as in *The Cenci*, to reinforce his conviction that evil is organic, that it is communicable, like an infectious disease, and that unless it is properly destroyed, the forces of good can never be asserted.

Shelley emphasized the one aspect of the myth that Byron in *Manfred* had tried to downplay, namely that the vampire is the devil incarnate in a sinner's body and that unless annihilated the fiend will wreak eternal havoc. He maintains, however, the popular superstition that the vampire first attacks next of kin. This point, lost in our twentieth-century retelling of the myth, was a most important part of the Romantic version, as seen for instance in Byron's *Giaour*. Here is the famous Giaour curse, which seems an obvious influence on a number of other aspects of *The Cenci* as well:

> But first on earth, as Vampyre sent,
> Thy corpse shall from its tomb be rent;
> Then ghastly haunt thy native place,
> And suck the blood of all thy race;
> There from thy daughter, sister, wife,
> At midnight drain the stream of life;
> Yet loathe the banquet, which perforce
> Must feed thy livid living corse,
> Thy victims, ere they yet expire,
> Shall know the demon for their sire;
> As cursing thee, thou cursing them,
> Thy flowers are withered on the stem.
> But one that for thy crime must fall,
> Thy youngest, best beloved of all,

Shall bless thee with a father's name—
That word shall wrap thy heart in flame!
Yet thou must end thy task and mark
Her cheek's last tinge—her eye's last spark.
And the last glassy glance must view
Which freezes o'er its lifeless blue;
Then with unhallowed hand shall tear
The tresses of her yellow hair,
Of which, in life a lock when shorn
Affection's fondest pledge was worn—
But now is borne away by thee
Memorial to thine agony!
Yet with thine own best blood shall drip
Thy gnashing tooth, and haggard lip;
Then stalking to thy sullen grave
Go—and with Ghouls and Afrits rave,
Till these in horror shrink away
From spectre more accursed than they.   (ll. 755–86)

I would not contend that Count Cenci is an actual practicing vampire any more than Manfred, only that Shelley has slipped the vampire image in behind his character to show how evil is generated, transferred, and destroyed. The most obvious use of the myth is in Act I, where Cenci twice celebrates a perverse eucharist. Here he is, first celebrating the deaths of his sons:

(*filling a bowl of wine, and lifting it up*) Oh, thou
   bright wine whose purple splendour leaps
And bubbles gaily in this golden bowl
Under the lamplight, as my spirits do,
To hear the death of my accursed sons!
Could I believe thou wert their mingled blood,
Then would I taste thee like a sacrament,
And pledge with thee the mighty Devil in Hell,
Who, if a father's curses, as men say,
Climb with swift wings after their children's souls,
And drag them from the very throne of Heaven,
Now triumphs in my triumph—But thou art
Superfluous; I have drunken deep of joy,
And I will taste no other wine to-night.   (I, iii, 76–89)

Although Cenci claims he will drink no more—that he is sated with evil for awhile—this is not to be. For later that evening, after Beatrice has initiated a confrontation at the party, he again returns to the communion wine:

> (*Exeunt all but Cenci and Beatrice.*)
> My brain is swimming round;
> Give me a bowl of wine!   (*To Beatrice.*)
>   Thou painted viper!
> Beast that thou art! Fair and yet terrible!
> I know a charm shall make thee meek and tame,
> Now get thee from my sight!   (*Exit Beatrice.*)
>   Here, Andrea,
> Fill up this goblet with Greek wine. I said
> I would not drink this evening; but I must;
> For, strange to say, I feel my spirits fail
> With thinking what I have decreed to do.
>   (*Drinking the wine.*)
> Be thou the resolution of quick youth
> Within my veins, and manhood's purpose stern,
> And age's firm, cold, subtle villainy;
> As if thou wert indeed my children's blood
> Which I did thirst to drink! The charm works well;
> It must be done; it shall be done, I swear!   (I, iii, 163–78)

A number of important motifs are developed here in addition to the recurring image of wine as blood. When the count perceives Beatrice as viper-like, Shelley may be remembering Geraldine and her serpentine looks, but more peculiar is that, like Geraldine, who "seeks delay" (ll. 255–59, *Christabel*), the count also procrastinates. He is not all-powerful; his "spirits" fail; and although he is revived by the metaphorical blood, we get a definite sense of hesitation, almost as if part of him were unwilling. He repeats this hesitancy: ". . . I bear a darker deadlier gloom/ Than the earth's shade, or interlunar air,/ Or constellations quenched in murkiest cloud, In which I walk secure and unbeheld/ Towards my purpose.—Would that it were done!" (II, ii, 189–93). He is powerless to stop, however, for the count is truly a man possessed, and everyone, including himself, understands that—everyone, that is, except most twentieth-century critics who insist that he is consciously, and hence controllably, evil. In trying so to make Cenci fit into a paternalistic paradigm of tyranny that descends from the Pope, they oversimplify his character.[14] The other characters do not: Cardinal Camillo recognizes that Cenci harbors a "fiend within" (I, i, 45); his wife Lucretia can "see the devil . . . that lives in him" (II, i, 45); Beatrice realizes that only his death will " . . . dislodge a spirit of deep hell/ Out of a human form" (IV, ii, 7–8); and ironically even Cenci himself is aware that "I do not feel as if I were a man,/ But like a fiend appointed to chastise/ The offenses of some unremembered world" (IV, ii, 160–62).

14. For instance, G. Wilson Knight, in *The Golden Labyrinth* (New York: Norton, 1962), pp. 216–17, contends that God, the Pope, and the Cenci are all evil fathers, as does James Reiger in "Shelley's Paterin Beatrice," *Studies in Romanticism* 4 (1965): 173.

Another important motif, introduced in the count's communion speech, is that he knows a "charm" to make Beatrice "meek and tame" (I, iii, 167). What that charm is we are never told—for to tell that might make the vampirism not metaphorical but actual, a result Shelley understandably wanted to avoid. His drama is about evil and the transfer of evil, not about some gothic monster. Although we do not know the specific charm, we do know the means of transfer and its effect. The spell seems to be transferred through Cenci's eye, and is so powerful that when Beatrice attempts to recount what has happened, she can only mumble, "He said, he looked, he did . . ." (II, i, 76). The vampire eye is an important element of the play, for, as with Christabel, the once-innocent victim acquires the "chill glare" and serpentine aspect of her oppressor after she has been attacked. So later in the play, as Beatrice becomes desperate, Lucretia notices that her daughter's eyes " . . . shoot forth/ A wandering and strange spirit" (III, i, 81–82), and by the end of the play, when Beatrice is cornered by both Camillo (the church) and the judge (the state), she reportedly uses this hypnotic power to force her henchmen to remain quiet.

Finally the last motif introduced in Cenci's eucharist speech is that his heinous activity will take place at night. Cenci is a creature of the dark, not just because gothic monsters prefer evening work, but specifically because as a vampire—even a figurative vampire—he is photophobic. The daytime for him is "—garish broad and peering . . ./ Loud, light, suspicious, full of eye and ears,/ And every little corner, nook, and hole/ Is penetrated with the insolent light./ Come darkness!" (II, ii, 176–80). Little wonder then that he demands that Beatrice "attend me in her chamber/ This evening: . . . at midnight and alone" (I, i, 145–46). Their awful nocturnal conjunction is reminiscent of that part of the Giaour curse where the vampire must

> . . . ghastly haunt thy native place,
> And suck the blood of all thy race;
> There from thy daughter, sister, wife,
> At midnight drain the stream of life,
> Yet loathe the banquet, which perforce
> Must feed thy livid living corpse,
> Thy victims, ere they yet expire,
> Shall know the demon for their sire.   (ll. 757–64)

And now, with the overlapping of the incest motif, the central horror is increased, for as Count Cenci is draining goodness, he is not leaving behind an empty husk, but rather impregnating a neutralized life with evil. This Manichean transformation occurs before us as Beatrice, once goodness personified, is undone and then reconstituted as evil when she accepts the "pernicious error" of allowing the ends to justify the means. For when she decides to destroy her father she destroys herself, in a sense becoming the person she hates. The doppelgänger transformation of victim into vampire is central not only in the myth, but in Shelley's system of evil. At the end she is indeed her father's "wretched progeny," ironically, the child perpetuating the sins of the father.

The image that links these processes of transformation, vampiric and incestual, is the image of fluid, or more specifically, the two fluids central to each process— blood and semen. Admittedly much of the blood imagery in the play is hymeneal, showing the trauma of innocence when actually impregnated with evil, but equally often the images of blood are used to show, not how blood results from rupture, but rather how it has been drained from the characters by Cenci. Although all the characters in the Cenci family have been psychologically bled of the energy of goodness, Beatrice is most obviously described as pale and wan, especially after her encounter with her father (III, ii, 351). The same pallid condition is also true of her brother Bernardo (II, i, 123) and her mother Lucretia (II, i, 41–42). They are now only shells of their former selves, but the count has not seen fit—as will his literary descendant, Count Dracula—to make all his victims actively participate in evil. Only Beatrice will finally execute his will.

The image of blood is more than a metaphor of energy exchange; it also symbolizes initiation into Cenci's demonic world. Paradoxically, although Beatrice is unable to recount what has happened between her and her father, her organs of perception are colored with the satanic stain: "My eyes," she says, "are full of blood; just wipe them for me . . ./ I see but indistinctly . . ." (III, i, 2–3). And she continues:

> My God!
> The beautiful blue heaven is flecked with blood!
> The sunshine on the floor is black! The air
> Is changed to vapours such as the dead breathe
> In charnel pits! Pah! I am choked! There creeps
> A clinging, black, contaminating mist
> About me . . . . (III, i, 12–18)

Here Beatrice's transformation is literally occurring before not only her eyes but our own as well. Just as the vampire rises in mist from his "charnel pit," so evil clouds the inner world; the *modus operandi* of both external vampire and internal corruption is synchronized. This process is further developed when Cenci claims that Beatrice may well carry his child, an organic division of his demonic energy. He hopes his evil seed will develop into "a hideous likeness of herself, that as/ From a distorting mirror, she may see/ Her image mixed with what she abhors . . ." (IV, i, 146–48). Here again the incest and vampire motifs are dovetailed, for part of the superstition is that a vampire can cause hideous offspring if he even so much as looks at a fertile female.[15] Cenci is the incubus, the living nightmare, visiting evil and chaos on the unprotected and unwary. Not only does he drain goodness, he quite literally discharges evil in its place. The residue of this evil, the image of this

15. The relationship between the vampire and the fertile woman is discussed in Anthony Masters, *The Natural History of the Vampire* (London: Mayflower Books, 1974), pp. 91–92.

potentiality for disorder, is represented by the other important fluid in the play—semen.

The relationship between blood and semen is a close one as they are both life-giving or life-supporting fluids. Ernest Jones, the Freudian psychologist, contended that "in the unconscious mind blood is commonly an equivalent for semen," and Anthony Masters in his *Natural History of the Vampire* elaborates:

> There existed in vampire belief a very strong love motive which involved the vampire in having intercourse with a living woman. This belief probably grew up via the occasional erotic stimulant of blood-letting in intercourse, the breaking of virginity, and, on a more mystic level, the medieval succuba, an erotic demon who preyed upon and destroyed man's virility.[16]

Shelley depends on the blood/semen linkage to express almost subliminally not only the transfer of evil, but its organic development as well.

Shelley is concerned not only with the clash of good and evil but also with the consequences of this clash. The moral problem Beatrice faces is that once having been corrupted, having become literally a carrier of evil, she cannot escape. She recognizes that evil has her "enthralled," and cries out:

> O blood, which art my father's blood,
> Circling through these contaminated veins,
> If thou, poured forth on the polluted earth,
> Could wash away the crime, and punishment
> By which I suffer . . . no, that cannot be!   (III, i, 95–99)

Death, her own death, would seem to be the answer. In fact, Lucretia even tells her that "death alone can make us free" (III, i, 78), but Beatrice knows otherwise. Suicide is no palliative; it is, after all, one of the sins that created the vampire to begin with. Her religion (for she, like Cenci, is devoutly religious—he to the letter, she to the spirit) has forbidden this escape:

> Self murder . . . no, that might be no escape
> For Thy decree yawns like a Hell between
> Our will and it. . . .   (III, i, 132–34)

> I thought to die; but a religious awe
> Restrains me, and the dread lest death itself
> Might be no refuge from the consciousness
> Of what is yet unexplained.   (III, i, 148–51)

And here, as far as Shelley is concerned, she makes her mistake. For she will "expiate" the crime, she will assume the role Cenci has claimed for himself. As a

16. Ernest Jones, "On the Nightmare of Bloodsucking," from *On the Nightmare* (New York: Liveright, 1971), pp. 116–25, is still the best psychological interpretation of the vampire superstition. See also Masters, *Natural History of the Vampire*, p. 45.

"scourge," a redresser of wrongs, she will become the solipsist, the casuist, the Lady Macbeth. She decides to destroy not herself, but him, and in doing so ironically makes herself party to the same horrible processes that Cenci has initiated. She now faces the central problem of the play: how to develop the means to accomplish what all will agree is a noble end.

The problem of disposing of vampires is a complicated one. In nineteenth-century fiction it was usually a priest who destroyed the demon by driving an aspen, maple, hawthorn, or buckthorn stake through the fiend's heart; in twentieth-century cinema it is usually a doctor (chances are, a hematologist) who destroys the villain. In the folk tale it was the task of the vampire's child (usually a son) who, perhaps because he is a blood descendant, intuitively knew the father's weaknesses. The dhampire, by a complicated ritual, exorcises the parental demon, allows the soul to escape, and then destroys the now-neutralized husk of a body.[17] Shelley understandably does not emphasize this aspect, for again it would have made actual what he wanted metaphorical, but Cenci's death is nonetheless peculiar. Beatrice takes control, orchestrating the henchmen, who first refuse to kill the sleeping Cenci, but then are exhorted to finish the heinous task. They throttle the count and then heave the body over the parapet, where it is later found hanging (impaled?) on the branches of a tree (IV, iv, 73–77). Shelley thus only implies a death by staking.[18] But true to the myth, as soon as Cenci is killed, the spell on Beatrice seems broken; she feels that "My breath/ Comes methinks, lighter, and the jellied blood/ Runs freely through my veins" (IV, iii, 42–44). She is confident: "The spirit which doth reign within these limbs/ Seems strangely undisturbed. I could even sleep/ Fearless and calm: all ill is surely past" (IV, iii, 64–65).

But all ill is not passed. Her very act proves that Cenci has succeeded in corrupting her. In death he has achieved what he wanted in life, spiritual domination. The instant Beatrice acts as God's ministering angel she is tainted with the pride of her father, and in a fallen and scurvy world, she will have to pay the price of initiation. Shelley has so devised her plight that there can be no reprieve for evil regardless of intention. The ends simply cannot justify the means. She has met evil head on, and now there is no escaping its consequences. Suicide is ruled out (that would only lead to an eternity of suffering); exile is denied (witness the fate of her brothers); remaining to redress wrongs by patience will not work (she has the example of Lucretia)—she cannot go, she cannot stay. So at the end, battling like a cornered animal, she reverts to the same methods her father used: she employs the powers of evil and subterfuge.

This must have been a most difficult philosophical bind for Shelley to resolve. How much simpler to make her tragic, nobly accepting an unfair fate, but Shelley

---

17. The role of the "dhampire" is discussed in ibid., pp. 44, 143; and Nancy Garden, *Vampires* (New York: Lippincott, 1973), pp. 67–70.

18. In this context it is interesting that later when Beatrice has a vision of her own burial, it is "under the obscure, cold, rotting, wormy ground!/To be nailed down in a narrow place" (V, iv, 50–1). Is she to be staked into the earth like a lamia?

wants no martyr. He has gone to considerable pains to show us a Beatrice contaminated with evil; he has so fitted the vampire motif into both the artistic and philosophic structure of his work that ultimately we will not be able to understand the one without the other. Finally, once we understand how the vampire of evil works, we will be forced into disagreeing with those characters in the play (and critics as well) who insist on seeing Beatrice as a force of pure good. For what Giacomo, Bernardo, and Lucretia (all of whom are effusive in their praise of Beatrice) cannot see is that violence met with violence can only lead to violence. Evil can vamp the good, forcing it to resort to the very evil means it despises.[19]

Perhaps Orsino, with Iago-like insight, understands Beatrice best when he soliloquizes: "'Tis a trick of this same family/ To analyse their own and other minds./ Such self-anatomy shall teach the will/ Dangerous secrets . . .'" (II, ii, 108–11). Early on, Beatrice has analyzed herself and found only Innocence. She is then attacked by Evil, and for the rest of the play her primary concern is to return to that lost Innocence, that prelapsarian world. She, like Blake's Thel, has seen the ugliness of the fallen world and wants to return behind the Veil of Har. But it is too late. Instead of trying to live with sin, she must destroy it. "It is sufficiently clear," Shelley wrote elsewhere, "that revenge, retaliation, atonement, expiation are rules and motives, so far from deserving a place in any system of political life, that they are the chief sources of a prodigious class of miseries in the domestic circles of society."[20] Again it is Orsino who is able to apply this to the world of Realpolitik: " . . . he prospers best, Not who becomes the instrument of ill,/ But who can flatter the dark spirit, that makes/ Its empire and its prey of other hearts/ Till it be become his slave . . ." (II, ii, 157–61). Whereas Orsino seeks to use this knowledge for his own aggrandizement, it is also possible, as Shelley attempted to show in *Prometheus Unbound*, to use this wisdom for good.

Passive resistance would then seem the only alternative. And Shelley, at least at this time in his life, seriously promulgated it as the proper response to evil.

> And if then the tyrants dare
> Let them ride among you there,
> Slash, and stab, and maim, and hew,—
> What they like, that let them do.

19. This misunderstanding of Beatrice has continued until recently outside the play as well, with those critics who interpret her almost as an archetype of purity. So she has been variously labeled "an ennobling vision of maidenly purity," "a harrassed maiden," and "a feminine ideal," with the emphasis always on her ethical virginity. See E. S. Bates, *A Study of Shelley's Drama "The Cenci"* (New York: Columbia University Press, 1908), p. 80, and Bertrand Evans, *Gothic Drama from Walpole to Shelley* (New York: Macmillan, 1902), pp. 127–28. But this characterization is quite literally denied in the play—she is not pure, she is not a maiden, she is not ideal. Just as erroneous, however, are the interpretations of her as a pathetic victim, a personification of "oppression and female suffering." See Neville Rogers, *Shelley at Work* (Oxford: Clarendon Press, 1956), p. 202; or Newman Ivey White, *Shelley* (New York: Knopf, 1940), 2: 140. In either case, to assume she is goodness unfairly victimized or an object of masculine oppression denies her the very humanity that makes her benevolently mistaken.

20. *On the Punishment of Death*, in *The Complete Works of Shelley* (Julian ed.), 6:185.

With folded arms and steady eyes,
And little fear, and less surprise,
Look upon them as they slay
Till their rage has died away.   (*Mask of Anarchy*, ll. 340–47)

But Beatrice is not one who can stand by "with folded arms and steady eyes" and wait until evil has run its course. Like the Assassins in Shelley's unfinished novel, she is so convinced of her own innocence, so sure she can set things right, that she accepts any means for the "restitution" of justice. In so doing, she is consumed by the very thing she wishes to destroy. For again as Shelley wrote, "men, having been injured, desire to injure in return. This is falsely called a universal law of human nature; it is a law from which many are exempt and all in proportion to their virtue and cultivation."[21]

But Shelley's use of the vampire myth makes the exception to this "universal law" not just a matter of "virtue and cultivation," but one of almost superhuman fortitude as well. For once one has succumbed even unconsciously to evil, once Beatrice did indeed go to the Cenci "at midnight and alone," her fate was cast to the powers of darkness. She did not meet evil passively; rather, she allowed herself to be drawn in against it, and in so doing made herself party to it. It is here in this confrontation that the vampire myth resolves some of the ambiguity; for in being so intractable to evil, Beatrice has made herself easy prey. Admittedly if she did not act, Cenci might attack her again as he has planned, but if she passively resisted, he might have withered away. For Cenci realizes that he pushes best against people who shove back. He understands that "'tis her stubborn will/ Which by its own consent shall stoop as low/ As that which drags it down" (IV, i, 10–12). Evil does not want to destroy good (Cenci as vampire makes this clear: "I rarely kill the body, which preserves,/ Like a strong prison, the soul within the power . . ." [I, i, 114–15]), but Beatrice, so impatient to restore innocence, cannot withstand the onslaught of experience. Having been attacked, she retaliates and this action constitutes for Shelley her "pernicious mistake."[22]

The Cenci is thus one of the most philosophically intricate works Shelley ever wrote. It is intricate in that Shelley set for himself the complex task of reconstructing historical events in a form that demands sequential as well as imaginative cohesion, and it is philosophical in that he deals with the problem of casuistry, the use of evil means for good ends.[23] It is a drama that shows through a fiction the real workings of evil: how evil is generated, how it is transferred, and how it can destroy and be destroyed. While one could say the same thing about *The Cenci*'s compan-

---

21. *Philosophical View of Reform*, ibid., 7: 55.

22. Shelley expressed his own feelings about Beatrice's action in the "Preface" to *The Cenci*: "Undoubtedly no person can be truly dishonoured by the act of another; and the fit return to make to the most enormous injuries is kindness and forbearance, and a resolution to convert the injurer from his dark passions by peace and love. Revenge, retaliation, atonement, are pernicious mistakes."

23. For the best explanation of philosophical problems in *The Cenci*, see Earl Wasserman, *Shelley: A Critical Reading* (Baltimore: Johns Hopkins University Press, 1971), pp. 84–130.

ion piece, *Prometheus Unbound*, there is an important difference. *Prometheus Unbound* is a work, as Shelley himself said, of "pure idealism," while *The Cenci* is one of "sad reality." In artistic terms, this means that while in *Prometheus Unbound* Shelley can resolve casuistical problems by fiat (which he does by having Prometheus forgive Jupiter prior to the action of the drama), in *The Cenci* he must "work them out" through action and imagery within the play. In *The Cenci* there can be no apocalyptic resolution, no Act IV where cosmic harmonies are struck, no Spirits of the Mind floating out to milennial levels; instead, only the sad irresolution of Actuality.

The vampire myth almost mandates this sad irresolution, for although the myth may be melancholy it is never tragic. And it is rarely, if ever—at least until our generation—blatantly humorous. We now often make fun of the vampire either by mocking his ludicrous perversions or by reversing the roles so that we can actually sympathize with him. That we are able to do this attests to the currency of the story, for it means that the audience knows the tale so well that it can appreciate the parody. In fact, one of the best indications of the acceptance of a new mode or motif in literature is not so much that it becomes formulaic, but that the parodies of formula soon become more interesting than the straight renditions. Surely the Gothic provides adequate proof: Cobb's *The Haunted Twelve*, Barrett's *The Heroine*, Peacock's *Nightmare Abbey*, and Austen's *Northanger Abbey* are sometimes far more interesting than the genre they exaggerate. This is also true of the vampire story, for although there were plenty of hack renditions that approximated parody (most notably Thomas Pecket Prest's *Varney the Vampyre*), there was one supreme example in poetry that still baffles and amuses. And this parody is to be found ironically in a work that is one of the touchstones of English Romanticism, Keats's *The Eve of St. Agnes*.

A little over a decade ago Jack Stillinger wrote an article about *The Eve of St. Agnes* that has still not been fully assimilated into Keats criticism, although it has been often anthologized and much discussed.[24] Stillinger argues that Porphyro is no Prince Charming, Madeline is no Cinderella, and that the poem, rather than being an experiment in rhapsodic aestheticism, might better be considered a skeptical condemnation of the imagination gone awry. If a piece of criticism can be called scandalous, surely this is it. For Stillinger refutes the dominant Pre-Raphaelite response to the poem as a "gorgeous gallery of poetic pictures" that has filtered into the twentieth century through Amy Lowell, M. R. Ridley, and most recently Douglas Bush. This view is still popular, though somewhat out of favor.[25]

24. Jack Stillinger, "The Hoodwinking of Madeline: Scepticism in *The Eve of St. Agnes*," *Studies in Philology* 58 (1961): 533–55, rpt. in Stillinger's collection, *"The Hoodwinking of Madeline" and Other Essays on Keats' Poems* (Urbana: University of Illinois Press, 1971). Reprinted also in W. J. Bate, ed., *Keats: A Collection of Critical Essays* (Englewood Cliffs, N.J.: Prentice Hall, 1964) (abridged); and in Allan Danzig, ed., *Twentieth Century Interpretations of "The Eve of St. Agnes": A Collection of Critical Essays* (Englewood Cliffs, N.J.: Prentice Hall, 1971). My page references will be from Stillinger's own collection, *"The Hoodwinking of Madeline" and Other Essays on Keats*, and will be cited as *The Hoodwinking*.

25. The first major critic to praise the poem's lushness per se was Leigh Hunt, but it was William Michael Rossetti's *Life of John Keats* (London: W. Scott, 1887) that set the Victorian stance. Amy Lowell,

According to Stillinger, Porphyro does a number of things that make his motives suspect, and which simply cannot be overlooked. For instance, he insinuates his way into Madeline's chamber by intimidating Angela with threats of suicide (ll. 151–53); he flaunts his lover's plan as a "stratagem" (l. 139) which Angela recognizes as "cruel," "impious," "wicked" (ll. 140, 143); and even the genial narrator compares it to Merlin's pact with the devil (ll. 170–71). He seems a sorcerer, a "hoodwinker," who, if not actually, appears to be in league with the fairy legions of enchanters, more concerned with drugging his supposed love out of reality (l. 267) than with making their love part of a mutual reality. Keats emphasizes this theme by surrounding Madeline with aviary image-clusters of innocence being exploited. So she is "an afrighted swan" (variant lines to 196), "a dove forlorn" (l. 333), "a tongueless nightingale" (l. 206), while Porphyro is the nest robber. Porphyro is the snaky Geraldine and Madeline the dove-like Christabel.

The poem is admittedly a dense analogical mix of different mythic and allusive levels—the St. Agnes story; the allusions to Shakespeare, Boccaccio, Mrs. Radcliffe; the incorporation of Keats's psychological theories of the mind and imagination developed in the letters—but for Stillinger these are only the surface levels. The poem has a deeper structure built up on the deceit and hypocrisy of the central protagonist, Porphyro himself. For Porphyro is in reality a confidence man, a huckster of the worst sort, not peddling Confederate bonds to widows, but rather poisoning the punch of unsuspecting schoolchildren.[26] He promises Madeline what La Belle Dame promises the knight-at-arms and what Lamia promises Lycius: he promises escape from the mutable, finite world of suffering into the immortal world of dreams. But what he does not tell her (and what she does not wish to know) is that his dream world is ultimately self-annihilating.

This interpretation collides not only directly with the Pre-Raphaelite reading but also tangentially with the strain of criticism popular a decade or so ago and still the basis of much current scholarship. This other critical approach, stated by Earl Wasserman, basically upholds the validity of the visionary imagination, stressing Madeline's dream and Porphyro's ascent into her transcendent world. Porphyro is, according to these critics, moving up the Pleasure Thermometer as he makes his spiritual pilgrimage deeper and deeper into the castle until he finally reaches the *locus amoenus* of Madeline's boudoir.[27] But the one thing that Wasserman and

---

John Keats (Boston: Houghton Mifflin, 1925); M. R. Ridley, *Keats' Craftsmanship* (London: Oxford University Press, 1933); and W. J. Bate, *John Keats* (Cambridge, Mass.: Harvard University Press, 1963) modify this view somewhat but agree on the poem's sublimity of image and lack of profundity.

26. Stillinger summarizes his case: "I have presented him [Porphyro] as villain in order to suggest, in the first place, that he is not, after all, making a spiritual pilgrimage, unless the poem is to be read as a satire on spiritual pilgrimages; in the second place, that the lovers, far from being a single element in the poem, are as much protagonist and antagonist as Belinda and the Baron, or Clarissa and Lovelace; and in the third place, that no matter how much Keats entered into the feelings of his characters, he could not lose touch with the claims and responsibilities of the world he lived in." *The Hoodwinking*, p. 82.

27. Earl R. Wasserman, *The Finer Tone: Keats' Major Poems* (Baltimore, Md.: Johns Hopkins University Press, 1953), pp. 97–137; R. A. Foakes, *The Romantic Assertion* (London: Methuen, 1958), pp. 85–94; and more recently, although in more circumspect form, C. Douglas Atkins, "The Eve of St. Agnes Reconsidered," *Tennessee Studies in Literature* 18 (1973), 113–32. This kind of reading is usually

others do not comment on is the various eccentricities of Porphyro's character. In interpreting the poem primarily as a paradigm of the imagination and fitting it into the psychological schema Keats developed in *Endymion* and his letters, they overlook much of what is sinister in the character of Porphyro.[28]

Whereas many recent critics have attempted to use *The Eve of St. Agnes* as an "exemplum" of Keats's poetic philosophy, Stillinger is primarily concerned with what is actually in the poem itself. And it is on the basis of this internal evidence, rather than on what he finds outside the poem, that he concludes that Porphyro is indeed a Robert Lovelace out for no good other than his own. But I contend that Porphyro is worse than that—he is a destroyer, a villain of the first order, not an imaginary Adam in Madeline's Edenic dream, but rather the poisoner of the apple. He is, in short, the Satan of the piece. For the character of Porphyro may be drawn from the same source as Count Cenci's—the myth of the vampire.

That Keats was familiar with vampire lore is obvious in *Lamia* and more subtly implied in *La Belle Dame sans Merci*. In fact, he could hardly have avoided the myth, even if he had tried, for in 1819 vampire stories were certainly in fashion. The vampire was fast becoming, like the Wandering Jew and Don Juan, an archetype of a kind of Romantic consciousness; the solipsist gone berserk, ingloriously perverting all the cultural norms. Assuming that Keats had wanted a demon to satirize, he could not have picked a more current and popular evil-doer.

As with Shelley's *Cenci*, I think Coleridge's *Christabel* had the greatest influence on Keats. We know he read it, we know he was impressed by it, we know he picked up actual phrases and descriptions from it. According to Professor Rosemarie Maier's "The Bitch and the Hound: Generic Similarity in *Christabel* and *The Eve of St. Agnes*," it may be that Keats is consciously retelling Coleridge's poem.[29] Not only are actual passages lifted, but also the furnishings of Madeline's chamber, the time sequence, the watch dogs, the seduction scenes, the pairings of Beadsman/Sacristan, Angela/Christabel's mother, and the theme of innocence experienced—there is simply too much to attribute to the conventions of the genre. Although Professor Meier contends that Geraldine is a lamia (as has almost everyone else since A. H. Nethercot), she does not see that just as Keats lifted many of the trappings of Christabel's world, he also lifted the myth behind the protagonist. It is an understandable oversight, for Geraldine is a female vampire and there is therefore a level of sexual perversity in Christabel's world that is totally absent in Made-

---

based on two important Keats letters—one in which he compares the imagination with "Adam's dream" and another in which he compares life to a "Mansion of Many Apartments." See Hyder E. Rollins, ed., *The Letters of John Keats* (Cambridge, Mass.: Harvard University Press, 1958), 1: 185, 280–81.

28. How obvious Porphyro's villainy is has been questioned by C. Douglas Atkins in "The Eve of St. Agnes Reconsidered," p. 114, who concludes that "clearly there is no textual warrant for viewing Porphyro as a villain, despite Stillinger's claims," but one cannot remove parts of the protagonist's character by fiat, and Atkins nowhere proves his assertion, other than by contending that if Porphyro is a friend of Angela's and the narrator's, then he surely cannot be evil. The poem simply contradicts this argument.

29. Rosemarie Maier, "The Bitch and the Hound: Generic Similarity in *Christabel* and *The Eve of St. Agnes*," *Journal of English and Germanic Philology* 70 (1971): 62–75.

line's. But as we have seen in *Lamia* and *La Belle Dame sans Merci*, Keats was fascinated with the metaphor of vampire as lover, and love itself as an enervating process, and so he employed the vampire myth in a much more traditional way.

Armed with a rudimentary knowledge of vampires, and Professor Stillinger's revolutionary reading of the poem, let us retrace Porphyro's steps.[30] First it must be noted that the moon is full, the sky clear, and all the action takes place at night. Concerned with more than observing the Unities, Keats may also be keeping to the vampire's timetable. Before Porphyro is introduced, however, we are shown the necessary withdrawal of the beadsman from the chapel (usually situated in the Outer Bailey) back into the house proper. Wasserman and others have made much of the beadsman's representing an alternative lifestyle, an ascetic retreating style that is counterpoised to Porphyro's more aggressive and dynamic search for higher consciousness. But I think the explanation is much simpler if Porphyro, acting *as if* he were a vampire, can enter the house only after the Christian powers have been removed. For he may have the same problem getting into the mansion that Geraldine had crossing the threshold of Leoline's castle. After Porphyro has crossed the Outer Bailey he approaches the inner gate house of the mansion.[31] Here at the threshold he meets Angela:

> Ah, happy chance! the aged creature came,
> Shuffling along with ivory-headed wand,
> To where he stood, hid from the torch's flame,
> Behind a broad hall-pillar, far beyond
> The sound of merriment and chorus bland.   (ll. 91–95)

Angela is certainly a puzzling character. She seems to be in league with Porphyro (why is her cane a "wand"?), yet she also recognizes him as evil. For she leads him into "a little moonlit room,/ Pale, latticed, chill, and silent as a tomb" (ll. 112–13), and there, after hearing of his plans for Madeline, says, "Thou must hold water in a witch's sieve,/ And be liege lord of all the Elves and Fays,/ To venture so . . ." (ll. 120–22). As Stillinger pointed out, it is she who first tells us of Porphyro's real character. For he is not simply a teenage Lothario idly wandering about the moors on a winter evening; rather, he seems in league with the diabolical powers of the universe. He is, as La Belle Dame later will be, a "faery" in the malefic sense. The narrator, the only other relatively trustworthy source we have aside from Angela, will later reinforce this view by comparing Porphyro's dealings

30. It must be noted, however, that the action occurs on St. Agnes' Eve (20 January). Had Keats wanted to stress the diabolical side of the vampire motif, he might have set the time near Walpurgis Night (30 April), traditionally the vampire's favorite, as Coleridge had done in *Christabel*. Instead, he wished to stress another side of the myth, namely Madeline's virginity and its loss. For on one level the poem is about innocence deflowered, and the vampire is simply the metaphorical vehicle.

31. The modern reader may well miss the fact that Porphyro is here crossing a threshold, but as Arthur H. Bell, in "Madeline's House Is Not Her Castle," *Keats-Shelley Journal* 20 (1971): 12, has contended, Keats is not describing a castle but rather "a medieval manor house such as Great Chalfield Manor, Wiltshire" where there are a number of baileys or enclosed courts. Porphyro is moving from an outer court to an inner one, and it is here that Angela seems to assist him.

to Merlin's pact with the devil (l. 171). Admittedly the analogy is confusing, but it seems that Porphyro's magic may have come from a league with the powers of Darkness, just as Merlin's had in the Arthurian legend.[32]

After Porphyro tells Angela his "stratagem," she first balks, telling him:

> A cruel man and impious thou art:
> Sweet lady, let her pray, and sleep, and dream
> Alone with her good angels, far apart
> From wicked men like thee. Go, go!—I deem
> Thou canst not surely be the same that thou didst seem.　　　(ll. 140–44)

But he will not be dissuaded and threatens to call out the guard, which will not only mean his capture, but will also reveal Angela's complicity, so she relents. It is all a ruse, of course, and Angela should know better, for Porphyro needs her to gain access to Madeline's chamber, just as he needed her to cross the outer threshold. Once inside, however, vampires are rather like the police—easy to invite in, difficult to get to leave.

Soon the demon lover is in Madeline's closet and at the brink of success. Angela, her work done, is led away by an obliging Madeline; which may hint of Madeline's own complicity. Her zombielike movements are suspicous: she "rose, like a missioned spirit, unaware" (l. 193) to help Angela away. Perhaps, like Christabel, she is not as innocent as she seems. Porphyro meanwhile has been provided with assorted goodies with which to tempt his love. Admittedly this is part of the St. Agnes legend, but it may also prefigure La Belle Dame's exotic foodstuffs that are used to entice the knight, as well as Lamia's banquet feast.

What is still more intriguing is Porphyro's reaction to Madeline's undressing, for it is as central to this poem as it was in *Christabel*. On one level it is voyeurism to be sure, wonderfully erotic for "lover" and reader alike. But there is also the possibility that Porphyro is not as much excited by Madeline as he is perplexed by other powers in the room. For as Madeline prepares to pray, her breast and neck are bathed in blood-red light (l. 216) that is cast from the moon through the stained-glass windows. Then as she slowly kneels, he sees the light glance on her silvery cross, and immediately "Porphyro grew faint" (l. 224). One of the reasons crosses are worn is to protect the wearer from vampires and other devilish monsters, and here Keats may be punning with the symbolism. For on one level Porphyro is awed, as we are, with Madeline's heavenly beauty, but on another level he may be dumbstruck by the icon. In any case, her prayers finished, "his heart revives" (l. 226), and as she "unclasps her warm'd jewels one by one" (l. 228), presumably the cross is taken off. Madeline is no longer protected: Porphyro, the "famish'd pilgrim," can finally make his move.

It is midnight, and the moon dimly lights the room; Madeline lies in bed first in

---

32. For more on these two confusing lines (190–91), see Marion Cusac, "Keats as Enchanter: An Organizing Principle of *The Eve of St. Agnes*," *Keats-Shelley Journal* 17 (1968): 116, where the different critical views are reviewed.

a "wakeful swoon, perplexed" (l. 236), then falls into a charmed and spellbound sleep. Porphyro is gaining control. He goes to her side and, on her lute, carefully plays an ancient ditty that, I believe, a wryly clever Keats could not neglect naming. Porphyro plays "La Belle Dame sans Merci." Why this of all songs? It is usually glossed as Alain Chartier's medieval ballad, but possibly Keats has his own poem in mind. For here in late January to early February 1819 he may already be composing a poem that will be finished in April. If this is the case, and again I stress it is only conjecture, it is a sly and witty prefiguring of his own poetic work.

What happens next we are never told. The assumption has always been that Porphyro "sleeps" with Madeline, and naturally Keats could not include this if he expected Taylor to publish the poem. In fact, according to Woodhouse there was quite a discussion about this part of the poem, and Keats rewrote some eight lines.[33] Stuart Sperry goes so far as to contend that there is no physical union of the two lovers, for this scene "in no way resembles rape or even a seduction of any ordinary kind."[34] Porphyro's concern, Sperry continues, is to enter her dream-life without waking her—which is correct—but once again I believe Porphyro's motives are in no way amorous.

A careful look at the deleted lines may resolve the problem. Porphyro has hypnotized Madeline: she cannot move her eyes from his, she starts to moan, wakes, and notices how "pallid chill and drear" he is. The revised lines are:

> See, while she speaks his arms encroaching slow,
> Have zoned her, heart to heart—loud, loud the dark winds blow!

> For on the midnight came a tempest fell;
> More sooth, for that his quick rejoinder flows
> Into her burning ear: and still the spell
> Unbroken guards her in serene repose.
> With her wild dream he mingled, as a rose
> Marrieth its odour to a violet.
> Still, still she dreams, louder the frost wind blows.

There is no mention of sexual intercourse; in fact, we see only Porphyro moving to her burning ear. To comprehend the importance of whatever he is really doing we must remember that outside nature is moving in diabolical sympathy. Like the folk vampire he merges into her dream as he performs his sensual and hideous act. The midnight dream is becoming a nightmare: the dark winds blow, the tempest falls, the storm howls. In the original this action is somewhat blurred; Madeline cries out:

> ["]Oh leave me not in this eternal woe,
> For if thou diest, my love, I know not where to go."

33. Jack Stillinger explained the major textual problems in "The Text of *The Eve of St. Agnes*," *Studies in Bibliography* 16 (1963): 207–12, rpt. in *The Hoodwinking*, pp. 158–66.

34. Stuart M. Sperry, Jr., "Romance As Wish Fulfillment: Keats' *The Eve of St. Agnes*," *Studies in Romanticism* 10 (1971): 32.

> Beyond a mortal man impassion'd far
> At these volumptuous accents, he arose,
> Ethereal, flush'd, and like a throbbing star
> Seen mid the sapphire heaven's deep repose;
> Into her dream he melted, as the rose
> Blendeth its odor with the violet—
> Solution sweet: meantime the frost-wind blows . . . .   (ll. 314–22)

Keats, perhaps at Woodhouse's suggestion, finally restored the original lines, backing away not from the sexual, but rather from the vampiric. The mention of the midnight hour, the sympathetic howling of the "dark winds," the burning at her ear (perhaps the vampire kiss?), the hypnotic spell, and her deep dreaming—all of which appear in the revision—are absent in the final restoration. Perhaps the stanza was a too gothic and obvious intrusion of a diabolical process Keats wanted only metaphorically expressed.

Their "marriage" completed, the moon sets (l. 324) just as it had after Geraldine's encounter with Christabel. Porphyro realizes that his time before dawn is running out. He prepares to leave his "bride" (ll. 326, 334), and Madeline realizes:

> ["]Porphyro will leave me here to fade and pine.—
> Cruel! what traitor could thee hither bring?
> I curse not, for my heart is lost in thine,
> Though thou forsakest a deceived thing—
> A dove forlorn and lost with sick unpruned wing."   (ll. 329–33)

Somehow she has missed out on the transcendent, visionary experience which so many critics have claimed was hers; rather, she is now more like the dove in Bard Bracy's dream. Are these the hyperbolic words of a star-crossed Juliet, or are they the plaint of a gulled fool now pathetically dependent on her serpentine lover? Porphyro, after protesting that he will not "rob thy nest" (l. 340), relents: "Awake! arise! my love, and fearless be,/ For o'er the southern moors I have a home for thee" (ll. 350–51).

Critics, unable to see the malefic side of Porphyro, have understandably been confused by the next two stanzas.[35] For here we are told that the lovers pass what seem to Madeline to be "sleeping dragons all around" (l. 353), glide "like phantoms" (ll. 361–62) past a waking bloodhound, and then exit through a door that mysteriously opens. Keats has seeded these penultimate stanzas with hint after hint of Porphyro's demonic nature. First, we must remember that Porphyro's name itself

---

35. Stillinger, *The Hoodwinking*, p. 87, n. 24, gives the best general summary of the critical debate. Basically the optimists believe that all ends well—Porphyro and Madeline transcend the mutable world—while the pessimists contend just the opposite—the lovers descend from Madeline's chamber into a ferocious world they are not prepared to face. These points of view are best developed in (optimistic) Arthur Carr, "John Keats' Other 'Urn,'" *University of Kansas City Review* 20 (1954): 237–42; and (pessimistic) Herbert G. Wright, "Has Keats' *Eve of St. Agnes* a Tragic Ending?" *Modern Language Review* 40 (1945): 90–94.

is unique in literature, probably derived from "Porphyre," which from the sixteenth century onward was "a name applied to a kind of serpent."[36] Hence Madeline's initiation into this world of dragons and phantoms may well cause her to halluci-nate the sleeping dragons all around. Keats is hinting, I think, that it takes one to know one. She has entered Porphyro's spookish world, and has become, metaphor-ically at least, a part of it. Hence Madeline moves as he does, like a phantom.[37] Keats makes sure the reader does not miss this, for we are told it twice; they "glide, like phantoms, into the wide hall; / Like phantoms, to the iron porch, they glide" (ll. 361–63). But equally interesting is the possibility that Porphyro's name might come from "porphyria," which was a disease in which the victim became very sensitive to sunlight. A person with porphyria can look terrifying, for his teeth and nails take on a strange fluorescent glow. This disease became one of the major nineteenth-century explanations of vampirism and quite possibly was known to Keats as a young apothecary surgeon.[38]

Next the lovers pass the sleeping hound, a descendant of Christabel's "mastiff bitch" who earlier in English literature had recognized with an "angry moan" the demonic presence of that other vampire, Geraldine. And here again Keats may be punning with the image, for we are told that the dog is a bloodhound, and that he does not bark because he recognizes an "inmate" (l. 366). Which inmate—Made-line or Porphyro? Keats saves yet more enigmas for the concluding lines of the stanza. The door that was mysteriously left open for Porphyro to enter now myste-riously opens to let him leave: "By one, and one, the bolts full easy slide: / The chains lie silent on the footworn stones; / The key turns, and the door upon its hinges groans" (ll. 367–69). Just how is the door opened? By supernatural agency, or did Porphyro slide back the bolt? The door image does more than "frame" the poem; Keats focused on it because it is central to the vampire's entrance into and exit from a Christian household.[39]

The lovers flee to the south. It may be more than coincidental that we are earlier told that the beadsman moves north (l. 19), deeper into the manor, away from the raging storm, and that now we are told that the lovers flee south, into the world of mist and danger. The directions of heathen and Christian should be opposite. Be-hind them that night the baron and his court have nightmares of "witch, and de-mon, and large coffin-worm" (l. 374). Paradoxically, they, "the barbarian hordes" and "hyena foemen," are, like Bard Bracy, the ones with the true visionary imagi-nation, for they know what the real dreamers, Christabel/Madeline, will never understand. It is here at the end of the poem that we are given the dream/reality mix-up, not earlier in Madeline's hypnotized hallucination. It is the baron who, like Adam, will wake to find his dream has become reality. Madeline, however,

36. *Oxford English Dictionary* (Oxford: Clarendon Press, 1933; corrected re-issue, 1961), 7: 1132.
37. Phantoms are ghosts, spirits of the dead, as are vampires. Ibid., 7:765.
38. Nancy Garden, *Vampires* (New York: J. B. Lippincott Co., 1973), p. 112.
39. The "device of doors" is clearly important if only because the poem opens and closes with the opening and closing of the front door. See W. S. Ward, "A Device of Doors, in *The Eve of St. Agnes*," *Modern Language Notes* 73 (1958): 90–91.

will quite possibly never wake; she may well join the knight-at-arms, enthralled to the horror of the living dead.

Admittedly, this is a grisly reading, and certainly it is at loggerheads with all but Stillinger's and perhaps Bate's interpretations. But when we think of what Keats was concerned with in 1819—as is made progressively clearer in *La Belle Dame* and *Lamia*—it does seem possible. In fact, the parallels with *Lamia* are more striking than those with *La Belle Dame sans Merci*: the danger of dreams as escape, the vampire lover enervating the love-victim, the lushness of deceit, and even the obvious architectural similarities between Madeline's castle and Lamia's palace.[40] And for those who wince at this gothic kind of reading, saying Keats could never have intended such a dreadful level in the poem, we need only recall his other "smokable" companion poem, *Isabella*. Is the scene where Isabella digs up Lorenzo, severs his head, and then brushes the dirt from his eyelids any less macabre than the love scene in *The Eve of St. Agnes*? There is much "wormy circumstance" in both poems, except that in *The Eve of St. Agnes* it is almost all below the surface.

But as distinct from *Isabella*, these three strange love poems of 1819, *The Eve of St. Agnes*, *La Belle Dame*, and *Lamia* may be more profound than macabre. For they are all love poems, explaining the enervating side of love, love as possession. They are all poems about youthful "enthrallment." Keats did not use that word, but surely that is the predicament he is describing. The dreaming knight in *La Belle Dame* is warned by death-pale warriors that she "Hath thee in thrall" (l. 40); Lycius is first entranced by Lamia, just as Madeline is spell-bound by Porphyro. In each case the more powerful lover magically dominates the "victim" and "gains" strength as the partner weakens. One "self" is metaphorically consumed by another in a kind of psychic cannibalism. In a sense this is Keats's realization of the other side of "unreflecting love," for this adolescent, unconsidered love is potentially dangerous. It can easily run off center and leave one of the lovers pathetically weak and dependent. In these three poems that is precisely what happens. The knight is forever woebegone, Lycius and Lamia intrude into each other's psychic privacy, and Madeline's fate, although uncertain, is possibly quite horrible.

This ultimately raises, I suppose, the biographical question of why Keats had such a difficult time writing a straight romance. In *Isabella*, he is of course bound by Boccaccio, but not so with these other poems. Here he is on his own. Perhaps, although this is a dangerous kind of guess, the recent wasting away of his brother Tom in December 1818 and the alternating love affair with Fanny Brawne were somehow linked in his mind. For the process of wasting away, of growing "pale, and specter-thin," of being consumed by tuberculosis, is close to the vampiric process of enervation—so close, in fact, that in the early nineteenth century tuberculosis was often thought to be caused by a vampire's attack.[41] And this process of energy loss is metaphorically similar to what the lover feels as the love affair turns

40. Richard E. Johnson, "Architectural Imagery in *The Eve of St. Agnes* and *Lamia*," *Xavier University Studies* 5 (1966): 3–11.

41. Garden, *Vampires*, p. 113.

pernicious and one's selfhood is absorbed into another's. To describe this process, most clearly in *Lamia*, more subtly in *La Belle Dame*, and opaquely in *The Eve of St. Agnes*, Keats used an incredibly bold analogy—the metaphor of the lover as vampire.

So far in Romantic poetry the male vampire had not been a character of much independence or substance; in fact, he has hardly been a character at all. At best, the myth has been used as a metaphor, a way of discussing the aberrant personality traits of a protagonist. Manfred, Cenci, and perhaps Porphyro are vampiric only in that they stretch an already extant stereotype, the Byronic Hero, into hyperbole. The male vampire, at least to the male poet, is simply not much of a poetic character; rather, as we shall see, he is intrinsically prosaic. Perhaps predictably, just the reverse is true with the lamia in poetry, for here the lamia attacks the young, usually male, victim with excesses of love and initiates him into the world of truth. The female victims of the attacking male, Astarte, Beatrice, and perhaps Madeline, are all debilitated by their nocturnal lovers; they are used by Manfred, Cenci, and Porphyro and then presumably discarded. But the victims of a lamia attack are given wisdom, albeit short-lived, for their participation: Christabel, the knight, and Lycius do achieve insight into how things are put together. Admittedly the androgynous Christabel is in desperate shape, the knight horribly dependent on his vision, and Lycius finally destroyed (by Apollonius, not by Lamia), but at least they have knowledge. Astarte, Beatrice, and Madeline learn nothing; they are simply the objects of male aggression and aggrandizement. Manfred has his way, and suffers only the desire for oblivion; Cenci is ultimately successful in corrupting goodness, and Porphyro has also gotten what he wanted. In essence the lamia may be heartless but rarely cruel; the vampire is heartless and always cruel.

Is this situation the result of a male fantasy, that he should see himself as a destroyer of women but unable to be destroyed by them? Or is there something in the myth itself that precludes his own victimization? Here the example of Bertha Rochester (the only lamia created by the female artist) is of key importance. Bertha is vampiric only to Jane, and although the objects of her attacks are men, her real victim is Jane herself. The tearing of Jane's wedding veil is a wonderfully apt image of the power she has: she can exclude other women from her man; she can keep them isolated and single. Hence she is the only lamia who is not described as the femme fatale; she is rather, at least to Jane, ugliness and carnality and bestiality personified. Such speculations about the deep structure of the myth are beyond the pale of this work; they are more appropriately the subject of a study of human consciousness. What we do know, however, is that when the male vampire moves from poetry into prose fiction, he gains real cultural potency for the first time. He becomes not the mechanism to explore interpersonal states, but rather a dynamic, forthright, and potentially complex protagonist. He becomes for the first time an end, not the means. Again, interestingly enough, when the male vampire is created by a female consciousness, as he is in Emily Brontë's Heathcliff, he at last becomes poetic—that is to say, metaphoric and symbolic. Heathcliff is by far the most complex and exciting of all the vampires in Romantic prose, precisely because we see him at last from the female point of view. To this day, however, our cultural vampire is the vampire of masculine fiction, specifically of nineteenth-century prose, and so it is to those works, Polidori's *The Vampyre*, Prest's *Varney the Vampyre*, and Stoker's *Dracula*, that we now turn.

4. The Vampire in Prose

*With a plunge he seizes her neck in his fang-like teeth—a gush of blood,
and a hideous sucking noise follows. The girl has swooned, and the
vampyre is at his hideous repast!*

—Varney the Vampyre

How often are we ever able to determine precisely when a mythic figure enters the
cultural milieu and is a subject for literary treatment? When, for instance, was the
figure of Prometheus or Don Juan or the Wandering Jew first used by an artist?
Who told the first ghost story? When did the dandy first appear? Who was the first
wicked stepmother? In almost all cases where the archetype has gained a broad
currency, it is nearly impossible to determine exactly when it moved from what
T. S. Eliot called "primordial image" into conscious artistic use. In other words,
we can never be sure when we stop dreaming about an image and start consciously
recreating it. The vampire is an exception; for although we are unsure about his
entrance into poetry, we know exactly when he burst from mythic imagination into
prose.

As we have seen, around the turn of the nineteenth century the English and
German Romantic poets were experimenting with the vampire myth as a metaphor
for the psychology of human interactions, but it was not until 1819, when an
irascible Scotsman, John Polidori, published his novella, *The Vampyre*, that the
myth was finally exploited for its own sake. Polidori's work set off a chain reaction
that has carried the myth both to heights of artistic psychomachia and to depths of
sadistic vulgarity, making the vampire, along with the Frankenstein monster, the
most compelling and complex figure to be produced by the gothic imagination.

Had the first vampire novel been written by some hack novelist, some nameless
drudge, the fiend might have roamed for centuries more in the dreamscapes of folk
consciousness. Paradoxically, the book was written by a kind of John Doe, except
that this John Doe was traveling with the most influential literary figure of the early
nineteenth century, Lord Byron. In addition, *The Vampyre's* original reading public
believed it to be a work not by Polidori, but by Byron. From this case of purpose-
fully mistaken identity the vampire was not just born in the novel but given an
instant popular audience. Polidori had been vilified (vehemently in the 1820s) for
what were thought to be his conscious sins of commission; supposedly his vampire
tale was a plagiarism of a story by Lord Byron, but in retrospect this is not so clear.

In fact, what happened has never been entirely understood, although recently there has been a revival of interest in putting the pieces back together again.[1]

It is important to know something of the historical background, for *The Vampyre* is not just an important gothic novella; it is also a roman à clef of some complexity. In 1816 Lord Byron was in a terrible predicament: his wife, Annabella Milbanke, had learned of what he himself prated as his own gross infidelities, the most shocking of which was the assertion of incest with his half-sister Augusta Leigh. Whether or not incest actually occurred, or whether she found out instead about her husband's homosexual activities, is still disputed; but the result was that the same London society that had just lionized Byron, now cast him out. As he earlier "awoke to find [himself] famous," now he woke to find himself infamous. He was exiled from drawing rooms, spat upon in the streets, and cast in the role of social pariah, almost a vampire among men.

Byron was genuinely shocked. His rise to prominence, his shining, and then this evaporation and fall had been so sudden and so definite. Paradoxically, in his social demise he created his most lasting impression, for Byron's ostracism forced him into living the role he had artistically created. And he lived it almost better than he wrote it. In 1816 he was no longer just writing about the melancholy outcast, the lusty libertine in the open shirt whose peculiarities made him live forever on the fringe of lawlessness; he had overnight become that character, and he played it in wondrous style. Life had become theater.

Byron cast about for a physician to accompany him on his hegira to the Continent. It was a common enough procedure for English nobility to travel with their own medical attendants, especially when their parties had grown as large as Byron's retinue of servants and friends had by April 1816. The man who finally got the job was almost as unusual as his employer. John Polidori (1795–1821) was an Italian Scotsman, a combination Byron doubtless thought would prove explosively entertaining. Polidori was precocious—the youngest man ever to receive a medical degree from the University of Edinburgh—and was eager for travel and excitement. Traveling with the most infamous man in England was incentive enough, but sweetening the proposition was a promise by John Murray to pay handsomely (five hundred pounds or guineas, depending on the version) for a full account of Byron's continental activities. Although Polidori proved to be no Boswell, he fleshed out the myth of Byron as prepotent Lothario. For instance, his diary records, along with much insignificant minutiae, such indiscreet scenes as Byron's arrival at the Cour Imperiale: "As soon as he reached the room Lord Byron fell like a thunderbolt upon the chambermaid."[2] But his diary was soon neglected as other matters, less literary, took precedence.

1. James Rieger, "Dr. Polidori and the Genesis of *Frankenstein*," *Studies in English Literature* 3 (1963): 461–74; Robert R. Harson, "A Profile of John Polidori with a New Edition of *The Vampyre*" (Ph.D. dissertation, Ohio University, 1966); Christopher Frayling, "Introduction" to *The Vampyre: A Bedside Companion* (New York: Charles Scribner's Sons, 1978); and especially Henry R. Viets, "The London Editions of Polidori's *The Vampyre*," *Papers of the Bibliographical Society of America* 63 (1969): 83–103.

2. *The Dairy of John Polidori*, ed. William Michael Rosetti (London: Elkin Mathew, 1911), p. 33.

Eight days after the Byron entourage left England, Percy Shelley, Mary Godwin, their infant son William, and Claire Clairmont set sail in remarkably similar circumstances. Shelley's exile was also self-imposed: his marriage, too, was floundering (he was now living with a woman not his wife); William Godwin, his future father-in-law and past friend, was angry with him; his own father had attempted to settle his inheritance prematurely; and his poem *Alastor* had been a critical disaster. He was, like Byron, an outcast. As the Shelley company calmly moved toward Switzerland, the Byron party took a more circuitous route. Byron and his physician were not getting along well: Polidori soon proved cantankerous, moody, petulant, and terribly jealous of his employer. By the time the Byron entourage reached Geneva on 25 May 1816, the rift was becoming a split. For instance, just before arriving at Lake Geneva, Byron and Polidori had been sitting at a window overlooking the Rhine. Polidori turned to his employer and abruptly demanded, "What is there, excepting writing poetry, that I cannot do better than you?" To which Byron replied, "First . . . I can hit with a pistol the keyhole of that door—secondly, I can swim across that river to yonder point—and thirdly, I can give you a d———d good thrashing." Polidori, so the story goes, skulked away.[3]

With the coming of the Shelleys to Lake Geneva Polidori was for the first time since the trip began the odd-man-out, the exile from the exiled. Byron's friendship with the Shelleys and his amorous relations with Claire Clairmont piqued Polidori, who fancied himself both a poet and lover. By the time of the famous evening pact to write a horror story (sometime between June 15–17), Polidori must have been feeling the strain, for even Mary Shelley, who had the least reason to dislike Polidori, seems almost to have patronized his pretentions.[4] In her account of the results of the bargain, she recalls that Byron wrote a fragment of a story, Shelley produced something based on childhood experiences, but

> Poor Polidori had some terrible idea about a skull-headed lady, who was so punished for peeking through a keyhole—what to see I forget—something very shocking and wrong of course; but when she was reduced to a worse condition than the renowned Tom of Coventry, he did not know what to do with her, and was obliged to dispatch her to the tomb of the Capulets, the only place for which she was fitted.[5]

So Polidori's story was not a vampire tale. In fact it was once thought to be a plan for his future novel, *Ernestus Berchtold, or the Modern Oedipus*, but a reading of this novel about the incestuous affairs of a young Swiss patriot makes one wonder.[6] In the Introduction to this novel, however, Polidori outlines Byron's story, which was supposedly about a vampire:

3. For further gloss, see Leslie Marchand, *Byron: A Bibliography* (New York: Alfred A. Knopf, 1957), 2: 619.

4. The confusing chronology of this famous pact to write a horror story is best explained in Harson, "Profile of John Polidori," pp. 25–36, 55–74.

5. Mary Shelley, "Introduction to the Third Edition of *Frankenstein*," *Frankenstein: or the Modern Prometheus*, ed. James Rieger (1818; rpt. New York: Bobbs-Merrill Company, 1974), p. 225. Mr. Rieger makes the case that this introduction was primarily composed by Percy Shelley. "Introduction," p. xviii.

6. See Harson, "Profile of John Polidori," p. 65.

Two friends were to travel from England into Greece; while there one of them should die, but before his death, should obtain from his friend an oath of secrecy with regard to his decease. Some short time after, the remaining traveller returning to his native country, should be startled at perceiving his former companion moving about in society, and should be horrified at finding that he made love to his former friend's sister.[7]

Apparently Byron had discussed his story with his doctor, then had written it down in his notebook (that infamous notebook that was once his wife's account book) and put it away. This summary is not much of a story, but Polidori, ever mindful of both Byron's genius and his own reportorial assignment from Murray, salted it away.

Polidori might never have recalled Byron's outline from the brine of memory had the events of 1816 turned out differently. The same qualities that had made Polidori such an eccentric traveling companion soon grew into what Byron termed his "tracasseries." Polidori's feistiness, his curmudgeonly manner, and his quick wit that had been so entertaining grew tiresome, not just to Byron but to the Shelleys as well. When Shelley, who himself was no athlete, beat Polidori in a boat race, Polidori grew so testy that he challenged Shelley to a duel—hardly a heroic gesture, as Polidori knew that Shelley was a pacifist, at least in public. Shelley demurred, but Byron, who by this time was finding Polidori tedious, offered to fight in Shelley's stead. Although reckless, Polidori was no fool, and realizing that Byron was an excellent shot, he once again skulked off. Byron would later describe "Polly Dolly" as "exactly the kind of person to whom, if he fell overboard, one would hold out a straw to know if the adage be true that drowning men clutch at straws."[8] It came as no surprise that by the end of the summer Polidori had proved such a problem that he was dismissed.

This dismissal did not separate Byron and Polidori for long. The two men met again that fall in Italy. On 28 October at La Scala, the Milan Opera, Polidori insulted an Austrian officer for blocking his view of the stage. There was a challenge; Polidori was invited outside for what he thought was to be a duel, but instead turned out to be his arrest for disorderly conduct, and was thrown in jail. Byron, through his Italian friends, effected Polidori's release, which only infuriated him further; he left town in a huff, and by the spring of 1817 had returned to England. He returned home without money, without fame, without his detailed report of Lord Byron's daily affairs, but with a rough draft of Byron's projected horror story.

In the April 1819 issue of Colburn's *New Monthly Magazine*, the first vampire story in English prose appeared. Polidori was paid £30 for what in retrospect was the most influential horror story in English. From the Preface that introduced *The Vampyre* it appeared it might have been written by a "Lord B.," a state of affairs Mr. Colburn did little to change; in fact, he may even have written it. About two weeks

7. "Introduction" to *Ernestus Berchtold* (London: Longman, Hurst, Rees, Orme, and Brown, 1819), pp. v–vi.

8. As related in Thomas Moore, *Letters and Journals of Lord Byron* (London: John Murray, 1830), 2: 29.

after publication John Murray wrote to Lord Byron to explain that he had acquired

> . . . a copy of a thing called The Vampire, which Mr. Colburn had had the
> temerity to publish with your name as its author. It was first printed in the
> New Monthly Magazine, from which I have taken the copy which I now
> enclose. The Editor of that Journal has quarrelled with the publisher, and has
> called this morning to exculpate himself from the baseness of the transaction.
> He says that he received it from Dr. Polidori for a small sum, Polidori saying
> that the whole plan of it was yours, and that it was merely written out by him.
> The Editor inserted it with a short statement to this effect; but to his astonish-
> ment Colburn cancelled the leaf on the day previous to its publication, and
> contrary to, and in direct hostility to his positive order, fearing that this state-
> ment would prevent the sale of this work in a separate form, which was sub-
> sequently done. He informs me that Polidori, finding that the sale exceeded
> his expectation, and that he sold it too cheap, went to the Editor, and declared
> he would deny it. . . .[9]

In the following issue of the *New Monthly Magazine* Polidori admitted that
while *The Vampyre* was based on Byron's idea, the telling of it was his own invention. Byron also wrote a letter to *Gallignani's Messenger* (a Paris magazine that had
printed an announcement of *The Vampyre* at the end of April), reiterating that the
idea might have been his, but the execution was not. Neither of these disavowals
moved Colburn from his public insistence that Byron indeed had been the author.
And so when *The Vampyre* promised to be so successful that still more money
could be made by publishing it separately as a book, the same printing plates were
used, except that Byron's name was deleted in the second printing. For Colburn
had learned that the laws governing books were much stricter than those concern-
ing magazines.[10]

Whether or not *The Vampyre* would have survived on its own, had it not appeared to be Byron's work, is of course a moot point. It surely would not have
gained such a wide readership, both in England and on the Continent (Goethe, for
instance, claimed it was the best thing Byron ever wrote!), but it might well have
launched the vampire into prose nonetheless.[11] For it is a well-made tale, full of
biographical intrigue, local color, melodrama, suspense, and, most important, a
dynamic new protagonist who prefigures the wonderfully morose Melmoth the
Wanderer. Polidori carefully prepares his reader for this new human terror by providing a brief history of the vampire and a catalogue of his peculiarities. In his
Introduction he explains the rise of the vampire belief as it parallels the growth of
Christianity, its use as a tool of territorial expansion and consolidation, and the

9. "John Murray to Lord Byron, April 27, 1819," in *The Works of Lord Byron*, ed. Roland Prothero
(London: John Murray, 1900), 4: 286.
10. See Harson, "A Profile of John Polidori," p. 72, and especially Viets, "The London Edition of
Polidori's *The Vampyre*," pp. 83–103.
11. E. M. Butler, *Byron and Goethe* (London: Bowes & Bowes, 1956), p. 55.

physical characteristics of the vampire, embellishing the goriest parts: "[Once fed,] their veins become distended to such a state of repletion, as to cause the blood to flow from all the passages of their bodies, and even from the very pores of their skins."[12] But his best argument is the stock of any ghost story—the teller's assertion and then proof that the demon he will describe is not imaginary but real. Polidori relates the history of Arnold Paul, a Hungarian vampire whose strange story had already been told in the 1732 *London Journal*. Paul, a Hungarian soldier, returned from the dead to ravage friends and family alike for some twenty days until he was finally disinterred, staked, decapitated, and burned. This is all a matter of record, says Polidori, and so begins his tale.

Just the briefest summary of Polidori's story will exonerate him from charges of plagiarism for, if anything, *The Vampyre* is more a slander of Byron than a plagiarism. Polidori's vampire is named Lord Ruthven, a name that had earlier been coined by Lady Caroline Lamb to satirize Byron in her novel *Glenarvon*. This novel, incidentally, had been published by the same Mr. Colburn in May 1816 and had caused Byron some initial anxiety, at least until he had read it. Polidori surely must have known how Byron would react to seeing that name, and doubtless thought it a clever send-up of his old employer. As we first meet Lord Ruthven in England he is a lady-killer in both the metaphorical and literal sense. His current victim is one Lady Mercer, who bears notorious resemblance to Byron's most eccentric pursuer, Lady Caroline Lamb (who had dressed in a page's uniform to insinuate her way into Byron's household):

> Lady Mercer, who had been the mockery of every monster shewn in drawing-rooms since her marriage, threw herself in his [Ruthven's] way, and did all but put on the dress of a mountebank, to attract his notice—though in vain;—when she stood before him, though his eyes were apparently fixed upon hers, still it seemed as if they were unperceived;—even her unappalled impudence was baffled, and she left the field. (p. 265)

As Lord Ruthven is quite literally dispensing with Lady Mercer, Mr. Aubrey, an idealistic ingenu, enters London society, seeking a place in the world. He is an orphan far from home and needing the guidance of a mature teacher. Unfortunately—for he is very impressionable—he meets the strange, melancholy Ruthven, and they become like father and son. Soon, however, Ruthven suffers some "nameless embarrassments" and hastily plans to leave England. Aubrey now too feels the need for a change of scenery and suggests that they set off together. Ruthven agrees, and they travel to the Continent, one for escape, the other ostensibly "to perform the Tour."

So far there seems little doubt that Polidori is paralleling his own fortunes with Aubrey's, and Byron's with Ruthven's. The comparison continues when Aubrey and Ruthven reach the Continent, for just as Polidori and Byron had grown irri-

---

12. John Polidori, *The Vampyre*, in *Three Gothic Novels*, ed. E. F. Bleiler (1819; rpt. New York: Dover Publications, 1966), p. 261. Henceforth page numbers will appear parenthetically in the text.

tated with each other, Aubrey now finds his companion not at all what he expected. For instance, Ruthven's acts of generosity are strangely ambivalent:

[He] was profuse in his liberality;—the idle, the vagabond, and the beggar, received from his hand more than enough to relieve their immediate wants. But Aubrey could not avoid remarking, that it was not upon the virtuous, reduced to indigence by the misfortunes attendant even upon virtue, that he [Ruthven] bestowed his alms;—these were sent from the door with hardly suppressed sneers; but when the profligate came to ask something, not to relieve his wants, but to allow him to wallow in his lust, or to sink him still deeper in his iniquity, he was sent away with rich charity. (p. 267)

By the time they reach Rome, Aubrey's suspicions become justified. Letters arrive from his guardians insisting that he part from his companion, for

It had been discovered, that his [Ruthven's] contempt for the adultress had not originated in hatred of her character; but that he had required, to enhance his gratification, that his victim, the partner of his guilt, should be hurled from the pinnacle of unsullied virtue, down to the lowest abyss of infamy and degradation: in fine, that all those females whom he had sought, apparently on account of their virtue, had, since his departure, thrown even the mask aside, and had not scrupled to expose the whole deformity of their vices to the public gaze. (p. 269)

On the biographical level we are never told who this "adultress" is. Polidori seems content to let us have our choice: perhaps Lady Caroline Lamb, or even Annǎbella Milbanke. Aubrey, however, loses no time in severing the friendship and moves to other apartments. However, before he goes he informs Ruthven's current inamorata that she is in great danger. She too severs affairs with Ruthven, which only infuriates the literal lady-killer still more. We will never know whether Polidori had Claire Clairmont in mind as the continental victim of Ruthven/Byron, but since the other pieces so neatly fit, it is almost irresistible to so speculate.

Aubrey soon heads off to Greece, meeting on the way Ianthe, a sprightly young beauty who lives with her parents at the edge of the dark woods. It is Ianthe who first tells Aubrey of vampires, how they feed "upon the life of a lovely female," how they slowly destroy their victims, how they are totally without principle or compassion. She even describes their features: the hollow eyes, penetrating stare, pallid skin, lanky frame—all those features that Aubrey soon realizes apply to Lord Ruthven. But like the innocent adolescent of folklore, he is unable to anticipate consequences of an evil that he only intellectually knows exists.

One day Aubrey prepares to go off on an excursion and Ianthe, realizing that he will have to return through the woods at night, pleads with him to spend the night on the far side of the woods and not risk a possible vampire attack. Aubrey laughs at her suggestion, a laugh that has been since heard in almost every vampire story and film. It is the laugh of the foolish youngster who, once warned of the vampire, insists such things can never happen to him. Aubrey crosses the woods by day and starts to return that evening. Halfway through the forest he hears the "shrieks of a woman mingling with the stifled, exultant mockery of a laugh." He rushes to the source, a small dark cabin, heaves open the door, and is accosted by the blurred form of a man who throws him to the ground. Aubrey hears these muffled words, "Again baffled," but he does not understand the meaning. We do, for although Aubrey does not now realize it, the stranger is Ruthven and his "again baffled" refers to the fact that this is the second time that Aubrey has thwarted his desires. Aubrey would doubtless have been murdered were it not for the timely arrival of the local posse armed with torches. Fearing the bright lights, the mysterious figure departs, leaving behind a dazed Aubrey, a bejeweled dagger, and the body of a beautiful girl:

> There was no colour upon her cheek, not even upon her lip; yet there was a stillness about her face that seemed almost as attaching as the life that once dwelt there:—upon her neck and breast was blood, and upon her throat were the marks of teeth having opened the vein:—to this the men pointed, crying, simultaneously struck with horror, "A Vampyre! a Vampyre!" (p. 274)

The mutilated girl was Ianthe. What she was doing in the same woods that she knew to be haunted by vampires is anyone's guess.

Her parents are inconsolable, and die heartbroken; Aubrey weakens and soon becomes bedridden. Now, for some unaccountable reason, in a state of delirium he asks that Ruthven be sent for to nurse him back to health. The victim, like the moth to the flame, seems pathetically drawn to the source of his destruction. As it happens, Ruthven "chanced at this time to arrive at Athens" and is more than happy to aid a companion, even one who had earlier spurned him. As Aubrey improves, however, he is continually horrified by the weird juxtaposition of the sight of Ruthven on the one hand and his memory of the vampire on the other. But he is powerless to send the fiend away, either in memory or in reality.

Ruthven is hale and hearty while Aubrey recovers, but once Aubrey's convalescence is finished Ruthven returns to his original emaciated state. Whether or not Polidori is here introducing a psychological explanation of vampirism is unclear. As far as we know, Ruthven never actually drains Aubrey of blood; instead there is a continual battle for energy: Ruthven grows strong as Aubrey weakens, then Aubrey stabilizes and Ruthven slowly pales. Still, Aubrey never completely recovers his former strength, for he is forever haunted by the memory of his encounter with the vampire. Finally, hoping to dispel these unpleasant memories, he proposes to Ruthven that they visit some out-of-the-way sights in rural Greece. Ruthven naturally accedes.

While traveling through some nameless but remote spot, Aubrey and Ruthven are waylaid by robbers. Ruthven is badly wounded in his shoulder and two days later calls Aubrey to his side. Here he extracts a deathbed promise from Aubrey, a promise that has become a donnée of Gothic fiction:

"Swear!" cried the dying man, raising himself with exultant violence, "Swear by all your soul reveres, by all your nature fears, swear that for a year and a day you will not impart your knowledge of my crimes or death to any living being in any way, whatever may happen, or whatever you may see."—His eyes seemed bursting from their sockets: "I swear!" said Aubrey; he sunk laughing upon his pillow, and breathed no more. (p. 276)

The next day, when Aubrey goes to bury the body, he finds that it has somehow mysteriously disappeared. He later learns that Ruthven had contracted with robbers to drag his corpse to a nearby mountain where it should be "exposed to the first rays of the moon." Once again, Polidori is introducing what will become a common-place of vampire fiction, for this is the first time in any vampire story that moonlight's rejuvenative powers are mentioned. While sorting out Ruthven's possessions, Aubrey finds a strangely shaped jeweled sheath made to hold a dagger of the same size as the one he found next to Ianthe. Aubrey then finds an identical dagger, with caked blood still on it, and realizes the awful truth, the truth he has tried so hard not to admit—that Ruthven is beyond any doubt the vampire.[13]

Aubrey never recovers from this shock. He returns to England for a long conva-lescence, a rest that is interrupted only by a "drawing room party" for his beautiful sister, the charming Miss Aubrey. Timidly standing at the edge of the festivities, he is seized by the arm. He turns—it is Lord Ruthven come back from the dead. Aubrey trembles; "Remember your oath," Ruthven whispers; and Aubrey becomes limp.

Polidori must have realized that the oath was the weakest link in the story, for to increase the pathos of Aubrey's condition, Polidori must make him an honorable man whose word is his bond, yet he must be courageous enough to realize that there can be no honor when dealing with fiends. Nobly Aubrey decides to break his oath and tell all about Ruthven, but ironically his own physical state is so pathetic and his powers of concentration so weak that all who hear the story, in-cluding the same trustees who had earlier warned him of Ruthven, consider it the tale of a madman.

As time passes Aubrey's condition worsens until he is revived by the news of his dear sister's impending wedding to a certain Earl of Marsden. Since he thinks she is free of Ruthven's attentions, his spirits are buoyed; however, chancing upon his sister's locket he finds that her intended husband is no other than the demonic Ruthven, now masquerading as the earl. Aubrey flies into a rage, ranting on about how his sister must forswear this demon, but his outburst only confirms what all have suspected—that Aubrey is insane.

As the wedding day approaches, Aubrey is placed in protective confinement. He bribes one of the servants to carry a last desperate appeal to his sister, but alas, the

---

13. This is admittedly confusing, for a vampire has little need for daggers to ply his trade, but Polidori, perhaps more aware of the Gothic tradition than of the vampire myth, included the dagger—a vestige of the literary tradition.

servant delivers the note to the very doctor who has confined him. The next day, in desperation, Aubrey escapes from his room, rushes downstairs to the ceremony. All set to blurt out the truth, he is clutched once again by his tormentor, who whispers,—"Remember your oath, and know if not my bride today, your sister is dishonoured. Women are frail!" (p. 283). Aubrey is no longer able to contain himself. With hideous appropriateness he bursts a blood vessel and is taken back to bed. He is incoherent until midnight; then exactly a year and a day after his oath, he calmly explains Lord Ruthven's true nature to the now-believing guardians. They rush to protect the innocent bride, "but when they arrived, it was too late. Lord Ruthven had disappeared, and Aubrey's sister had glutted the thirst of a VAMPYRE!" (p. 283).

So ends the first vampire story ever told in English prose. It is, finally, a far cry from Byron's projected story, yet Polidori seems to have Byron's outline in mind, at least in the beginning. He has introduced additional characters, new locations, and vivid details. And, with the exception of the oath, the story has a momentum of its own that is quite sufficient to carry even the most skeptical reader past such contradictions as why a vampire need carry a dagger, or what Ianthe is doing out in the woods at night. *The Vampyre* is also a far cry from the usual Gothic novel. There is none of the trite disinheritance plot and creaking cellar doors that had become almost a staple of the pulps; there is some "local color," and even an attempt at verisimilitude by having much of the action occur in Greece (considered a favorite ground for vampires); and there is no attempt to explain away terror with elaborate ratiocinations, but instead an acceptance of the supernatural on its own terms. Polidori's most important innovation, however, is the introduction of an active villain, a villain as eager to suck the life from his fictional compatriots as is the author to scare the life out of his audience.

Not only was Polidori the first to use the figure of the vampire in prose, but he also seems, like Coleridge and Keats, one of the first to understand its psychological possibilities. For Polidori seems to use the myth in part as an analogy to explain how people interact. To Ianthe and Miss Aubrey, Lord Ruthven is an actual vampire, a horrid demon, but to Aubrey, Ruthven is a parasite of a different sort, a psychological sponge. Ruthven never "attacks" Aubrey, never sucks his blood; yet there does seem to be some energy exchange between the two men. At their first meeting Aubrey is robust, Ruthven pale and thin. Ruthven then strengthens as the relationship deepens and becomes positively "healthy" on the continent, when he dispenses his perverse charity to those he knows will misuse it. But most interesting is what happens when Aubrey is taken ill, for it is Ruthven who nurses him back to health, letting energy now flow from strong character to weak. Polidori explains this strange energy flux:

His lordship [Ruthven] seemed quite changed; he no longer appeared that apathetic being who had so astonished Aubrey; but as soon as his convalescence began to be rapid, he again gradually retired into the same state of mind, and Aubrey perceived no difference from the former man, except that at times he was surprised to meet his gaze fixed intently upon him, with a smile of malicious exultation playing upon his lips: he knew not why, but this smile haunted him. During the last stage of the invalid's recovery, Lord Ruthven was apparently engaged in watching the tideless waves raised by the cooling breeze, or in marking the progress of those orbs, circling, like our world, the moveless sun;—indeed, he appeared to wish to avoid the eyes of all. (p. 274)

It is almost as if Ruthven were "playing with his food." The relationship between Aubrey and Ruthven becomes still more macabre when one considers the familial overtones. We are told that Aubrey comes to London to learn about the world. He is seeking a teacher, someone he can trust, a father. He is an orphan, and the paternal figure he finds is Lord Ruthven. Still this symbiosis between parent and child is never fully developed in Polidori's novella, as it is in, say, Coleridge's *Christabel*—there is only the hint of reciprocity, only the inkling of the interdependence between parent and child.

Ultimately Polidori's novel is remembered (if remembered at all) not for its possibly sophisticated psychology, but for two more mundane reasons. First, by the 1820s it had formally launched the vampire into prose fiction and drama; and second, its appearance under Byron's name had made it a "literary event." Soon after its initial appearance, *The Vampyre* was in such demand that the publishing firm of Sherwood, Nelly, and Jones issued it as a book, which in two years went to six printings and was translated into three French versions and two German ones. In retrospect, however, what made the book so sensational now seems best forgotten. The charge of plagiarism, made by people like Hobhouse and Murray, and buttressed by such statements from Byron as "I was never so disgusted with any human production than with the eternal nonsense . . . emptiness and ill humor, and vanity of that young person [Polidori]," overlooked Byron's insistence that "I have . . . a personal dislike to 'vampires,' and the little acquaintance I have with them would by no means induce me to divulge their secrets."[14] Yet Polidori never escaped censure and a few years later, at the age of twenty-five, committed suicide. Paradoxically a close comparison of the two stories exonerates Polidori, for, if anything, he had written a more interesting, imaginative, and compelling tale than Byron's "Fragment of a Novel" ever promised to be.

Byron's "Fragment," published by John Murray in 1819, was attached to the end of *Mazeppa*, apparently more to prove Byron's wavering claim of being first to write a vampire story than to assert its literary importance. In Byron's story the ingenu is not only a participant, like Polidori's Aubrey, but narrator as well. He tells of his travels to the East accompanied by one Augustus Darvell. This Darvell is a man of fortune and family who, like Ruthven, is slightly older than the hero, and serves as both literal and figurative guide. As they travel, Darvell, who already was "prey to some curious disquiet," becomes "daily more enfeebled" until he seems almost to "waste away." The young narrator is understandably concerned as his companion

14. "Letter to John Murray, June 17, 1816," and "Letter to the Editor" of *Gallignani's Messenger*, 27 April 1819 in *The Works of Lord Byron*, 4: 140, 288.

becomes progressively more withdrawn and silent, but they still continue eastward. When they arrive at the ruins of Ephesus in Turkey, Darvell is simply too weak to continue, and so they camp near a cemetery. Here within sight of this "city of the dead" Darvell asks for water, but no water can be found. Darvell then, almost in a stupor, describes the exact spot of a concealed well not a hundred yards distant. The young narrator queries: "How did you know this?" and Darvell replies, "From our situation; you must perceive that this place was once inhabited, and could not have been so without springs: I have also been here before" (pp. 289–90). Although Darvell is too weak to explain how or when he has been here before, he is strong enough to extract a promise from the narrator that he will never tell anyone of his death. As the young man swears a complex and solemn oath, Darvell removes a "seal ring" from his finger and gives it to his companion, telling him to fling it into the salt springs of the Bay of Eleusis at noon of the ninth day of the month and then to go to the ruins of the temple of Ceres and wait an hour. "Why?" both reader and narrator ask, but we are never told.

Now, inexplicably, a stork with a snake in her beak comes to perch on a grave-stone near the expiring Darvell. When the young narrator tries to frighten the bird away, she only returns to the same spot. Strangely, the stork never eats her prey, and when Darvell is asked to explain he only replies, "It is not yet time." Just as he speaks the bird flies away and, as the narrator turns to tell his companion, he finds him dead. The body now, in most un-vampire-like fashion, starts rapidly to decom-pose, and so the narrator quickly starts digging at the appointed spot. As he does, "the earth suddenly gave way, having already received some Mahometan tenant" (p. 291). The narrator is bewildered, as we are too, for here Byron's fragment ab-ruptly ends.

It is admittedly unfair to judge a completed work like Polidori's with a fragment like Byron's, but certain comparisons can be made. The stories do share Byron's projected outline: two friends travel from England to Greece, one dies and obtains from the other an oath of secrecy; but here the stories break apart. Byron's story is incomplete, while Polidori's has the young man return to England and later meet his former companion. So in a sense Polidori follows Byron's chronological out-line, but he makes a crucial change with regard to character. Polidori's Ruthven is a vampire; Byron's Darvell simply is not. Nowhere in Byron's work is there anything other than a vague suggestion that Darvell is "a being of no common order." Twen-tieth-century critics have still echoed the nineteenth-century contention that Byron was going to write a vampire story, the rough draft of which is his "Fragment." But Byron never said he was going to write a vampire story, and the text of the "Frag-ment" seems to bear him out. [15]

15. See, for instance, Anthony Masters, *The Natural History of the Vampire* (London: Mayflower Books, 1972), p. 201; Margaret L. Carter, *Shadow of a Shade: A Survey of Vampirism in Literature* (New York: Gordon Press, 1975), p. 22; Nancy Garden, *Vampires* (New York: Lippincott, 1973), p. 72; Christopher Frayling, "Introduction" to *The Vampyre: A Bedside Companion*, and James Rieger, "Intro-duction" to Mary Shelley's *Frankenstein* (New York: Bobbs-Merrill, 1974), p. xvii.

Had Byron wished to write a vampire story, one would expect him to have seeded his fragment with more substantial hints of Darvell's true character. Actually, Darvell seems simply another Byronic Hero who, like Lara or the Corsair or any of a host of others, is driven by some inner demon, some mysterious force, into a life of exile. And the central image in Byron's story—the stork with the snake in her beak—is nowhere to be found in vampire lore; it seems more reminiscent of Mayan or Aztec folklore than of middle European. Additionally, when the young narrator is told to fling the ring into the Bay of Eleusis "on the ninth day of the month at noon precisely (what month you please, but this must be the day)" and then to repair to some ruins and wait an hour, we are as baffled by this mumbo-jumbo as is the narrator. We know from such poems as *The Giaour* (ll. 755–86) that Byron was familiar with vampire lore, so presumably he must have intended these instructions for some still unknown purpose. Finally the most crucial bit of evidence that Darvell is not a vampire is the rapid decomposition of his body, for this decay violates the most important principle of the vampire myth, namely the awful imperishability of the flesh.

So I suspect that Byron was not the originator of the vampire story, either in intention or execution. True, the general idea of the story was his, but the character of the vampire was not. Here history may have done Polidori an injustice, on the one hand exonerating him from the charge of plagiarism, while still maintaining that the introduction of the character was Byron's. Since the travelers, the oath, and the return from the dead, were all presumably Byron's ideas, it is understandable to conclude that the characterizations were also, but quite the opposite seems true. The characters—Ruthven, Aubrey, Lady Mercer, and Ianthe—are all clearly Polidori's, and so too is the literal and figurative use of the vampire. Polidori's innovation in the Gothic novel has been unfairly neglected, and while it may be hyperbolic to claim that had Polidori lived he "might now hold a place in the 19th century literary hierarchy slightly above Charlotte Brontë," it is certainly true that Polidori was able to add a character to the dusty pantheon of Gothic villains.[16]

To a considerable extent, the vampire's subsequent durability in both the novel and the cinema is a testament to how Polidori first cast him in prose. It would be a mistake, I think, to see Polidori working outside the tradition of the Gothic, for although the publishing history of *The Vampyre* is startling, the work itself is solidly within the tradition of the Romantic schauerroman. In fact, Ruthven, apart from his Byronic correspondences and blatant vampirism, might well have come from the pen of Walpole or Beckford or Godwin. Indeed, there is a character in fiction two decades earlier who seems to prefigure Ruthven, and that is Schedoni from Mrs. Radcliffe's *The Italian* (1797). In retrospect, it seems almost amazing that Schedoni is not a vampire, for here is the cold, cruel, unrepentant perversion of humankind, an agent of the diabolical who knows no feeling, yet is able to produce feeling in others of the most excruciating kind. Schedoni murders and tortures and

16. James Rieger, "Dr. Polidori and the Genesis of *Frankenstein*," p. 404.

infects without remorse. He is a demon who even looks surprisingly like the vampire Ruthven:

> Among his associates no one loved him, many disliked him, and more feared him. His figure was striking, but not so from grace; it was tall, and, though extremely thin, his limbs were large and uncouth, and as he stalked along, wrapped in the black garments of his order, there was something terrible in its air; something almost superhuman. His cowl, too, as it threw a shade over the livid paleness of his face, increased its severe character, and gave an effect to his large melancholy eye, which approached to horror. His was not the melancholy of a sensible and wounded heart, but apparently that of a gloomy and ferocious disposition. There was something in his physiognomy extremely singular, and that cannot easily be defined. It bore the traces of many passions, which seemed to have fixed the features they no longer animated. An habitual gloom and severity prevailed over the deep lines of his countenance; and his eyes were so piercing that they seemed to penetrate, at a single glance, into the hearts of men, and to read their most secret thoughts; few persons could support their scrutiny, or even endure to meet them twice.[17]

Schedoni also looks surprisingly like another character in late Gothic fiction, Emily Brontë's Heathcliff. Indeed, Heathcliff is a lineal descendant of the Gothic antihero who has as his grand progenitor Milton's Satan, and was carried through Romanticism in such characters as Radcliffe's Schedoni, Blake's Devil, Shelley's Cenci, the Byronic Heroes, Polidori's Ruthven, Lewis's Ambrosio (again almost but not quite a vampire), until finally dissipating into Varney the Vampyre of the "penny dreadful." Before the midcentury doldrums, however, the vampire reached an artistic peak in the demon-cum-vampire figure of Heathcliff.

To contend that Heathcliff acts like a vampire seems the height of critical folly. For in this century we have lifted *Wuthering Heights* from its Gothic context, preferring to see it as a work existing apart from any tradition, a literary enigma, sui generis. I think this is a mistake, although an understandable one. The Renaissance Italians had an explanation for this process by which succeeding generations can rarify a work of art out of context. The first generation, so they said, sees what is in the foreground. The second, as if to show its heightened sensibilities, only sees what is in the background, and the third, not willing to be denied the last word, sees what is not there. Nowhere do we more clearly see this process than in the criticism of *Wuthering Heights*.

Witness, for example, what has happened to Heathcliff. To the first generation of critics he was a "fiend," "an incarnation of evil qualities," filled with "implacable hate," as well as "ingratitude, cruelty, falsehood, selfishness and revenge." He was a devil, "impelled to evil by supernatural forces."[18] A strain of this kind of criticism

17. Ann Radcliffe, *The Italian* (1796; rpt. London: Oxford University Press, 1968), pp. 34–35.
18. For instance, see "Currer Bell," *Palladium* (Sept. 1850), p. 12; "A Strange Book," *Examiner* (8 Jan. 1848), p. 31; or almost any contemporary review as well as "Humanity in Its Wild State," *Britannica* (15 Jan. 1848), p. 16.

still continues today, with Mary Visick calling Heathcliff "a skinflint and a bully," but the old venom has somehow disappeared.[19] The second generation of critics saw Heathcliff not in black but in shades of gray. So to Dorothy Van Ghent he represented "a part of nature which is 'other' than the human soul"; or for David Cecil and V. S. Pritchett, he was the principle of storm, acting, as Cecil said "involuntarily under the pressure of his own nature."[20] Then there was David Wilson, who saw Heathcliff as part of "the social struggle of Brontë's time."[21] For these more subtle interpreters, Heathcliff ceased to be human (and hence culpable), and was part of a social or natural process in which he was pathetically powerless. All that was left for the next generation—our generation—was to see Heathcliff as a mortal, fallible man who does his best in a scurvy world, and recently Larry Champion has put forth just that argument. In the fallen world of Wuthering Heights, Champion contends, Heathcliff constructs his own value system and heroically sticks to it. In doing this, Champion concludes,

> There can be little doubt that the author has intended Heathcliff to be, not a devil or a bully or an elemental symbol, but a credible protagonist. Emily Brontë has carefully and methodically created an atmosphere in which sympathy for his revenge can be achieved and has so manipulated the surrounding characters and events that transfer of sympathy becomes a virtual impossibility.[22]

So here we have in microcosm the whole critical circle. Heathcliff has gone from devil to tragic hero in three generations of critics. Perhaps it is now time to reconsider the merits of seeing him as devil. To do so is difficult because so many of the other characters have lost their relative status in Heathcliff's rise to sympathy. First to go was Nelly Dean, who was the one "moral," "normal," "practical" person in the novel, but who now, according to James Hafley, has displaced Heathcliff to become "the villain."[23] And when she fell (for indeed Hafley makes an impressive case), she took Catherine with her. In fact, it is now Catherine, in her refusal to be honest with her own feelings (marrying Edgar when she didn't love him), who forces poor Heathcliff into taking revenge. The problem has become still more complex, for with the defrocking of Nelly we have lost the only witness to much of what has occurred.

I must say that I cannot resolve this bind. All we can do now is take what Nelly says, weigh it carefully, and then accept it only if it is borne out by the observations of other characters. I make this point because, although Nelly never says so, there is much in her story to suggest that Heathcliff acts as if he were a vampire. This is

19. Mary Visick, *The Genesis of "Wuthering Heights"* (Hong Kong: Hong Kong University Press, 1958), p. 6.

20. Dorothy Van Ghent, *The English Novel: Form and Function* (New York: Rinehart, 1953), p. 164; and David Cecil, *Early Victorian Novelists* (Indianapolis: Bobbs-Merrill Co., 1953), p. 174.

21. David Wilson, *The Critic* 1 (1947): 44.

22. Larry Champion, "Heathcliff: A Study in Authorial Technique," *Ball State University Forum* 9 (1968): 25.

23. James Hafley, "The Villain of *Wuthering Heights*," *Nineteenth-Century Fiction* 13 (1958): 199.

not to imply that Heathcliff is a vampire, only that his relationships with other people can be explained metaphorically. All we need do is listen to Nelly as she muses about Heathcliff near the end of her tale:

> "Is he a ghoul, or a vampire?" I mused. I had read of such hideous, incarnate demons. And then, I set myself to reflect, how I had tended him in infancy; and watched him grow to youth; and followed him almost through his whole course; and what absurd nonsense it was to yield to that sense of horror.
>
> "But, where did he come from, the little dark thing, harboured by a good man to his bane?" muttered superstition, as I dozed into unconsciousness. And I began, half dreaming, to weary myself with imaging some fit parentage for him; and repeating my waking meditations, I tracked his existence over again, with grim variations; at last, picturing his death and funeral of which, all I can remember is, being exceedingly vexed at having the task of dictating an inscription for his monument, and consulting the sexton about it; and, as he had no surname, and we could not tell his age, we were obliged to content ourselves with the single word, "Heathcliff." That came true; we were. If you enter the kirkyard, you'll read on his headstone, only that, and the date of his death.
>
> Dawn restored me to common sense. I rose, and went into the garden, as soon as I could see, to ascertain if there were any footmarks under his window. There were none. (p. 280)[24]

Nelly may "protest too much" about her superstitions, for she is still—even after Heathcliff's death—checking for footprints. Emily Brontë obviously wanted the reader to feel the same uneasiness, for although Heathcliff is never shown as an active vampire (for that would have ruined our superstitions), we are shown an occasional footprint or two, just enough to keep us checking.

First, as Nelly says above, we know nothing about Heathcliff's parentage. He comes to Wuthering Heights with no surname, no age, no identification whatsoever, yet we do know that he immediately stirs revulsion. Even Mr. Earnshaw realizes this. He tells his wife, "See here, wife;.I was never so beaten with anything in my life, but you must e'en taken it as a gift of God; though it's as dark almost as if it came from the devil" (p. 30). And Nelly continues:

> We crowded round, and, over Miss Cathy's head, I had a peep at a dirty, ragged, black-haired child; big enough both to walk and talk—indeed, its face looked older than Catherine's—yet, when it was set on its feet it only stared round, and repeated over and over again some gibberish that nobody could understand. I was frightened, and Mrs. Earnshaw was ready to fling it out of doors. . . . (p. 30)

---

24. Emily Brontë, *Wuthering Heights* (Boston: Houghton Mifflin, 1956). Page numbers will appear in parentheses after quotations in the text.

Admittedly Nelly is prejudicial in retrospect, but again and again Heathcliff is referred to by the other characters as an "imp of Satan" (p. 33) or "a charge of the devil" (p. 93), for "truly it appeared as if the lad *were* possessed of something diabolical" (p. 55). These accusations are never really taken seriously, however. They are, as it were, only footprints to be followed or not.

Emily Brontë seems content to let us slide the vampire legend behind Heathcliff, almost as if it were a metaphor to explain his peculiar behavior. Whether or not he actually does suck blood, he acts *as if he were* vamping other characters. It is especially in periods of great stress that Heathcliff assumes vampiric characteristics to heighten the reader's reaction. For instance, after Lockwood tells his dream in which he rubs Catherine's wrist over broken glass until it bleeds, Heathcliff reacts by "crushing his nails into his palms and grinding his teeth to subdue the maxillary convulsions" (p. 21). Are we to believe that if Heathcliff did not grind his teeth together, perhaps he would be involved in some paroxysm of biting?

We will never know exactly what the relationship was between Heathcliff and Catherine, for much has wisely been left out. Nevertheless, it seems that Catherine is the one he "vamps," perhaps only in the psychological sense, but even that is left ambiguous. By their late teens these two seem to have established a peculiar kind of symbiosis, living off the metaphorical blood/energy of each other. By the time Cathy proclaims, "I *am* Heathcliff" (p. 70), the transfusion seems complete; in fact, she may be quite literally stating the truth.

If this symbiosis is the case and neither can live without sustenance from the other, it may be instructive to look again at the last love scene between Heathcliff and Catherine. Heathcliff has sneaked into Thrushcross Grange and rushes immediately into Catherine's arms. Nelly reports:

> He neither spoke, nor loosed his hold, for some five minutes, during which period he bestowed more kisses than ever he gave in his life before, I dare say; but then my mistress had kissed him first, and I plainly saw that he could hardly bear, for downright agony, to look into her face! The same conviction had stricken him as me, from the instant he beheld her, that there was no prospect of ultimate recovery there—she was fated sure to die. (p. 135)

Why is she now "fated sure to die"? How do both Nelly and Heathcliff know this? Of course, when Catherine dies, she will carry Heathcliff's blood-sustenance with her, and she makes it a point to remind him, "You have killed me—and thriven on it, I think. How strong you are! How many years do you mean to live after I am gone?" Heathcliff responds characteristically: "Don't torture me till I am as mad as yourself," cried he, wrenching his head free and grinding his teeth" (p. 135). This macabre scene continues:

> Her present countenance had a wild vindictiveness in its white cheek, and a bloodless lip, and scintillating eye; and she retained, in her closed fingers, a portion of the locks she had been grasping. As to her companion, while raising himself with one hand, he had taken her arm with the other; and so inade-

quate was his stock of gentleness to the requirements of her condition, that on his letting go, I saw four distinct impressions left blue in the colourless skin.

"Are you possessed with a devil," he pursued, savagely, "to talk in that manner to me, when you are dying?" (pp. 135–36)

This passage must have been the most difficult of all for Emily Brontë to write, for Nelly must be able to report the goings-on without actually having seen their vampiric overtones. Still Brontë must let us see them. The scene rises to another climax when Catherine asks Heathcliff to "embrace her again":

At that earnest appeal, he turned to her, looking absolutely desperate. His eyes wide, and wet, at last, flashed fiercely on her, his breast heaved convulsively. An instant they held asunder; and then how they met I hardly saw, but Catherine made a spring, and he caught her, and they were locked in an embrace from which I thought my mistress would never be released alive. In fact, to my eyes, she seemed directly insensible. He flung himself into the nearest seat, and on my approaching hurriedly to ascertain if she had fainted, he gnashed at me, and foamed like a mad dog, and gathered her to him with greedy jealousy. I did not feel as if I were in the company of a creature of my own species; it appeared that he would not understand, though I spoke to him; so I stood off, and held my tongue in great perplexity. (p. 137)

An understandably shaken Nelly concludes the scene by spotting the congregation gathering outside Gimmerton Chapel, and tersely announces to the loving pair, "Service is over."

After Catherine's death the suggestions become more pronounced as Heathcliff's behavior grows more and more macabre. The farewell scene retold above occurred on 19 March. Catherine died a day later, and she was buried, as is stressed again and again, just outside the pale of the churchyard on 24 March 1784. In 1801, after the death of Edgar Linton, Heathcliff tells Nelly what he did on the night of Catherine's burial. He feverishly reports that he dug down to her coffin and was all set to throw it open when he felt her warm breath above him, and realized that "Cathy was there, not under me, but on the earth" (p. 245). This makes little sense to either the reader or Nelly, but he tells us no more. He throws the dirt back into her grave and returns to Wuthering Heights. In his own words now:

Having reached the Heights, I rushed eagerly to the door. It was fastened; and, I remember, that accursed Earnshaw and my wife opposed my entrance. I remember stopping to kick the breath out of him, and then hurrying upstairs, to my room, and hers—I looked around impatiently—I felt her by me—I could *almost* see her, and yet I *could not*! I ought to have sweat blood then, from the anguish of my yearning, from the fervour of my supplications to have but one glimpse! I had not one. She showed herself, as she often was in life, a devil to me! (pp. 245–46)

To find out how he really returned home we need to consult Isabella's letter to Nelly, for only Isabella can tell us what he was like that night. According to her, after his midnight revels, Heathcliff returned home and found the door locked. Isabella describes seeing him through the open casement: "His hair and clothes were whitened with snow, and his sharp cannibal teeth . . . gleamed through the dark" (p. 150).

When we put the whole story together—part told by Heathcliff, part by Isabella, none by Nelly—we may have a picture of Heathcliff's demonic nature. He has suppressed the essential nature of his experience at Catherine's grave and Nelly draws no conclusions, but his appearance to Isabella gives him away.

This is only the first time that Heathcliff goes to Catherine's grave. The second occurs on the day of Edgar Linton's interment. This time Heathcliff bribes the sexton to let him open Catherine's coffin and pry loose one side. Nelly asks if it isn't wicked to disturb the dead:

> "I disturbed nobody, Nelly," he replied; "and I gave some ease to myself. I shall be a great deal more comfortable now; and you'll have a better chance of keeping me underground, when I get there. Disturbed her? No! She has disturbed me, night and day, through eighteen years—incessantly—remorselessly—till yesternight—and yesternight, I was tranquil. I dreamt I was sleeping the last sleep, by that sleeper, with my heart stopped, and my cheek frozen against hers." (p. 244)

Apparently having gathered strength from his second trip to Catherine, Heathcliff continues his diabolical ways until November, when Lockwood comes to call, finds Catherine's diary and has the dream of Catherine's bloody hand which triggers Heathcliff's "maxillary convulsions" (p. 21).

About five months later Heathcliff is running low on energy: he is losing his life, for his source of sustenance has been depleted. He cannot strike the young Catherine (p. 272); he can no longer enjoy the process of destruction (p. 274), and he even must remind himself to breathe (p. 274). He goes out every midnight, and returns each morning, pale, with a "strange joyful glitter in his eyes" (p. 277). Where has he been? What has he done? We are never told. Nelly offers him food but he cannot eat. He seems so calm "it was unnatural—[the] appearance of joy under his black brows; the same bloodless hue: and his teeth visible, now and then, in a kind of smile; his frame shivering, not as one shivers with chill or weakness, but as a tightstretched cord vibrates—a strong thrilling, rather than trembling" (p. 278).

Night after night he is off on the prowl: day by day he abstains from food. His cheeks grow hollow and his eyes turn red (p. 282). Then one morning Nelly notices his window open and the rain driving in. She peeks into his room:

> Mr. Heathcliff was there—laid on his back. His eyes met mine so keen, and fierce, I started; and then he seemed to smile.

I could not think him dead—but his face, and throat were washed with rain; the bed-clothes dripped, and he was perfectly still. The lattice, flapping to and fro, had grazed one hand that rested on the sill—no blood trickled from the broken skin, and when I put my fingers to it, I could doubt no more—he was dead and stark!

I hasped the window; I combed his black hair from his forehead; I tried to close his eyes—to extinguish, if possible, that frightful, life-like gaze of exultation, before anyone else beheld it. They would not shut—they seemed to sneer at my attempts, and his parted lips, and sharp, white teeth sneered too! (p. 284)

Eyes open, half-smile, bloodless cut, drawn-back lips, gleaming teeth—Doctor Kenneth may not be able to make the diagnosis, but the nineteenth-century reader could.

What such a reading does, of course, is to return Heathcliff to the way he was viewed by the first generation of critics. He is the scourge, the infector carrying the plague to all he meets. He may be pathetic in that he is trapped into passions he cannot overcome, but he is in no way tragic. For as we have seen, Emily Brontë went to considerable lengths to make vampirism a possible explanation for his aberrant behavior. That she was able to succeed in portraying Heathcliff as at least metaphorically vampiric depended on her midcentury audience's ability to supply what was missing—they had to know enough about vampires to fill in the blanks around Heathcliff's unexplained character. Certainly Charlotte Brontë's characterization of Bertha Rochester shows that the myth was current in Yorkshire; still if additional proof be necessary to show how knowledgeable that audience was, it is amply provided in a work first published serially seven years before *Wuthering Heights* and *Jane Eyre*—the incredibly popular and lurid and tedious *Varney the Vampyre, or the Feast of Blood*.

Varney the Vampyre was justifiably the most celebrated of the mid-nineteenth-century "shockers," for it carried the schaurroman to levels of splendid excess. It is also celebrated because it is so often referred to in criticism of the "popular novel," yet so seldom read; for as E. F. Bleiler has contended, "[*Varney*] may well qualify as the most famous book that almost no one has read."[25] In part this is because until recent times the book simply could not be found, even though great numbers were published serially in the 1840s and then in book form several years later. *Varney* seems to have been a work that was read literally into dust. In the 1930s Montague Summers tried to purchase a copy, but none could be found in the private market. Then a decade ago there was sufficient interest to photoduplicate one of the two extant copies held in the British Museum, and now there is no excuse for not reading it. No excuse, that is, except for one's sanity. For the complete *Varney* (almost complete—a few chapters and pages are missing, or at least seem that way!)

25. E. F. Bleiler, "Introduction" to the Dover edition of *Varney the Vampyre* (New York: Dover Publications, 1973), p. viii.

is one of the most redundant, exorbitant, digressive, thrilling, tedious, and fantastic works ever written.

Varney's oxymoronic nature is a result of both composition and audience: it was written for the first of the mass-market audiences by one of the most prosperous Grub Street publishing houses, the House of Edward Lloyd. *Varney* was written episodically and in a hurry, printed on the first of the great steam presses, typeset on assembly line, hawked in the streets, then read into scraps. Although we know how *Varney* was written and printed, no one knows who wrote it, for as with many other works produced by Lloyd, it seems the result of composite authorship. In the Lloyd offices off Salisbury Square a small factory of hacks turned out reams of these proletarian potboilers. In fact, *Varney* may be best appreciated in the context of what else was being spewed out from the presses between the 1840s and the 1860s. Just a few titles of this ludicrous gore will suffice: *Wagner the Were-Wolf; The Coral Island, or The Hereditary Curse; The Bronze Statue, or The Virgin's Curse; Pope Joan, or the Female Pontiff; The Greek Maiden, or The Banquet of Blood; Ada the Betrayed, or The Murder at the Old Smithy; The Child of Mystery, or The Cottager's Daughter; The Hebrew Maiden, or The Lost Diamond; The Maniac Father, or The Victim of Seduction; Ernestine de Lacy, or The Robber's Foundling; Almira's Curse, or The Black Tower of Bransdorf; The Skeleton Clutch, or The Goblet of Gore; The Death Ship, or The Pirate's Bride and the Maniac of the Deep; Sawney Bean, The Man Eater of Midlothian. . . .*

Not only were there scores of these "bloods" produced weekly, but often a number of authors would collaborate simultaneously on different works. So just as there is no consistency within the genre, there is often no consistency within the individual work. For instance, in places *Varney* is well written (as in the first chapter or in the introduction of Baron Stolmuyer), while in other places it rises only to fall to bathos (as the chapters following p. 127, where the new authors seem to forget what had earlier been written). Likewise there is little internal consistency about *Varney*'s past: we are told he became a vampire for killing his wife and then later for killing his son. Or we are informed that he has lived since the age of Henry IV, but later that he became a vampire during the Restoration, and still later that he was a contemporary criminal who turned into a vampire after being hanged. In one chapter we are told that he cannot eat meat; then a few pages later he is seen having a steak dinner. The evidence of different hands is especially apparent in the second half, when *Varney* starts a series of episodic and almost unconnected adventures in Italy and England. In fact, the only part of the novel that seems to bear the mark of a single hand is the first third, and the hand seems to be that of James Malcolm Rymer rather than that of Thomas Pecket Prest, as Montague Summers so confidently contended.[26] But no matter, *Varney* is the important transitional work be-

---

26. This problem of authorship is discussed by E. F. Bleiler, in "A Note on Authorship" in the Dover edition of *Varney the Vampyre,* pp. xvii–xviii. Louis James, working from Rymer's proof copy and scrapbooks, seems now to have established "majority authorship" as James Malcom Rymer, *Fiction for the Working Man 1830–1850* (London: Oxford University Press, 1963), p. 36.

tween the Romantic vampire tales and Bram Stoker's *Dracula*, and since reading its 868 pages of double-columned miniscule print is something only the zealous would attempt, I have summarized the plot in an appendix (see page 207). Admittedly much is lost in such a summary, but at least not the reader's eyesight.

Varney is really unparalleled even in vampire lore: part melodrama, part picaresque novel, part theodicy, part parody, part travesty—it is proof, if any really be needed, of the popular acceptance of the myth, for *Varney* deals with all the clichés in the most unselfconscious manner. There is no pretense, no purpose, no art; just a rollicking story. As opposed to its earlier, more sombre treatments, the vampire myth in *Varney* is not the means of telling the story, but the story itself; and *Varney*, for all its vulgarity, established the vampire solidly in the culture of the most common reader, where he has still continued to thrive. There is so little art in *Varney* that even other "penny-dreadfuls," such as *Knight's Penny Magazine* (1846), found it tiresome. It made no difference, of course; while *Varney* was still coming out in penny parts, the Bannerworth episode was being dramatized and rushed to the stage. If there is any deep truth in *Varney*, it is surely that one must never allow a vampire too much moonlight and one must never pay writers by the word.

Still, one cannot dismiss *Varney*, especially because of its clear and continuing impact on the vampire stories of the midcentury, to say nothing of our own cultural resurrections of the vampire. The initiation of the heroine through sex, the vampire's middle-European background, the quasi-medical-scientific explanations, the midnight vigils, the mob scene (which became so stylized in James Whale's horror films at Universal Studios), the hunt and the chase, all these and more are in *Varney*. They have all become clichés today, not because we have sifted through the story to find the moments of impact, but rather because our great-grandparents did. In fact, much of the credit we give Bram Stoker really belongs to the authors of *Varney*.

There are two other works that need be mentioned before discussing *Dracula*, if only because they both show inventive variations with the same material: Edgar Allan Poe's *The Fall of the House of Usher* and J. Sheridan LeFanu's *Carmilla*. Neither is as obstreperous as *Varney*, and both happily are far more sophisticated.

It is one of the paradoxes of literary scholarship that often a minor aspect of a work, especially if it has some odd peculiarity, will receive an inordinate amount of criticism as scholars tend to be more tantalized by this eccentricity than by the work itself. So with Poe's *The Fall of the House of Usher*, where one of the most peripheral instances of vampirism has sparked considerable discussion. This began in the early 1960s when two critics, Lyle Kendall and J. O. Bailey, almost simultaneously followed the general arguments of D. H. Lawrence and Allen Tate to the same, or nearly the same, conclusion; namely, that something or someone is vampiric in Poe's story. Neither critic, however, was absolutely sure who or what it was or, more importantly, why it was of any significance.[27]

27. The vampirism in "Usher" was discussed almost simultaneously a decade ago by Lyle H. Kendall, Jr., in "The Vampire Motif in *The Fall of the House of Usher*," *College English* 24 (March 1963): 450–53;

In the 1920s D. H. Lawrence had discussed the story, as was his wont with most of Poe's works, in terms of character, using such favorite concepts as "sympathetic vibration," "destructive interference," or "resonance" to describe interactions between Madeline and Roderick. His thesis, simply put, was that these two protagonists vibrated so long against each other that when one (Madeline) ceased resisting, the other (Roderick) lost harmonic balance and "identification with the beloved became a lust."[28] It is therefore the story of a lover driven mad by the lack of resistance. In addition, according to Lawrence, Poe made this love incestuous to show how important barriers must be if both parties are to remain sane. In Lawrence's own words:

> In the human realm, Roderick had one connection: his sister Madeline. She, too, was dying of a mysterious disorder, nervous, cataleptic. The brother and sister loved each other passionately and exclusively. They were twins, almost identical in looks. It was the same absorbing love between them, this process of unison in nerve-vibration, resulting in more and more extreme exaltation and a sort of consciousness, and a gradual break-down into death. The exquisitely sensitive Roger [sic] vibrating without resistance with his sister Madeline more and more exquisitely, and gradually devouring her, sucking her life like a vampire in his anguish of extreme love. And she asking to be sucked.[29]

Allen Tate in "Our Cousin Mr. Poe" agreed with Lawrence about how the process of spiritual love gone awry becomes vampiric, but wondered why Poe "did not explicitly use the universal legend of the vampire."[30] His answer was simply that Poe needed both aesthetic distance and freedom from the vampire's all-too-prescribed lifestyle. So Poe deliberately blurred the myth to make it more a general statement of human condition than a consistent parallel. The vampire thus became a metaphor to express the human desire for primal unity. Poe's lovers do consume each other in a psychological and intellectual sense; there is no eroticism, rather "love" is always a desire for domination. However, Tate, as opposed to Lawrence, does not see Roderick as the vampire, but rather Madeline. Roderick has attempted to possess Madeline, to destroy her independence: he has attempted to suffocate her being, but she will not be so easily debilitated, so she finally returns lamialike from the tomb to "suffocate" him in the vampire's embrace. Did Poe know what he was doing? Did he know he was using a century-old analogy of the lover as vampire? Tate suspects not. Once again, as opposed to Lawrence, he believed that it was Poe's genius not to know what he was doing; rather to be so intuitive that he could use the myth unaware. For as Tate contends:

---

and more completely in J. O. Bailey, "What Happens in *The Fall of the House of Usher*," *American Literature* 35 (Jan. 1964): 445–66.

28. D. H. Lawrence, *Selected Literary Criticism*, ed. Anthony Beal (1932; rpt. New York: The Viking Press, 1966), p. 341.

29. Ibid., p. 343.

30. Allen Tate, "Our Cousin, Mr. Poe," in *The Forlorn Demon* (Chicago: Regnery, 1953), p. 84.

By these observations I do not suggest that Poe was conscious of what he was doing; had he been, he might have done it even worse. I am not saying, in other words, that Poe is offering us, in the Lady Madeline, a vampire according to Bram Stoker's specifications. An imagination of any power at all will often project its deepest assumptions about life in symbols that duplicate, without the artist's knowledge, certain meanings, the origins of which are sometimes as old as the race. If a writer ambiguously exalts the "spirit" over the "body," and the spirit must live wholly upon another spirit, some version of the vampire legend is likely to issue as the symbolic situation.[31]

Although recent critics have given Poe more credit for being conscious of what he was doing, there is still no consensus about who is vamping whom. Where D. H. Lawrence contended that Roderick was sucking life from a willing Madeline, and Tate believed that Roderick "possessed" his sister and she returned "like a vampire" to destroy him, Lyle Kendall in "The Vampire Motif in *The Fall of the House of Usher*" made the point that Madeline is a succubus, or a lamia, who has already been attacking her brother prior to the narrator's arrival.[32] Hence Roderick suffers from what appears to be pernicious anemia, but is in truth blood loss caused by the voracious Madeline. Kendall's evidence is Roderick's unexplained pallor, the perplexity of the physician, the brother-sister/parasite-host references, and Roderick's own pathetic attempts to protect himself from the she-vampire by reading books on exorcism and demonic defense. Poe lays all these hints before us, Kendall contends, so that we may piece together a parable of evil, a story that shows through the vampire myth how evil is self-defeating, literally self-consuming.

A still more imaginative interpretation is J. O. Bailey's "What Happens in *The Fall of the House of Usher.*" Bailey accepts the same documentation of the details as do the other critics, except that he is more concerned with the documentor than with the details. It is essential in Bailey's view to realize that the narrator is not common sense personified; rather, he is obtuse, ignorant, and occasionally blind to knowledge that is right before him. For instance, he implies that Roderick is both an opium eater and a drunkard, hence hardly a credible witness, but nowhere do we ever see an addicted Roderick. The narrator goes to considerable lengths to tell us that Roderick is mad, but once again, nowhere is this shown. Perhaps, says Bailey, we had best suspend judgments about the narrator and Roderick and Madeline, if only because none of them is in a position to know the complete story.[33] When we do this, we are left with the two languorous and pale Ushers, and one hyperactive and erratic narrator.

Or are we? Bailey contends that there is another character as well, a character whose presence pervades the whole story, including the title—*The House of Usher*. For the house, as both a family edifice and as an archetype of family, is a dominant

31. Ibid., p. 88.
32. Lyle H. Kendall, "The Vampire Motif in *The Fall of the House of Usher*," *College English* 24 (March 1963): 450–53.
33. J. O. Bailey, "What Happens in *The Fall of the House of Usher*," pp. 445–66.

theme. It is the house that has imprisoned Madeline and Roderick; it is the house that figures as the psychic oppressor in the central poem, "The Haunted Palace"; and it is the house that finally comes tumbling down after the mutual extinction of Madeline and Roderick. The literal house of Usher falls when the figurative house of Usher, Madeline and Roderick, prove unregenerative. This interchange between house and family or, in the story's terms, the "sentience of all things," is Poe's theme, and all the hints of vampirism (the threshold scene, the full moon, the Hallowe'en time, the violent localized storm, the repetition of "incubus,") are simply parts of this larger analogy.

So in a sense critics have found vampirism in every character: in Madeline, in Roderick, and even in the House of Usher itself. As if these were not enough, I should now like to propose a fourth alternative, the only one left—the narrator himself. Professor Bailey has already called into question the narrator's veracity, but he did not take the next step to contend that the narrator might well be the villain of the piece. I don't really want to go that far either, but I do think it important that we remember the narrators in Poe's earlier stories, for they certainly are a sorry lot. In *Berenice*, in *Morella*, and in *Ligeia* the narrator has been an addict of some kind, and this addiction has blurred his ability to recount the truth. Usually this truth is that he himself has been the perpetrator of some heinous act in which he has enervated a loved one. I think the narrator in *The Fall of the House of Usher* can also be viewed in this context.

There is some indication in the text of the narrator's suspicious and even demonic manner. Ostensibly he has come to help a fellow in distress, but one wonders by his all-too-eager participation in such hideous acts as the entombment of Madeline whether he is not somehow more deeply involved than he wishes us to realize. From the outset he hardly fills us with confidence. For instance, when describing the House of Usher from a distance, he compares his feelings to "the afterdream of the reveller upon opium" (p. 115), and later uses the same general terms to describe Roderick's voice:

> . . . that leaden, self-balanced and perfectly modulated guttural utterance, which may be observed in the lost drunkard, or the irreclaimable eater of opium, during the periods of his most intense excitement. (p. 119)[34]

Why should he use this pharmacological analogy, unless he himself has experimented with mind-altering drugs, or at least wants us to think so? Like the earlier narrators in *Berenice*, *Morella*, or *Ligeia*, he simply cannot be counted on to tell the truth. He even makes some judgments that are simply not borne out in fact; for instance, he implies that the family surgeon is a perfidious character: "On one of the staircases, I met the physician of the family. His countenance, I thought, wore a mingled expression of low cunning and perplexity" (p. 118). This is almost a throwaway scene, for we never meet the doctor again, yet it may well hint of the

34. Page numbers in parentheses after quotations will be from *The Fall of the House of Usher* in *The Selected Poetry and Prose of Edgar Allan Poe*, ed. T. O. Mabbott (New York: Modern Library, 1951).

narrator's duplicity, for if the narrator were metaphorically vampiric, the doctor would be his natural enemy. Also, the narrator sets forth a litany of evidence that points to Roderick's and Madeline's mutual degradation: Roderick's cadaverous appearance, Madeline's ghastly pallor, Roderick's ghoulish poem and demonic reading list, Madeline's wasting away, and her subsequent entombment in the dark vault—all these things he describes as a detached and impartial observer. But he is not as detached as he appears to be; as a matter of fact, he is quite involved with the central action. On the night of Madeline's entombment as he is lying in bed,

> an irrepressible tremour gradually pervaded my frame; and, at length, there sat upon my very heart an incubus of utterly causeless alarm. Shaking this off with a gasp and a struggle, I uplifted myself upon the pillows, and, peering earnestly within the intense darkness of the chamber, hearkened—I know not why, except that an instinctive spirit prompted me—to certain low and indefinite sounds which came, through the pauses of the storm, at long intervals, I knew not whence. (p. 126)

He rises from bed, ostensibly because he is possessed by this "incubus"; but could it not be that as a creature of the night himself he has his own plans for the Ushers? I would never say this had he stayed on the fringe of the story and simply reported, but instead he actively participates. He goes downstairs where Roderick is going through the trials of the damned, or at least that is the way it is described: actually, a close look at the final scenes makes things far more confusing. In the living room Roderick hears the sounds of his sister's footsteps coming closer and closer; then he hears the beating of her heart; then he suddenly turns to the narrator:

> "Will she not be here anon? Is she not hurrying to upbraid me for my haste? Have I not heard her footsteps on the stair? Do I not distinguish that heavy and horrible beating of her heart? MAD-MAN!" here he sprang furiously to his feet, and shrieked out his syllables, as if in the effort he were giving up his soul—"MAD-MAN! I TELL YOU THAT SHE NOW STANDS WITHOUT THE DOOR!" (p. 130)

Who is this "madman"? Is it just an antecedentless reference, or is he referring specifically to the narrator? Since Roderick buried his sister with the narrator's seeming willingness, the idea might have been the narrator's—a stratagem we were understandably not informed of. In this case it makes some sense that Roderick might lash out and condemn the narrator, who now neglects to explain Roderick's actions to us. Madeline arrives with blood on her robes, blood that the narrator claims was evidence of some bitter struggle, yet again he neglects to name the combatants. This narrative process is so reminiscent of what happens in *Berenice*, where the narrator does not bother or remember to tell us how he got blood and gore all over his clothing. The two pathetically enervated Ushers now die in each other's arms, and the narrator, possible catalyst of their destruction, simply packs up and rides off into "the blood red moon." All crumbles behind him, leaving us as perplexed at the end as we were at the beginning.

If such a reading of the narrator as vampire is possible, it would show Poe working in a frame very much like Coleridge in *The Rime of the Ancient Mariner*, or Henry James in *The Sacred Fount*. For it is the narrator, the displaced artist himself, who may be the culprit in his own tale. As we shall see in *The Oval Portrait*, the exchange of energies between creator and created, artist and artifact, is very much on Poe's mind during the early 1840s. It is also very much in the spirit of Romanticism, for the Romantic artist was nothing if not the continual observer of his own creations, the taker of his own artistic pulse. This is not, of course, to deny that the other characters, Roderick, Madeline, and even the House, are vampiric, for indeed they may well be, but only to stress that vampirism as a mode of discussing energy exchange is a more complex aspect of the story than has been critically acknowledged.

J. Sheridan LeFanu has been called the "Irish Edgar Allan Poe" with some reason, for he too found in the macabre the means to explore human interaction, and, like Poe, many of his stories have been read and enjoyed simply for their scary effects. As early as 1880, when Henry James described a night in an English countryhouse, he included "the customary novel of LeFanu at the bedside, ideal for after-midnight reading."[35] Although LeFanu did more than write midnight tales— for he was a writer of amazing versatility (historical romances, comical local color stories, ballads, poetic dramas, reviews)—he is still best known for these bedside thrillers, the most famous of which is *Carmilla*.

As a vampire story *Carmilla* is less diffuse than *Dracula*, less frothy than *Varney*, less dull than *The Vampyre*; it is, in fact, a masterful little tale. It owes its mastery in part to LeFanu's conscious attempt to render Coleridge's *Christabel* into prose, especially the descriptions of the psychodynamics of perversion. For *Carmilla*, like *Christabel*, is the story of a lesbian entanglement, a story of the sterile love of homosexuality expressed through the analogy of vampirism. And as such, it has become the copytext of a subgenre in the cinema that rivals *Dracula* in numbers if not in redundancy. From Carl Dreyer's masterful *Vampyr* (1932), there has been a spate of female vampire movies: *Blood and Roses*, *The Vampire Lovers*, *Lust for a Vampire*, *Twins of Evil*, and others—all based on *Carmilla*.

Briefly, this is LeFanu's story. Laura, who is now almost thirty, is writing of what happened to her a decade ago. At that time she was living with her father in a castle somewhere in the forests of middle Europe. The setting is all very gothic—stone castles, dark woods, evening mist, full moon, hanging plants—all the shades and shadows of Mrs. Radcliffe's world. One night a black stagecoach comes thundering out of the forest, overturns near a stone cross and disgorges a young lady about Laura's age onto the siding. The girl is injured, and her black-garbed mother, ob-

35. Henry James, "The Liar," in *The Complete Tales of Henry James*, ed. Leon Edel (New York: J. B. Lippincott, 1963), 6: 383.

viously in a hurry, asks Laura and her father if the young lady can stay at their castle. Of course she can, replies Laura's father, lifting the injured girl and carrying her back across the threshold into the castle.

The girl is Carmilla, and like her literary predecessor Geraldine, she is extraordinarily vague about her past, saying only that she is duty-bound to silence. However, she surprises Laura by claiming that as a child she had a dream in which they—she and Laura—had embraced. Laura is especially surprised because she has had exactly the same dream, although for her it was a nightmare. Thus begins a pattern of attraction and repulsion that continues until the very end. Laura is repeatedly befuddled by these ambivalent feelings:

> Now the truth is, I felt rather unaccountably towards the beautiful stranger. I did feel, as she said, "drawn towards her," but there was also something of repulsion. In this ambiguous feeling, however, the sense of attraction immensely prevailed. She interested and won me; she was so beautiful and indescribably engaging. (p. 23)

.   .   .   .

> It was like the ardour of a lover; it embarrassed me; it was hateful and yet overpowering; and with gloating eyes she drew me to her, and her hot lips travelled along my cheeks in kisses; and she would whisper, almost in sobs, "You are mine, you shall be mine, and you and I are one for ever." Then she has thrown me back in her chair, with her small hands over her eyes, leaving me trembling. (pp. 26–27)[36]

Finally Carmilla's magnetic pull draws her in. It is an erotic love she offers Laura, yet as with the Poe stories there is no hint of sex; rather, it is a slow gravitation toward the sensual and forbidden.

As this adduction progresses, it becomes clearer that Carmilla is a lamia: she sleeps until noon, is languid, has dark eyes and hair, eats nothing, never prays, is cold to the touch, becomes disconcerted when Laura starts singing hymns, has supernatural strength in her hand, and even has fangs, or at least front teeth so sharp and long that an itinerant peddler offers to dull them. Carmilla attacks Laura by first appearing in her erotic dreams; then she transforms herself into a cat to bite her, not on the throat but on the breast. Nowhere in Romantic literature has the myth been this frank: the element of sexual delight in sucking is here almost uncensored. Additionally LeFanu is the first author to describe in detail the process of these attacks as they appear to the victim. It is here that he (surely unknowingly) unfolds the adolescent and erotic nature of the myth:

> Certain vague and strange sensations visited me in my sleep. The prevailing one was of that pleasant, peculiar, cold thrill which we feel in bathing, when we move against the current of a river. This was soon accompanied by dreams

36. Page numbers in parentheses after quotations are from J. Sheridan LeFanu, *Carmilla and the Haunted Baronet* (New York: Warner Paperback Library, 1974).

that seemed interminable, and were so vague that I could never recollect their scenery and persons, or any one connected portion of their action. But they left an awful impression, and a sense of exhaustion, as if I had passed through a long period of great mental exertion and danger. After all these dreams there remained on waking a remembrance of having been in a place very nearly dark, and of having spoken to people whom I could not see; and especially of one clear voice, of a female's, very deep, that spoke as if at a distance, slowly, and producing always the same sensation of indescribable solemnity and fear. Sometimes there came a sensation as if a hand was drawn softly along my cheek and neck. Sometimes it was as if warm lips kissed me, and longer and more lovingly as they reached my throat, but there the caress fixed itself. My heart beat faster, my breathing rose and fell rapidly and full drawn; a sobbing, that rose into a sense of strangulation, supervened, and turned into a dreadful convulsion, in which my senses left me, and I became unconscious. (p. 44)

As Laura steadily weakens from these "attacks," we learn that Carmilla is mysteriously disappearing at night, and soon there are reports that other neighborhood children have been attacked. True to the Gothic conventions, Laura's father explains away her midnight wanderings as sleepwalking, and so, of course, it is for the local doctor to make the proper bedside diagnosis.

"Now you can satisfy yourself," said the doctor. "You won't mind your papa's lowering your dress a very little. It is necessary, to detect a symptom of the complaint under which you have been suffering."
I acquiesced. It was only an inch or two below the edge of my collar.
"God bless me!—so it is," exclaimed my father, growing pale.
"You see it now with your own eyes," said the doctor with a gloomy triumph.
"What is it?" I exclaimed, beginning to be frightened.
"Nothing my dear young lady, but a small blue spot, about the size of the top of your little finger." (p. 51)

This bit of voyeurism reinforces the subliminal sexual content of the story, as no previous vampire in literature (with the possible exception of Coleridge's *Christabel*) had touched so close to the breast. The good doctor leaves, presumably to seek aid, advising the family to keep watch on Laura and protect her.

Here the story takes a peculiar twist, for instead of duly protecting Laura, her father plans a picnic trip to Karnstein, a ruined castle nearby. En route they meet a General Spielsdorf, who tells them of the strange fate of his daughter. It seems that a short while ago a strange woman in a black coach had left her daughter (named Mircalla—this anagram foreshadows the connection) with the general while leaving for pressing business elsewhere. Mircalla acted just like Carmilla— eating no food, disppearing at night—and the general's daughter was soon attacked and wasted away. The general is now going to Castle Karnstein because he believes that somehow the Karnsteins and Mircalla are related. His suspicions prove well-founded, for when he arrives at the ruins he recognizes Carmilla (who has travelled in a different coach) as Mircalla. He grabs an axe and gives chase, but the lamia is too fleet for him, and escapes into the ruins. All agree that it is time to call in the proper vampire-destroyer, the local clergyman.

We soon learn from various sources who conveniently pass by that Carmilla/Mircalla is actually the Countess Karnstein, who has been ravaging the area for centuries. The next day the grave of the Countess is opened and all recognize the culprit.

> The features, though a hundred and fifty years had passed since her funeral, were tinted with the warmth of life. Her eyes were open: no cadaverous smell exhaled from the coffin. The two medical men, one officially present, the other on the part of the promoter of the inquiry, attested the marvellous fact, that there was a faint, but appreciable respiration, and a corresponding action of the heart. The limbs were perfectly flexible, the flesh elastic; and the leaden coffin floated with blood, in which to a depth of seven inches, the body lay immersed. Here then, were all the admitted signs and proofs of vampirism. (p. 78)

The lamia is done away with in the proper manner, but true to the gothic tradition the last word is never written. The story returns now to the present where Laura, now at thirty, still has momentary reveries in which she fancies she hears "the light step of Carmilla at the drawing room door" (p. 82).

Ten years later that light step is heard again in the English novel as Dracula comes creeping out from Transylvania. Except that this time the light step will become a thunderous rumble, for in Dracula's path will follow the thousands of vampires who now inhabit every dark corner of the popular media. Ironically, *Dracula*, the greatest vampire novel, is the work of fiction that takes the vampire out of literature and returns him to folklore. As a literary work *Dracula* has suffered from this achievement, for although the novel has been exceedingly popular, there have been few critical commentaries about it. This is certainly because the vampire and Dracula have become synonymous, and the vampire is hardly considered a scholarly subject, but it is also because the book appeared in 1897, at the height of literary Realism and Naturalism. Had it been written in 1820, I suspect that it would have been hailed, as *Frankenstein* is, as a Romantic milestone. As Royce MacGillivray says, "Had *Dracula* come to literary life in the age of Romanticism and the Gothic novel, one imagines it would have been received rapturously into the literary tradition of western Europe instead of being sternly restricted, as it has been to the popular imagination."[37] One need only remember the literary reception of Polidori's *The Vampyre* to realize this statement is not extravagant. Instead, it has

37. Royce MacGillivray, "*Dracula*: Bram Stoker's Spoiled Masterpiece," *Queens Quarterly* 79 (Winter 1972): 520.

only been in the last decade that *Dracula* has finally been taken seriously, both as popular novel and serious art.[38]

It is rare that an almost century-old book can achieve such commercial success without scholarly approbation. Most books that "earn their keep" on publishers' lists do so because they are continually being revived in classrooms. *Dracula* is an exception; any publisher can make money with it. Why has this misplaced Gothic novel lasted in the popular marketplace while the works of Walpole or Lewis or Radcliffe or Maturin have gathered dust, to be opened only in classrooms and then primarily for purposes of literary history? Part of the reason must be that *Dracula* is, first of all, a good story, complete with a lusty villain, damsels in distress, and haunted castles. The earlier Gothics (even *Varney the Vampyre*) had all this as well, yet they had something else—they made everything sensible. Unlike its early predecessors, *Dracula* seems to depend on its very inexplicableness, its nonsensibleness, to generate a kind of tension that is unrelieved and ultimately unexplained.

What sets *Dracula* apart then, is that it is primarily a story of psychological terror, not physical violence. True, the earlier Gothics were not exactly action-packed, at least by our kinetic standards, but in *Dracula* there is hardly any action at all. Partly this lack of immediate and close-up action is because of the epistolary method, and partly because Bram Stoker knew that action itself is always explainable. Dracula, unlike his literary brother the Frankenstein monster, simply cannot be explained. There is no calculating scientist who created him—he just is. Where does he come from? What does he do? And more important, why does he choose these specific victims? All this is never sufficiently answered to give us a sense of causality and predictability. In the earlier Gothic novels precisely the opposite happened: everything was finally explained, whether it needed to be or not—the creaking door, the misplaced baby, the recognition scenes. These occurrences are simply nowhere to be found in *Dracula*. Dracula is just a monster who attacks people: he is our mythic Grendel returned.

And so to what, if *Dracula* does not operate like the traditional Gothic novel, may we attribute its phenomenal success? Again, it is easier to answer in the negative. *Dracula's* success is certainly not due to its organization and style. The book is cumbersomely plotted around five central events: (1) the "initiation" of Jonathan Harker into Dracula's world; (2) Dracula's pursuit of Lucy; (3) the staking of Lucy; (4) the staining of Mina; and (5) the pursuit of Dracula. The middle three of these sections are overlong and detract from the work's rising tension, while other parts, such as the correspondence between Mina and Lucy, are unnecessarily tedious. The style, too, is redundant and occasionally absurd—for instance, Van Helsing's annoying accent. Admittedly some of this awkwardness is a result of Stoker's working in a structure, the epistolary novel, that depends on the author's ability to vary

---

38. Just a few of the book-length studies include Raymond McNally and Radu Florescu, *In Search of Dracula* (New York: Warner, 1973); Leonard Wolf, *A Dream of Dracula: In Search of the Living Dead* (New York: Popular Library, 1972); and Gabriel Ronay, *The Truth about Dracula* (New York: Stein and Day, 1974).

styles, making each one fit a specific character. Stoker is not Wilkie Collins—he is best, I think, with the initial Jonathan Harker episodes and understandably less successful with Mina and Lucy. Because he is not a master of style, the secondary characters are often stilted or even superfluous. The central characters, Van Helsing, Renfield, Lucy, Mina, and of course Dracula himself, do indeed have distinct and memorable personalities (although one wonders about the credibility of Renfield), but the "boys"—Jonathan Harker, Quincey Morris, Lord Godalming, and John Seward—all seem fitted to the same pattern. They are stout, honest, loyal, brave—in short, good scouts all, and, unfortunately, dull.

If *Dracula's* claim on our attention is not its historical importance or its artistic merit, then its power is derived from something below the surface, something carried within the myth itself. *Dracula* is the consummate retelling of the vampire story; all the pieces are used and all the pieces fit. Stoker had no artistic pretensions, no deep truth to plumb; the vampire is there to frighten and shock, to make us jealous, not to enlighten. If the book is poetic and powerful, it is because Stoker was wise enough never to dilute the psychological content of the legend; in fact, if anything, he made it more potent. Dracula is terrifically alluring; he has everything we want: he has money and power without responsibilities; he parties all night with the best people, yet he doesn't need friends; he can be violent and aggressive without guilt or punishment; he has life without death; but most attractive of all, he has sex without confusion (i.e., genitalia, pregnancy . . . love). It's all take, no give. If only he didn't have those appetites!

The story of Stoker's *Dracula* is this: a band of boys, a gang if you will, under the direction of a wise father-figure/priest/doctor must destroy a demon who has been ravaging their women. It is more than a dragon-destroying quest, however; for this demon is articulate, shrewd, decidedly upper-class, intelligent, and sexually potent. There is no mention of this sexual potency, no mention of his incredible erotic power, but in every instance we are aware it is there. Dracula is evil, yes, but he knows how the world is put together and he knows how to get what he wants. What he wants is exactly what the "boys" want as well—women.

As an ancillary theory to the Oedipus complex, Freud, in *Totem and Taboo*, postulated that far in our cultural past the dominant male of the family, the father-figure, subjugated the weaker males by hoarding the women. In Freud's psycho-biological scheme the sons had to overthrow the father to continue their own genetic lines, as well as to express themselves sexually, and so they "displaced" the older male, perhaps even killing him. It is this removal (whether actual or imaginative makes no difference) that caused the sons to feel first exultation and then grief and then guilt, for they had destroyed their own progenitor. For this act they did penance by creating certain totems to alleviate guilt, while at the same time protecting themselves from being likewise displaced by the next generation of young men. The latter part of Freud's "primal horde" hypothesis need not concern us; rather, it is the gang killing of the father that seems to form the psychic core of the story of *Dracula*. This psychological interpretation was first proffered by the English anthropologist Maurice Richardson in "The Psychoanalysis of Ghost Stories" and has since become almost a donnée of *Dracula* criticism.[39]

It has also been pointed out that Dracula is as much a father-figure as Van Helsing, and that the central action of the book concerns the young boy's acceptance of the good father (Van Helsing) in order to destroy the evil father (Dracula).[40] Dracula does exert an almost patriarchal influence: he is older than the boys, living eternally at a dignified retirement age; he is the lord of the castle; he is wealthy; he has his own women, to whom Jonathan Harker, at least, is attracted; and he is about to add new women (Lucy and Mina) to what he refers to as "my family." Van Helsing, on the other hand, has a wife (she is now institutionalized) and can promise the boys nothing except knowledge. It is this knowledge, however, that is power, for it will allow the boys to destroy the father/demon to achieve "justice" (read "women") at last.

Lest there be any doubt as to the sublimated sexuality of the story, let me briefly point to a few central events.[41] First, it must be noted that all the central characters, with the exception of the evil totem, Dracula, appear to be models of chastity and Victorian virtue. Appearances are deceiving, however, as early in the story Jonathan Harker, one of the few young males already married, falls to the blandishments of Dracula's women. In Dracula's castle we see the young married male hesitatingly respond to wondrous temptation:

> In the moonlight opposite me were three young women, ladies by their dress and manner. I thought at the time that I must be dreaming when I saw them, for, though the moonlight was behind them, they threw no shadow on the floor. They came close to me, and looked at me for some time, and then whispered together. Two were dark and had high aquiline noses, like the Count, and great dark piercing eyes, that seemed to be almost red when contrasted with the pale yellow moon. The other was fair, as fair as can be, with great wavy masses of golden hair and eyes like pale sapphires. I seemed somehow to know her face, and to know it in connection with some dreamy fear, but I could not recollect at the moment how or where. All three had brilliant white teeth that shone like pearls against the ruby of their voluptuous lips. There was something about them that made me uneasy, some longing and at the same time some deadly fear. I felt in my heart a wicked, burning desire

39. Although the application of this Freudian theory to explain the psychological action of *Dracula* was first proposed by Maurice Richardson in "The Psychoanalysis of Ghost Stories," *Twentieth Century* 166 (1959): 428, it has since been reaffirmed in MacGillivray, "*Dracula*," p. 523, and Wolf, *A Dream of Dracula*, p. 314, n. 28.

40. A number of critics have claimed that Dracula is a "father-figure": Richards, "The Psychoanalysis of Ghost Stories," p. 427; MacGillivray, "*Dracula*," p. 522; and Wolf, *A Dream of Dracula*, chap. 6.

41. Many critics have commented on the sublimated sexuality of *Dracula*: Wolf, ibid.; C. F. Bentley, "The Monster in the Bedroom: Sexual Symbolism in Bram Stoker's *Dracula*," *Literature and Psychology* 22 (1972): 27–34; Joseph S. Bierman, "*Dracula*: Prolonged Childhood Illness, and the Oval Triad," *American Imago* 29 (Summer 1972): 186–98; Phyllis R. Roth, "Suddenly Sexual Women in Bram Stoker's *Dracula*," *Literature and Psychology* 27 (1977): 113–21; and Carrol L. Fry, "Fictional Connections and Sexuality in *Dracula*," *Victorian Newsletter* 42 (Fall 1972): 20–22.

that they would kiss me with those red lips. It is not good to note this down, lest some day it should meet Mina's eyes and cause her pain; but it is the truth.

.   .   .   .

The fair girl advanced and bent over me till I could feel the movement of her breath upon me. Sweet it was in one sense, honey-sweet, and sent the same tingling through the nerves as her voice, but with a bitter underlying the sweet, a bitter offensiveness, as one smells in blood.

I was afraid to raise my eyelids, but looked out and saw perfectly under the lashes. The girl went on her knees, and bent over me, simply gloating. There was a deliberate voluptuousness which was both thrilling and repulsive, and as she arched her neck she actually licked her lips like an animal, till I could see in the moonlight the moisture shining on the scarlet lips and on the red tongue as it lapped the white sharp teeth. Lower and lower went her head as the lips went below the range of my mouth and chin and seemed to fasten on my throat. Then she paused, and I could hear the churning sound of her tongue as it licked her teeth and lips, and I could feel the hot breath on my neck. Then the skin of my throat began to tingle as one's flesh does when the hand that is to tickle it approaches nearer—nearer. I could feel the soft, shivering touch of the lips on the super-sensitive skin of my throat, and the hard dents of two sharp teeth, just touching and pausing there. I closed my eyes in languorous ecstasy and waited—waited with beating heart. (pp. 46–47)[42]

If there ever was an example of Coleridge's "desire with loathing strangely mix'd," this is it, for Jonathan Harker is a willing/unwilling co-conspirator. The count, who is somehow related to these women, arrives like a good parent to stop the scene, but even so, as Professor C. F. Bentley has pointed out in "The Monster in the Bedroom: Sexual Symbolism in *Dracula*," the damage has been done. Bentley claims that to understand the extent of this damage we should treat the incident as "the masturbatory fantasy of an erotic dream," recalling Ernest Jones's words:

The explanation of these phantasies is surely not hard. A nightly visit from a beautiful or frightful being, who first exhausts the sleeper with passionate embraces and then withdraws from him a vital fluid; all this can point only to a natural and common process, namely to nocturnal emissions accompanied with dreams of a more or less erotic nature. In the unconscious mind blood is commonly an equivalent for semen.[43]

If this is true, it sheds important light on other more central actions, especially the transfusion of blood from the young boys into the body of Lucy. Lucy herself is as extraordinary a character as Dracula. At first she is the giggly and silly ingenue,

---

42. Page numbers in parentheses refer to Bram Stoker's *Dracula* (1897; rpt. New York: Dell Paperback, 1973).

43. Ernest Jones, *On the Nightmare* (1931; rpt. New York: Liveright, 1971), p. 119.

but after her encounter with the father/demon, Dracula, she is transformed into a highly erotic and captivating woman. Her "new life" is maintained, however, only by repeated infusions of the blood of Arthur, Quincey, and Drs. Seward and Van Helsing. She is the queen maintained by the boys—a queen to King Dracula. Hence it may be of more than passing interest that John Seward and Quincey Morris were previously her rejected suitors, and that in a sense through these transfusions they married her by the mingling of blood. Van Helsing even admits as much when he tells Seward not to mention to Arthur, Lucy's present fiancé, that he, Seward, has participated in one of the transfusions. After Lucy's death, in which Arthur has to drive a stake through his love's body (the phallic symbolism here, claims Bentley, is too obvious to miss), we are told that because of the transfusions "he felt as if the two had been really married, and that she was his wife in the sight of God" (p. 195).

If Professor Bentley is correct in believing, along with Ernest Jones, that blood is a metaphor for semen and that then these transfusions are, in a sense, analogies for the sexual act, it is possible to explain how the "boys" may participate without guilt. But what of Van Helsing? He should know better, for as the father-protector, the most perceptive of the Western males, he is aware of the psychological consequences. And indeed he seems to be, for when Van Helsing recalls his own participation in the transfusions, he suddenly changes from a most rational and controlled man into a hysterical maniac. This realization and transformation occurs in the puzzling "King Laugh" episode of chapter 13. All of a sudden Van Helsing, after thinking about what has happened, starts babbling about how in times of stress "King Laugh" starts shouting "Here I am! Here I am!" in his ear. Van Helsing's decompensation makes no sense at all until he later explains that when things are the most psychologically traumatic "King Laugh" comes to break them apart with comedy, i.e., in times of greatest pressure we laugh instead of cry. Dr. Seward understandably asks precisely what kind of situation needs this explosion, and in broken English Van Helsing replies that since the transfusion represents "marriage," then Mina "is a polyandrist, and me, with my poor wife dead to me, but alive by church's law, though no wits, all gone—even I, who am faithful husband to this now-no-wife, am bigamist" (p. 197). Worse still are the possible incestuous overtones, as Lucy has been "almost a daughter" to him.

If such a symbolic link exists between transfusions and marriage, or blood and semen, it may be worthwhile to examine the novel's other central scene, in which Dracula ravages and "initiates" Mina Harker into his family. It is such a crucial scene that we are given a number of versions, the first of which appears in Dr. Seward's diary. Seward recalls how he and Van Helsing burst into the Harkers' room, finding the count holding

> both Mrs. Harker's hands, keeping them away with her arms at full tension; his right hand gripping her by the back of the neck, forcing her face down on his bosom. Her white nightdress was smeared with blood, and a thick stream

trickled down the man's bare chest which was shown by his torn-open dress. The attitude of the two had a terrible resemblance to a child forcing a kitten's nose into a saucer of milk to compel it to drink. (p. 313)

We later have Mina's version:

With that he pulled open his shirt, and with his long sharp nails opened a vein in his breast. When the blood began to spurt out, he took my hands in one of his, holding them tight, and with the other seized my neck and pressed my mouth to the wound, so that I must either suffocate or swallow some of the—Oh, my God! my God! what have I done? What have I done to deserve such a fate, I who have tried to walk in meekness and righteousness all my days. God pity me! (p. 319)

Certain peculiarities of this scene are startling, the most striking of which is that Dracula is reversing the vampiric process by having Mina drink from his body as he presumably has drunk from hers. There is no precedent for this in vampiric folklore, although it seems a logical enough part of the story. The strain of sexual violation, which is already so prominent in the myth, is here given added hints of fellatio. That Stoker then compares this process to a kitten being forced to drink milk from a saucer may well reinforce the seminal imagery. So too does Mina's reaction, for she is horrified to admit to her spouse what she has done.

She shuddered and was silent, holding down her head on her husband's breast. When she raised it, his white nightrobe was stained with blood where her lips had touched, and where the thin open wound in her neck had sent forth drops. The instant she saw it she drew back, with a low wail, and whispered, amidst choking sobs:

"Unclean, unclean! I must touch him or kiss him no more. Oh, that it should be that it is I who am now his worst enemy, and whom he may have most cause to fear." (p. 315)

Later we are told that "she began to rub her lips as though to cleanse them from pollution" (p. 320). Surely Leslie Fiedler is correct when he contends that she has experienced "the ultimate sexual encounter" and is now to suffer the pangs of Victorian guilt.[44]

While it would be a mistake to force the blood/semen analogy too far, it may account for the book's almost clairvoyant insight into the dynamics of the myth. It is our horror (and the Victorian horror) of such sexual activity that may well draw us to the sublimated reenactment of what is forbidden. It is our "desire with loathing strangely mix'd" that makes both the myth and the book so compelling. In this context it is interesting that nowhere in the contemporary reviews of *Dracula* is there mention of anything morally objectionable. In point of fact the one charac-

44. Leslie Fiedler, *Freaks: Myths and Images of the Secret Self* (New York: Simon and Schuster, 1978), p. 344.

teristic of *Dracula* criticism is its remarkable tameness. Soon after publication the *Athenaeum* reviewer recognized the book's problems, and his comments have been echoed ever since:

> *Dracula* is highly sensational, but it is wanting in the constructive art as well as in the higher literary sense. It reads at times like a mere series of grotesquely incredible events; but there are better moments that show more power, though even these are never productive of the tremor such subjects evoke under the hand of a master. At times Mr. Stoker almost succeeds in creating the sense of possibility in impossibility; at others he merely commands an array of crude statements of incredible actions. . . . Still, Mr. Stoker has got together a number of horrid details, and his object, assuming it is to be ghastliness, is fairly well fulfilled.[45]

The only critic who has strayed from this path is Richard Wasson, who (writing just after the Second World War) contended that the book was a parable of Old Central Europe destroying New Western Europe.[46] Taking his cue from the fact that Dracula supposedly descended from Attila the Hun, and that he came West to find new blood, Wasson concluded that Stoker unconsciously realized the threat of the Axis powers. For Wasson, Dracula is the Fascist whose first victim is the appropriately named Lucy Westenra (Light of the West). To destroy her, however, he must battle the Alliance of Free Men. These free men personify occidental culture: Van Helsing, the Catholic from the Netherlands; Lord Godalming, the monied British nobility; Quincey Morris, the Winchester-packing American; Mina Harker, the archetypal mother/sister/female friend; and finally the two youthful Englishmen representing Law (Jonathan Harker) and Science (John Seward). Wasson's article is a critical tour de force, made perhaps risible by his contention that if such a reading were not true, how could we explain the fact that the United States army issued free copies of the book during World War II? Surely the army knew what the critics in ivory towers could never see; Count Dracula is the Nazi war lord; he is Hitler.

One more recent interpretation need be mentioned, as it attempts to synthesize the psychological, anthropological, and literary views of the novel. In "*Dracula*: the Gnostic Quest and the Victorian Wasteland," Mark Hennelly argues that *Dracula* is indeed a quest romance in which the boys, or as he calls them "the questing knights," must pass between the rival cultures of the Victorian Wasteland of England and the "demiurgic world of vampires" until they establish their own kingdom at the end with the birth of Quincey Harker.[47] In this context Dracula is the Fisher King who must be destroyed if the grail (the women) is to be retained. Hennelly's article makes wonderful reading and shows how easily the views of Fra-

45. *Athenaeum* review as quoted in Donald F. Glut, *The Dracula Book* (Metuchen, N.J.: The Scarecrow Press, 1975), p. 71.
46. Richard Wasson, "The Politics of *Dracula*," *English Literature in Transition* 9 (1966): 24–27.
47. Mark Hennelly, Jr., "*Dracula*: The Gnostic Quest and Victorian Wasteland," *English Literature in Transition* 20 (1977): 13–26.

zer, Jessie Weston, and Freud can be applied when the work of art is sufficiently vague and ambiguous. As Maurice Richardson said some twenty years ago, it will be only a matter of time until some Marxist tells us that Dracula is the extension of the feudal *droit du seigneur* in which the evil lord starves the peasants and the bourgeoisie while sucking the children's blood.[48]

For whatever *Dracula* may or may not be, one thing is certain: the book represents the culmination of the Romantic interest in the vampire. Dracula deserves his rightful place beside the other mid-nineteenth-century fictional solipsists— Count Cenci, Heathcliff, Manfred—as an example of the overreacher gone berserk, Faust gone awry. In a sense I suppose our century has witnessed life imitating art as this fictional character did indeed become real. The anti-hero/vampire in fiction became Nietzsche's Superman in philosophy, who became Adolf Hitler in fact. This process may in part account for the myth's rapid return from serious literature to popular culture, for once monsters become real, fiction can only pale in comparison.

There have been many twentieth-century novelists (Ray Bradbury, Robert Bloch, E. F. Benson, Agatha Christie, Virginia Coffman, H. P. Lovecraft, Richard Matheson, Peter Saxon, John Rechy, Fred Saberhagen, Colin Wilson, Desmond Stewart, Anne Rice, to name only a few) who have dealt with the vampire, but none so strikingly as Stoker.[49] He made the mold. The interest in vampire fiction continues, but it seems doubtful that the myth will ever again achieve its earlier psychological impact. Instead, it seems now almost completely expropriated by the popular media, a subject more readily adapted to radio (Orson Welles's *Dracula*), the stage (Edward Gorey's 1977 production of *Dracula* or the off-Broadway *The Passion of Dracula*), television ("Dark Shadows," "Night Stalker"), the movies (*Blacula* and some 120 Dracula films, including the recent parody *Love at First Bite*), or comics ("Vampirella," "Tales of Dracula"). In an appropriate way, the electronic media have returned the vampire to the folk who created him and made him once again an object of envy and terror. Perhaps it is just that things have come full circle, yet for insight into the possibilities of the myth one must return to the works of Ro-

48. Richardson, "The Psychoanalysis of Ghost Stories," p. 430.

49. The following is by no means a comprehensive listing, but it does testify to the vampire's current good health: Ray Bradbury has written a number of vampire stories ("The Crowd," "The Man Upstairs," "Homecoming," for example) and a novel (*Something Wicked This Way Comes* [New York: Simon and Schuster, 1962]); Robert Bloch has also written many stories (see "The Bat Is My Brother," "The Living Dead"); E. F. Benson's "Mrs. Amworth" is a small classic in the genre; H. P. Lovecraft wrote many vampire stories that appeared in *Weird Tales*, such as "The Thing on the Doorstep" or "The Case of Charles Dexter Ward"; Richard Matheson's "I Am a Legend" is often anthologized as an excellent example of a compact and terrifying vampire story; Peter Saxon has written many vampire novels (e.g., *The Darkest Night, Scream and Scream Again, Vampire's Moon*) that are forgettable, as is Virginia Coffman, *The Vampire of Moura* (New York: Ace Books, 1970). The best vampire novels are recent: Thomas Sturgeon, *Some of Your Blood* (New York: Ballantine Books, 1961); John Rechy, *The Vampires* (New York: Grove Press, 1971); Fred Saberhagen, *The Dracula Tape* (New York: Warner Paperback, 1975); Desmond Stewart, *The Vampire of Mons* (New York: Harper & Row, 1976); Colin Wilson, *The Space Vampires* (New York: Random House, 1976); Steven King, *Salem's Lot* (New York: New American Library, 1975); Chelsea Quinn Yarboro, *Hotel Transylvania* (New York: New American Library, 1978); and Anne Rice, *Interview with the Vampire* (New York: Knopf, 1976).

manticism. For the vampire had a still more profound role to play in nineteenth-century literature than its fictional adaptations would so far indicate. As we have seen, the vampire had been used metaphorically to express the dynamics of inter-personal relationships, but the Romantics would also use the myth to explore the varying relationships among the artist, the work of art, and the audience. In works as disparate yet central to Romanticism as Coleridge's *The Rime of the Ancient Mariner*, Wordsworth's *Resolution and Independence*, Poe's *The Oval Portrait*, Wilde's *The Picture of Dorian Gray*, and James's *The Sacred Fount*, the vampire myth reached its most sophisticated level of adaptation. And it is to these works that we now turn.

5. The Artist as Vampire

> *The true artist will let his wife starve, his children go barefoot, his mother drudge for his living at seventy, sooner than work at anything but his art. To women he is half vivisector, half vampire. He gets into intimate relations with them to study them, to strip the mask of convention from them, to surprise their inmost secrets, knowing that they have the power to rouse his deepest creative energies, to rescue him from his cold reason, to make him see visions and dream dreams, to inspire him, as he calls it.*
>
> —G. B. Shaw, *Man and Superman*

Had the vampire been simply a recurring motif in nineteenth-century art, it would be an interesting but at best tangential aspect of Romanticism. Perhaps the most scholars could say of this Gothic disorder was that the vampire was a lingering remnant of the Graveyard school, or that it was a curious prefiguring of the late Victorian interest in ghost and ghoul stories. But the vampire was more than an unfixed image or motif; as we have seen, it often became a serious analogue for the process of energy exchange involved in human interactions. In addition, it occasionally became an elaborate metaphor of the relationship between artist, artifact, and audience. Although Shaw's mouthpiece Jack Tanner says the words above about what he takes to be the behavior of the "true artist," the substitution of "Romantic artist" would make better sense. For Tanner's definition of the artist as psychic parasite, more than willing to use the energies of others for the advancement of his art, is a central theme in nineteenth-century literature.

In no other movement has the artist been so aware of his inner self and of his exchanging of energies, not only with those around him, but with the work of art as well. He is both enervated and energized by the art of creation. Likewise we in the audience feel both catharsis and rejuvenation in the process of experiencing his art. Hence, vampirism, simply as a process of energy exchange, is implicit in the creative process. For the Romantic artist this "process" usually involves four relatively stable parts: the artist, the audience, the object of art (artifact), and the subject of art. Creation at its simplest involves the movement of energy (life, imagination, attention) from one part to another. Although individual Romantic artists believed the process worked in different ways, they agreed that when art succeeded, the resultant energy in the system was greater than the initial charge. It is almost as if they saw art reversing the second law of thermodynamics, turning entropy around, moving toward lucidity instead of confusion.

Analogues between art and electricity are second nature for us in the twentieth century, for concepts of energy dynamics are an integral part of our folklore. When a work of art fails we can describe it in terms of a short circuit in the process; when it succeeds it is as if we have experienced a "positive charge." But witness Henry James (who had no such ready metaphors) describing the plight of the errant artist when his process has gone awry: "[Creation] is like the greedy man's description of the turkey as an 'awkward' dinner dish. It may sometimes be too much for a single share, but it's not enough to go round." (*The Sacred Fount*, chapter 2). Surely nothing can be more homely than seeing artistic creation as a turkey dinner; even the vampire analogy seems positively elegant in comparison.

It may be interesting to note in passing that as the Romantic artist became more self-consciously aware of his own dynamism, the critic became more and more a figure of contempt. The critic, who had had a most important (albeit much abused) role as commentator to the Neoclassicists, became a freeloader to the Romantics. He became the pilot-fish who drains not just the work of art, but the artist as well. He is the bloated leech. Shelley certainly invokes this role for the critic in *Adonais*, but it was Byron in *Don Juan* who specifically coupled it with the vampire:

> This [the role of the critic] is the literary *lower* empire,
>   Where the praetorian bands take up the matter;—
> A "dreadful trade," like his own "gather samphire,"
>   The insolent soldiery to soothe and flatter,
> With the same feelings as you'd coax a vampire.
>   Now, were I once at home, and in good satire,
> I'd try conclusions with those Janizaries,
> And show them *what* an intellectual war is.   (Canto II, stanza 62)

Today the role of the critic has now come full circle, as the French structuralists are co-opting for themselves a role similar to that demanded by the Romantic artists. The critic has been made artist once removed, and the unknowing artist now depends upon him for information and sustenance, as well as the reverse.

We can see these various positions being established in the Romantic movement. In five central works, *The Rime of the Ancient Mariner, Resolution and Independence, The Oval Portrait, The Picture of Dorian Gray*, and *The Sacred Fount*, we see Coleridge, Wordsworth, Poe, Wilde, and James manipulate various analogies to express their views of the creative process—what it entails, what it costs, what it results in. In a sense these works are all about the creation of these works; they are works of art about works of art, but there is, alas, no consensus, no "Romantic view." They all share, however, either explicitly or implicitly, the view that art, if properly created, generates or releases energies that are somehow organic, energies which continue to grow and interanimate the parts long after the artist has removed himself. They key word here is, of course, "properly," for in some of the Romantic versions such as *The Picture of Dorian Gray* or *The Sacred Fount*, creation goes awry, and energies become wildly destructive. Still these works are as insightful by their example of what not to do as they are in prescribing what to do.

Let me reiterate this process by example. In each of the above works there is an implicit parable of creation that somehow involves precise interactions between artist, audience, artifact, and subject matter. Often these various parts are reduplicated within the works, for in a sense, they are all works of art about the workings of art. So we find an artist like Coleridge creating a surrogate artist (the Ancient Mariner) who in turn creates a work of art (the *Rime*) to be heard by an audience (the Wedding Guest). The process is finally completed when this artifact (*The Rime of the Ancient Mariner*) is at last experienced by us—the real audience. So in *The Rime of the Ancient Mariner*, the Ancient Mariner is the "inside" teller of the tale, the Wedding Guest is the "inside" audience, the action of the youthful Ancient Mariner is the "inside" subject, and the Rime (the actual story) is the object. In Wordsworth's *Resolution and Independence* the real inside artist is the Leech Gatherer, while the subject and inside audience are the same—the despondent poet/narrator. The artifact is their conversation. The situation is much simpler in Poe's *The Oval Portrait*, where the inside artist is the painter, the artifact is the painting, the subject is the female sitter, and the inside audience is the narrator. Not so simple, however, is *The Picture of Dorian Gray*, where the artist is Basil, the subject is Dorian Gray, the artifact is the actual "picture" of Dorian Gray, and the audience is Lord Henry. Also more complex is James's *The Sacred Fount*, where the narrator is the inside artist, or better yet the inside artist manqué, the subject of art is the interactions of the Newmarch guests, the object (what the narrator is trying to "make") is his theory of the sacred fount, and the inside audience is Ford Obert and, in a sense, Mrs. Brissenden.

What happens in each of these works is that certain parties become enervated while others become energized. In *The Rime of the Ancient Mariner* the Ancient Mariner seems to gain energy at the expense of the Wedding Guest. At the end the teller of the tale seems to have exchanged wisdom for energy, and the audience, the Wedding Guest, leaves weaker but wiser. In *Resolution and Independence* the melancholy young poet is figuratively a leech who gathers energy from proximity with the old Leech Gatherer. In *The Oval Portrait* it is the object of art itself, not the artist or the subject of art, which comes alive, while in *The Picture of Dorian Gray* the energies flow back from the artist (Basil) and the artifact (the painting) to the subject of art, Dorian Gray. Obviously, as we shall see, something terrible has happened here to set the process in reverse. Something terrible also happens in another ghost story, *The Sacred Fount*, where energies are pumped from the foolish artist and his subjects into an "object," namely a "scientific" theory of human behavior. To see exactly how these Romantic works use the vampire myth as analogy to show the interactions of subject/object/artist/audience, we need look carefully at the texts.

The Rime of the Ancient Mariner

Why will an artist change a work of art after it has been published? I realize that this sounds like a silly question, for the obvious answer is that there is something about it he no longer likes and wants improved. A poem, novel, or play is never "finished" until the creator lets it alone. From this comes the principle that the preferred text—all other things being equal—is the last version approved by the author or the last one printed in his lifetime. Surely this principle is true in the sister arts. There are few who would contend that a painter's cover-up paint be scraped off to give us an earlier version, or that a piece of sculpture be recast in discarded molds, or that music be played from a sloughed-off score, or that rejects on the cutting room floor be spliced back into a film.

But what if the artist changes his work not to improve it, but rather to satisfy the demands of the state, or some institution, or his publisher, or even some overbearing friend? Then what is the critic's responsibility? This is especially difficult when the work in question has been published. For the actual printing of the text reduces the critic's liability, as it implies that the author was—if only for a second—able to consider it "done."

The choice of a text is a real problem with the English Romantic poets because so much of their work was published when they were young and then quietly tampered with in old age. And so for aesthetic reasons we often look the other way, accept versions that violate our bibliographical principles and commit one intentional fallacy after another. For instance, good cases can be made for accepting the 1805 *Prelude*, the earlier version of *La Belle Dame sans Merci*, and a number of cast-off lyrics by Blake. Although it is not my intent to make the case for preferring an earlier version of *The Rime of the Ancient Mariner* (that has already been done in the recent Empson/Pirie eclectic text), it is my task to explain an intention of the 1798 poem and to argue that one of the poem's most interesting aspects was partially sabotaged by a hoodwinked Coleridge.[1]

Two questions need to be answered: (1) What was Coleridge's original intention? and (2) why did he repudiate it? I think it clear that Coleridge had no single overriding design: in fact, what we see in the revisions is that he was, like a water-bug, constantly changing direction. It is a critical cliché that in his revisions a maturing Coleridge was forcing out the pantheism and replacing it with orthodox Christianity. Still there are a number of themes that continue throughout the various versions from the 1798 *Lyrical Ballads* to the 1817 *Sibylline Leaves*: the guilt theme, the problem of sin and expiation, the concern with New World exploration, the interest in an organic universe, the construction of psychological drama, the interplay of the teller of the tale and the listener. But let me introduce an intention

---

1. William Empson and David Pirie, eds., *Coleridge's Verse: A Selection* (New York: Schocken, 1973).

that has gone unnoticed, perhaps because Coleridge tried so hard to change it. When Coleridge first sat down in 1797, he had planned to write a vampire poem.[2]

A key to unlocking the vampiric content of *The Rime* is to be found in a close reading of the poem's revisions. For although John Livingston Lowes claimed that the poem "comes down [through the revisions] mostly unchanged," we shall see that is not quite true.[3] *The Rime of the Ancient Mariner* that we usually read is from the *Poetical Works* of 1834, which is based on the 1817 *Sibylline Leaves* text, which has eighteen lines added and nine lines subtracted from the 1800 second edition of the *Lyrical Ballads* text. This 1800 version represents a removal of several dozen individual words and forty-six full lines and an addition of seven lines to the 1798 original poem.

Working backwards from the 1834 (in essence the 1817) text, let me just mechanically list the major cruxes that have never been completely resolved. We are never told what the purpose of the Mariner's voyage was—an unusual oversight. In all of literature I cannot think of a voyage of such importance in which no hint of goal, cargo, ports, etc. is given. Second, the Wedding Guest often interrupts the Ancient Mariner, mentioning that he believes that the old man may be possessed by fiends (l. 79ff).[4] The Ancient Mariner does have a "glittering eye" (ll. 15, 228), a "bright eye" (ll. 20, 40), and the Wedding Guest cannot choose but to hear. Perhaps Coleridge is experimenting with mesmerism, but perhaps not, perhaps he is really possessed.[5] Then again things may be more complex because the Ancient Mariner himself cannot remove his eye from the eyes of the dead sailors in the moonlight (l. 440). The men "curse" the Ancient Mariner with their eyes (l. 215) and *he* is powerless to move. Surely these references to sight—eyes are mentioned twenty times—cannot be explained away by surface plot.

Most critics have believed that the shooting of the albatross and the blessing of

2. Here, in brief, is Coleridge's access to vampire lore: we know that on 20 April 1798 he checked out volume 2 of the *Memoirs of the Literary and Philosophical Society of Manchester*. It is not known but suspected that he also leafed through volume 3 of these Manchester Memoirs because by 31 December 1796 he seems to have read an article that appears in this volume on animal vitality (Arthur H. Nethercot, *The Road to Tryermaine* [New York: Russell and Russell, 1962] p. 61). And if he did, he may have read the preceding article by John Ferriar, "On Popular Illusions and Particularly of Medical Demonology" (John Livingston Lowes, *The Road to Xanadu* [1930; rpt., Boston: Houghton Mifflin, 1964], p. 518). Lowes suspected this was the kind of article "Coleridge would never pass by," yet ironically Lowes himself passed it by, though Nethercot did not miss its significance. Near the end of Ferriar's compendious treatment of spirit life he devotes seven pages to the vampire, seven pages that condense the work of Voltaire (one of Coleridge's early favorites) and Dom Calmet, the French Jesuit whose pioneering work on vampires was to become influential in the vampire novels of the later nineteenth century (*Memoirs of the Literary and Philosophical Society of Manchester*, 3, first series [1790]: 84-91). Given Coleridge's desire to track down sources, he probably read both Voltaire and Calmet in the original.

3. Lowes, *Road to Xanadu*, p. 518.

4. I realize much of what I am suggesting as vampiric may also be attributes of "the Wandering Jew" theme (the powers of speech, the night wandering, etc.), and I don't deny its existence. The two need not be mutually exclusive; in fact, they may even complement each other. See O. Bryan Fulmer, "The Ancient Mariner and the Wandering Jew" *Studies in Philology* 66 (1969): 797-815.

5. Lane Cooper, "The Power of the Eye in Coleridge," in *Late Harvest* (Ithaca, N.Y.: Cornell University Press, 1952), pp. 65-96.

the watersnakes are the two central acts, but they may have neglected one which might be equally important. In part 3, when the Ancient Mariner sees the skeleton ship, he bites his arm and sucks the blood. This was, I suppose, a heroic act in 1834, as it would be today, but what is the reaction of his fellow sailors as he breaks the skin?

> Gramercy! they for joy did grin,
> And all at once their breath drew in,
> As they were drinking all. (ll. 164–66)

Is it the yelling or the sight of blood that brings the skeleton ship? The skeleton ship is tacking until the blood is drawn; then it immediately turns and comes straight on. Could it be that the Ancient Mariner is a willing participant in some weird process, otherwise, as Derek Roper has pointed out in his edition of the *Lyrical Ballads*, how does the Ancient Mariner recognize the ship before the lady gets close enough to be seen?[6]

> Alas! (thought I, and my heart beat loud)
> How fast she nears and nears!
> Are those *her* sails that glance the Sun,
> Like restless gossameres? (ll. 181–84)

Has he seen her before? Certainly, as David Pirie says, "The later statement that she 'thicks men's blood with cold' implies that he has met or at least heard of her on occasion."[7]

After the dice game won by Life-in-Death (l. 197) the Ancient Mariner says that by nightfall his "life blood seemed to sip" (l. 205). He explains it was drunk away by fear. Or again is he trying to explain it away? This is additionally perplexing because the dream lady is called "The Night-mare Life-in-Death" (l. 192). In the nineteenth century a nightmare was a female (a succubus) who was supposed "to set upon people and animals at night and produce a feeling of suffocation" (we may well recall Fuseli's "The Nightmare"); however, the second half of her name, Life-in-Death, is reminiscent of the usual title of vampires, the "Walking Dead" or the "Living Dead."[8]

Blood seems to be almost a totemic symbol in the poem. For instance, the sun is not yellow or red; it is blood red (ll. 98, 112) and when the Polar Spirit lets the ship go, the Mariner faints and the blood is flung into his head (l. 391). He then claims that he heard some voices before his "living life" returned. What does he mean by "living life"? Is there some other kind? He finally "wakes" (l. 430), but by l. 470, when he is back home, he says, "O let me be awake my God/Or let me

---

6. As quoted by Empson, "Introduction" to *Coleridge's Verse*, p. 29. Malcolm Ware, in "Coleridge's 'Specter-Bark': A Slave Ship?" *Philological Quarterly* 60 (1961), believes the ship is a slaver, and this view fits metaphorically into a vampire reading, for the men will indeed become enslaved.

7. Pirie, "Notes" to *Coleridge's Verse*, p. 229.

8. *Oxford English Dictionary* (Oxford: Clarendon Press, 1961), 7:196.

sleep alway." Again what is he talking about? Was he in some kind of trance that he's not telling us about? Could he still be in this trance while he tells the story? And when the Ancient Mariner tried to pray, no prayer "gusht" from his heart (l. 245) because his heart was as dry as "dust" (l. 246). Martin Gardner explains away this imperfect rhyme as Coleridge's attempt to "suggest the Mariner's halting efforts to pray."[9] I agree that Coleridge is trying to draw our attention here, but I suspect he is trying to show us how the Ancient Mariner has been (metaphorically?) bled. This is especially interesting since the act of "forgiveness" is later described with the same trope: "A spring of love gushed from my heart,/And I blessed them unaware" (ll. 284–85). The only point I am trying to make is that the process of blood flowing seems important, if only as an analogy for some other process.

Aligned with the image of blood is the color red, which is clearly the most important color in the poem. Maud Bodkin sees it as partly representing the blood of communion, and she is quite close to what I think Coleridge intended.[10] But red is tied to more than the blood of communion; it is also blood in general. It is interesting that the moon (not the blood-red sun) casts red shadows (l. 271). Lowes suggests that this is plankton "burning" with phosphorescence, but it might just be a reference to blood.[11] When the ship comes home, the Ancient Mariner sees "crimson shadows" cast near the ship (l. 484). The plankton phenomenon was common to the seas near Tierra del Fuego, not to a harbor port on the other side of the world. Martin Gardner believes that crimson here "symbolizes perhaps the albatross's blood and the blood of Christ by which he [the Ancient Mariner] is cleansed of sin"; but couldn't it just as easily symbolize the Ancient Mariner's blood?[12] Admittedly, here there is real confusion that will be cleared up when we look at what Coleridge had in mind in the 1798 version. It is interesting to note that the men can rise to sail the ship only at night (ll. 329–40), which supports R. P. Warren's more general contention that "good" things happen during moonlight, while the sun is the implacable enemy of the Ancient Mariner.[13]

Some of the minor characters of the poem may hold the key to unlock this poetic china box. First the crew: vampires are spirits who take over the dead bodies of men, thereby denying their souls access to the heavenly world. Something like this may be happening in the crucial central scene when the men won by Death in the dice game are apparently revivified (l. 337ff). The 1834 Gloss reports that they were "inspired," but we must be careful because the first printing of the Gloss in the 1817 *Sibylline Leaves* uses the word "inspirited." Although the words may have the same root, they are different. The crew is not "inspired" but rather has been taken

9. Martin Gardner, *The Annotated Ancient Mariner* (New York: Clarkson N. Potter, 1965), p. 70.
10. Maud Bodkin, "A Study of *The Ancient Mariner* and the Re-Birth Archetype" in *Archetypal Patterns in Poetry* (London: Oxford University Press, 1934), chap. 2, pp. 26–88.
11. Lowes, *Road to Xanadu*, pp. 35–38, 41–42.
12. Gardner, *Annotated Ancient Mariner*, p. 92.
13. Robert Penn Warren, "A Poem of Pure Imagination," introductory essay to his edition of Coleridge, *The Rime of the Ancient Mariner* (New York: Reynal and Hitchcock, 1946).

over by spirits. This inspiriting is emphasized in l. 340 where they are called a "ghastly" crew, which means "ghostly," or that ghosts have taken over their bodies. Technically, these spirits are "revenants"—spirits who return to take over dead bodies. We are told later that these dead men belong in a "charnel-dungeon" (l. 436) rather than on shipboard. A charnel-house is where bodies are kept before burial. If they were dead, why did Coleridge not say that these men belong in graves? Is it because they are not really dead, but rather "still living dead"? Admittedly the 1834 (1817) version calls these revenants "a troop of spirits blest," and the Gloss adds that they were sent by the "guardian saint," but this may be a deception added to the poem in 1817 precisely to mask the original intention.

If the operations of the crew seem eerie and vague, we need only look at the hermit. Voltaire (whose entry on vampires in his *Dictionary* Coleridge had probably read) had said that the true vampires are monks "who eat at the expense of both kings and people," and in this context here is an unusual stanza about the hermit that has gone virtually unnoticed in criticism:

> He kneels at morn, and noon, and eve—
> He hath a cushion plump:
> It is the moss that wholly hides
> The rotted old oak-stump. (ll. 520–23)

What is he doing praying at the base of a rotted oak stump? The stump is perhaps an appropriate altar for a Druid, but not for a man of God. It may be more than coincidental that Christabel also "kneels beneath the huge oak tree,/And in silence prayeth she" (ll. 35–36), and we already know what happened to her. The hermit is also very eager to get on the ship; he forces the Pilot and Pilot's boy to board against their better judgment. And finally, when the hermit and the Ancient Mariner meet, the Mariner calls out:

> 'O shrieve me, shrieve me, holy man!,
> The Hermit crossed his brow.
> 'Say quick,' quoth he, 'I bid thee say—
> What manner of man art thou?'
>
> Forthwith this frame of mine was wrenched
> With a woful agony. (ll. 574–79)

Any schoolboy can tell that the sign of the cross is anathema to a vampire, and the Mariner (assuming now he is so tainted) seems to act accordingly.

If the hermit can be considered slightly tainted, then there are only three "normal" people left in *The Rime*: the Wedding Guest, the Pilot, and the Pilot's boy. I shall discuss the Wedding Guest later, but this is what happens to the Pilot and his boy. They have been goaded by the hermit to row out to the ship. The ship sinks and they pick up the Ancient Mariner. He lies in the boat until, in his own words,

> I moved my lips—the Pilot shrieked
> And fell down in a fit;
> The holy Hermit raised his eyes,
> And prayed where he did sit.
>
> I took the oars: the Pilot's boy,
> Who now doth crazy go,
> Laughed loud and long, and all the while
> His eyes went to and fro.
> 'Ha! ha!' quoth he, 'full plain I see,
> The Devil knows how to row.'
>
> (ll. 560–69)

Two points need mentioning: first, as the Ancient Mariner moves his lips what does the Pilot see that makes him shriek? Perhaps he is amazed, for he may have thought the Mariner dead, but why the *lips moving*, why not the eyes opening or the head twitching? Could it be that the Pilot sees the slightly extended teeth? And second, what of the boy's recognition of the Ancient Mariner as devil? The Ancient Mariner claims that the boy has gone crazy, but what else could he say? Perhaps the Mariner does not even recognize his own condition, but I doubt it; he may be covering up for the Wedding Guest. Kenneth Burke in his *Philosophy of Literary Form* says that the Pilot's boy

> cannot be understood at all, except in superficial terms of the interesting or the picturesque, if we do not grasp his function as a scapegoat of some sort— a victimized vessel for drawing off the most malign aspects of the curse that afflicts the "greybeard loon" whose curse has been effected under the dubious aegis of moonlight.[14]

Mr. Burke is on the right track, but he has things backward. The inclusion of the Pilot's boy who can see things as they really are is Coleridge's intrusion (and a typically Romantic one) of a youth who can see what his elders can't.

The Gloss was added in 1817 for no readily apparent reason. Probably Coleridge wanted to make his poem older, more realistic and Christian. Some critics even claim the prose in it is rather wonderful, but a good case can be made—as the Empson/Pirie text explains—asserting for the opposition that the Gloss rarely has anything to do with the poem. As Empson says, the Gloss "makes nonsense of nearly all the details of [the spirits] so nothing can be done to clarify the poem until this parasitic growth has been removed."[15] And David Pirie continues, saying that the Gloss "seriously perverts the original intention"; but he is really at a loss to say what that intention was.[16] Even B. R. McElderry, who usually praises Coleridge's additions to the poem, admits that here the Gloss has "all the appearance of an

14. Kenneth Burke, *The Philosophy of Literary Form* (Baton Rouge: Louisiana State University Press, 1941), p. 101.
15. Empson, "Introduction" to *Coleridge's Verse*, p. 43.
16. Pirie, "Notes" to *Coleridge's Verse*, p. 238.

afterthought."[17] As I intend to show later, for a number of internal and external reasons, Coleridge felt he had to get the vampire stuff, or whatever it was, out of the poem. In a sense, that is what the Gloss really does. Witness how it explains the "revenants" in part 5: "[The dead crew are revitalized] not by the souls of the men, nor the daemons of earth or middle air, but by a blessed troop of angelic spirits, sent down by the invocation of the guardian saint" (opposite l. 345). Now this is simply not in the poem. Nor is it in the poem, as the Gloss pretends, that the Polar Spirit obeys angels (opposite l. 135), nor that the Holy Mother helps out (opposite l. 295). In each instance it appears that the Gloss is added by an orthodox Coleridge to repair the excesses of youth.

All I have been trying to show so far is that certain peculiarities exist that *might* be explained in a certain way. Remember that so far we have dealt with only the 1834 (1817) text, and that much of what we might be seeing is the *pentimiento* of earlier versions. In other words, what we may be seeing in the 1834 text is the cover-up of the 1800 version, which in turn covers up the 1798 original poem. And so perhaps the place to start is with the first *Rime*, and then see how it was changed.

This is what Coleridge changed in 1800:

1. He deleted a number of archaisms.

2. He added seven lines. These are the most important, following l. 339 of the 1798 poem:

1798	1800
The body of my brother's son	The body of my brother's son
Stood by me knee to knee:	Stood by me knee to knee:
The body and I pull'd at one rope,	The body and I pulled at one rope,
But he said nought to me—	But he said nought to me.
And I quak'd to think of my own voice	'I fear thee, ancient Mariner!'
How frightful it would be!	'Be calm, thou Wedding-Guest!
	'Twas not those souls who fled in pain,
The daylight dawn'd—they dropped their arms	Which to their corses came again,
And cluster'd round the mast . . .	But a troop of spirits blest:
	For when it dawned—they dropped their arms
	And clustered around the mast . . .

The scene I think is clear enough. Coleridge wants to make sure we know that these spirits are *not* "revenants," but a "troop of spirits blest." In 1817 he glossed this with the same story, but it is interesting that he still has the crew working only at night, unable to endure sunlight. For in both versions they rise only when the moon is shining (ll. 335ff.).

3. He deletes forty-six lines, of which the following passages are the most important. In part 5 the ship is being moved by the Polar Spirit:

17. B. R. McElderry, Jr., "Coleridge's Revision of *The Ancient Mariner*," *Studies in Philology* 29 (1932): 90.

1798—text retained

It ceased: yet still the sails made on
A pleasant noise till noon,
A noise like a hidden brook
In the leafy month of June,
That to the sleeping woods all night
Singeth a quiet tune.

1798 text—omitted 1800

Listen, O listen, thou Wedding-Guest!
"Marinere! thou hast thy will:
For that, which comes out of thine eye,
    doth make
My body and soul to be still."

Never sadder tale was told
To a man of woman born:
Sadder and wiser thou wedding-guest!
Thou'lt rise to-morrow morn.

Never sadder tale was heard
By a man of woman born:
The Marineres all return'd to work
As silent as beforne.

The Marineres all 'gan pull the ropes,
But look at me they n'old:
Thought I, I am as thin as air—
They cannot me behold.

1798 text retained

Till noon we silently sailed on
Yet never a breeze did breathe:
Slowly and smoothly went the ship
Mov'd onward from beneath.

Two important things—obviously here the eye is actually projecting some kind of trance to the Wedding Guest, and secondly, the Ancient Mariner is invisible to the crew. Vampires have the power to dematerialize; that is, after all, how they get out of their buried coffins to walk about. The Ancient Mariner has returned home in part 6. He enters the harbor:

1798—text retained

The harbour bay was clear as glass,
So smoothly it was strewn!

And on the bay the moon light lay,
And the shadow of the moon.

1798 text—omitted 1800

The moonlight bay was white all o'er,
Till rising from the same,
Full many shapes, that shadows were,
Like as of torches came.

A little distance from the prow
Those dark-red shadows were;
But soon I saw that my own flesh
Was red as in a glare.

I turn'd my head in fear and dread,
And by the holy rood,
The bodies had advanc'd, and now
Before the mast they stood.

They lifted up their stiff right arms,
They held them straight and tight;
And each right-arm burnt as a torch,
A torch that's borne upright.
Their stony eye-balls glitter'd on
In the red and smoky light.

I pray'd and turn'd my head away
Forth looking as before.
There was no breeze upon the bay,
No wave against the shore.

1798—text retained

The rock shone bright, the kirk no less
That stands above the rock:
The moonlight steep'd in silentness
The steady weathercock.

This is the famous "Hand of Glory" passage that Lowes attempted to explicate. The superstition was that if the hand of a dead man were cut off, treated in a certain way, and then set afire, it would temporarily paralyze anyone who viewed the flame.[18] But I think it more plausible that the crew, having become vampires ("revenants") after the unexplained sucking-in of blood from the Mariner's forearm, are here being destroyed. We of course cannot expect the Mariner to explain how this destruction occurred, for that would surely lose the Wedding Guest; but Coleridge

18. Lowes, *Road to Xanadu*, pp. 250n., 509–11.

could be trying to show us the possibility of the Mariner's being a vampire (cf. ll. 163–65). Vampires may be destroyed by cutting out their hearts and then burning them. Coleridge, with good reason, spared us the former, but I think here he is showing us their consumption by fire. After the vampire bodies are burned the entrapped souls can escape, and indeed a few hours later they do.

There are other cuts in the 1798 version, but none so important. Here are the important 1817 changes: first Coleridge deletes an important passage in part 3 describing the spectre ship of Death and Life-in-Death. These are the parallel texts:

1798 text	*1817 text*

Alas! (thought I, and my heart
    beat loud)
How fast she neres and neres!
Are those *her* Sails that glance in
    the Sun
Like restless gossameres?
	Alas! (thought I, and my heart
	    beat loud)
	How fast she nears and nears!
	Are those *her* sails that glance in
	    the Sun,
	Like restless gossameres?

Are those her naked ribs, which
    fleck'd
The sun that did behind them peer?
And are those two all, all her crew,
That woman and her fleshless Pheere?
	Are those *her* ribs through which
	    the Sun
	Did peer, as through a grate?
	And is that Woman all her crew?
	Is that a Death? and are there two?
	Is Death that woman's mate?

His bones were black with many a crack,
All black and bare I ween;
Jet-black and bare, save where with
    rust
Of mouldy damps and charnel crust
They're patch'd with purple and
    green.
	Her lips were red, *her* looks were free,
	Her locks were yellow as gold:
	Her skin was as white as leprosy,
	The Night-mare Life-in-Death was she,
	Who thicks man's blood with cold.

Her lips are red, *her* looks are free, *Her* locks are yellow as gold: Her skin is as white as leprosy, And she is far liker Death than he; Her flesh makes the still air cold.	The naked hulk alongside came, And the twain were casting dice; 'The game is done! I've won! I've won!' Quoth she, and whistles thrice.
The naked Hulk alongside came And the Twain were playing dice; 'The game is done! I've won, I've won!' Quoth she, and whistled thrice.	
A gust of wind sterte up behind And whistled thro' his bones; Thro' the holes of his eyes and the hole of his mouth Half-whistles and half-groans.	

So in the first version Death has a "Pheere" or spouse while in the second, the reference to "mate" is ambiguous; he may be a mate only in the sense of a shipmate.

In the 1798 version Life-in-Death has perhaps—like the praying mantis—consumed her mate right down to the skeleton. There are more peculiar details as well. We recall that their ship was slowly *tacking* on the horizon until the Mariner bit his arm, and then the ship proceeded *straightaway* to the Mariner's ship. There was no wind. And it is interesting that while he (Death) is a mere skeleton, she is relatively robust. Life-in-Death is a harlot, a tramp, a whore, and she is also quite possibly a vampire. For vampires have red, puffy lips that draw back just as the deadly kiss is to be given the victim and that may be why Coleridge italicized "*His* bones" and "*Her* lips." Unfortunately, the italicized pronoun remains in the later versions—a vestige of the original intention but now no longer serving to heighten the counterpoint.[19]

The most important addition in 1817 was the Ancient Mariner's explanation that crewmates were animated not by malefic spirits but rather by the "angelic troop." Lowes correctly claims that this is a "radical modification," but he is at something of a loss to explain it.[20] Then to make doubly sure we don't mistake these spirits for demonic ones, Coleridge adds the Gloss. He did leave in the lines that began part 4, however, just after the crew had fallen:

> "I fear thee, Ancient Mariner!
> I fear thy skinny hand!
> And thou art long, and lank, and brown,
> As is the ribbed sea-sand.
>
> I fear thee and thy glittering eye,
> And thy skinny hand so brown."—
> Fear nor, fear not, thou Wedding-Guest!
> This body dropt not down.

I believe that Coleridge probably wanted these lines out as well, for they reinforce the vampire reading. The Wedding Guest is afraid that the Ancient Mariner may also be a ghost, and so the Mariner has to deny it straightaway. He must deny that he is possessed, for if the Wedding Guest had known the truth, he would have (if he could have!) high-tailed it into the next township.[21]

Coleridge must have thought that these changes and the addition of the Gloss (especially at the end of part 5) demythologized his poem, and of course he was

19. Coleridge insisted that the last of these stanzas be removed from the first edition of the *Sibylline Leaves*, but the printer overlooked his demands. Coleridge was furious and penned in the margin of his copy: "This stanza I had earnestly charged the printer to omit, but he was a coxcomb, and had an opinion of his own, Forsooth! The Devil daub him! (i.e., his own devil)." Lowes, *Road to Xanadu*, p. 533.
Understandably, Coleridge was mad, but should he have been *that* mad? I think it obvious that he now badly wants those stanzas out. They are, as Swinburne and others have noted, not very good poetry, but are they so terrible that Coleridge should have been this furious?

20. Lowes, *Road to Xanadu*, pp. 257, 258n.

21. I think Coleridge may have left the passage in while taking the others out because Wordsworth had added the last two lines of the first stanza. Coleridge may have felt nostalgic or simply intimidated by Wordsworth's presence in the poem.

partly right. They do make it Christian; they establish the primacy of good; they give the story a crime and punishment subject, and a moral theme. But they do not make it a better poem—only a different poem. But why did he want a different poem? B. R. McElderry believes that Coleridge simply wanted "to revive the creative joy of his youth; and by reviving *The Ancient Mariner* who could tell but that one day he might achieve something to stand beside it."[22] I don't entirely believe this. Rather I believe that he was embarrassed by his youthful foray into German Gothicism, and more importantly, that he was intimidated by Wordsworth.

This is what I think occurred: when the original version of *The Ancient Mariner* was composed, Coleridge was quite taken by the recent successes of German vampire poems and intended to capitalize on what he thought was a growing vogue. He conceived of a vampire poem in which a man spills the blood of a bird, and then excited somehow by this act, breaks his own skin and sucks the blood to find that it gives not only him, but also his crewmates, a new excitement. They come to share his blood-thirst. Later they will all suffer for it as they come under the sway of the demon queen, Life-in-Death, who locks them into her service. The Ancient Mariner breaks the spell by unconsciously blessing the same nature he had perversely and wantonly destroyed. His unconscious act calls forth the restorative powers of Christianity. Now, unlike Southey, who typically would leave the poem at this state, Coleridge then changes the vampire motif from real to metaphorical. The Ancient Mariner becomes a "psychic vampire," now sapping the energy of others with the story of what he had once experienced. Hence the introduction of the Wedding Guest—a tour de force. What the Ancient Mariner is telling the Wedding Guest is not necessarily the truth, for the surface "truth" in Coleridge's art is never really important. What is important is that as he is telling the story, he is sapping the energy of the Wedding Guest just as Life-In-Death had earlier sapped his blood (ll. 205 ff). The Wedding Guest's initial reluctance, his belief that the Ancient Mariner is possessed, and the hypnotic trance are all typical of the willing unwillingness of the vampire's victim. It calls for "a willing suspension of disbelief."

In other words, Coleridge is telling two stories of possession: one is the Mariner's tale, and the other we see right before our eyes with the Wedding Guest. No wonder the Wedding Guest left "like one who had been stunned,/ And is of sense forlorn," for he has been—as we the readers have been too—drained of energy after hearing the Mariner's tale. Coleridge is clearly using the word "forlorn" in the sense of being "deprived," for that is what art initially does—it leaves one "forlorn," deprived of a sense of well-being.[23] Just as the vampire draws his victim across into his world, so too does the artist draw the perceiver into his web of reality. The artist needs the perceiver's energy, just as the vampire needs his blood.

Although Coleridge appears less and less interested in the vampire *qua* vampire, as we see in the revisions, he remained fascinated by the psychological implications

22. McElderry, "Coleridge's Revision of *The Rime of The Ancient Mariner*," p. 91.
23. Gardner, *The Annotated Ancient Mariner*, p. 106.

not of the story, but in the telling of the story. For although "inside" the Ancient Mariner's tale the Mariner is made progressively less and less macabre, on the outside his relation with the Wedding Guest remains stable. In creating the relationship between the Ancient Mariner and the Wedding Guest, Coleridge moved the myth from actual to metaphorical, attempting not horror, but insight. For what the Ancient Mariner tells the Wedding Guest is important, to be sure, but it is not necessarily the truth. What it does to the Wedding Guest, however, is a different story, and it is that "truth" that Coleridge is finally interested in. For what we see in the revisions is that Coleridge is more fascinated with explaining the *affective* power of art than he is with telling a Gothic story. This was the case in *Christabel* as well, for in *Christabel*, Coleridge seems less interested in completing the tale (although he claimed he had written it entirely from beginning to end in his head) than in psychoanalyzing the interpersonal relationships between Geraldine and Christabel. So too in *The Rime of the Ancient Mariner* he seems as intrigued with explaining the relationship between teller and listener as with the tale itself.

In explaining the experience of art, Coleridge used a psychological aspect of the vampire myth which Ross Nichols, a British occult authority, here explains:

> On first thoughts, vampires would seem to be a ghoulish piece of romanticism . . . [but] move the idea of the vampire to the psychic intellectual plane and it is valid enough, and one begins to speculate whether the Dracula story is not a parable. Blood is a symbol of life, and psychic force and ideas are the life of the mind.
>
> Every public speaker knows the difference between a cooperative interested audience and one which in a passive way wants material given to it but gives nothing in return. The speaker is exhausted, whereas after talking to an actively interested audience, he is usually refreshed and satisfied. There are those who suck ideas, therefore, and this is a common experience.
>
> Less common, however, is the speaker who knowingly drains the vitality of his audience for psychic uses of his own. A process of mass and individual hypnosis takes place, wherein feelings of sympathy or enthusiasm for the speaker or a curse he represents flow towards him unguardedly.[24]

The Ancient Mariner is such a "psychic vampire," who saps the energy of the Wedding Guest just as Life-in-Death had earlier gained control of his own energy. The old man, the mythic artist, knows he can live only with the aid of an audience. Just as Keats's Grecian Urn demands completion by being viewed, so the "Rime" of the Mariner demands completion by being heard. As a symphony cannot be understood by a musician playing in the orchestra but only by a listener in the audience, so the introduction of the Wedding Guest is indeed an artistic triumph, for Coleridge has put us—the audience—as close as possible to the art. We are all

---

24. As quoted in Anthony Masters, *The Natural History of the Vampire* (London: Mayflower, 1974), p. 35.

guests at the wedding, the wedding of man and nature, and the wedding of artist and perceiver. We see in the Wedding Guest how we ourselves unconsciously react. He is the supernumerary on the stage, showing—not telling—our responses.

The question still remains as to why there has been such confusion in the texts. What I have to say is of course clearly conjectural, and it involves an acceptance of the internal vampire story, which is the weakest part of my argument. In 1798 the *Rime* appeared in first place in the *Lyrical Ballads*, while Wordsworth, Coleridge, and Dorothy were all fast friends. They each had a hand in the poem, although I think only Coleridge really understood what was going on. Wordsworth certainly wielded the power in the threesome, and he, doubtless unsure of his own poetic powers, may well have insisted that the *Rime* appear first almost as a gothic buffer for his more "revolutionary" poems. After publication Coleridge and the Wordsworths rushed off to Germany, making a point of not reading the reviews—at least not publicly. The reviews came in throughout 1798 and 1799 and were sent to Wordsworth, who must have agonized over them. The one thing that these 1798–99 reviews had in common was that they were singularly unimpressed with the *Rime*. It was obscure; it was extravagant; it was too long; it was a bore. Even Southey, who was working on his own high gothic poem, ridiculed the *Rime*.[25] *The Monthly Review* called it "a cock and bull story"; *The British Critic* said it was simply "[a] confusion of images which loses all effect from being not quite intelligible," and these reviews were not exceptions.[26] Wordsworth may well have thought that *The Ancient Mariner* was an albatross around his own poetic neck, and he may have made this clear to Coleridge. For Wordsworth could be testy when he felt secure, and the early praise for his own poems may have made him play on Coleridge's own insecurities. I think he told Coleridge to get the vulgar vampire nonsense out of the poem before the next edition.

I know this sounds harsh and catty, but look at what Wordsworth does to the *Rime* in the 1800 edition. First, he sets it at the very end, and second, he adds a note to the poem that is rather patronizing:

> Note to *The Ancient Mariner*.—I cannot refuse myself the gratification of informing such Readers as may have been pleased with this Poem, or with any part of it, that they owe their pleasure in some sort to me; as the Author was himself very desirous that it should be suppressed. This wish had arisen from a consciousness of the defects of the Poem, and from a knowledge that many persons had been much displeased with it. The Poem of my Friend has indeed great defects; first, that the principal person has no distinct character, either in his profession of Mariner, or as a human being who having been long under the controul of supernatural impressions might be supposed himself to partake of something supernatural: secondly, that he does not act, but is continually acted upon: thirdly, that the events having no necessary connection do not

---

25. *The Monthly Review* 29 (May 1799): 204.
26. *The British Critic* 14 (Oct. 1799): 365. Other negative reviews appeared in *The Critical Review* (Oct. 1798), and *The Analytical* (Dec. 1798).

produce each other; and lastly, that the imagery is somewhat too laboriously accumulated.[27]

I am not alone in believing this. Lowes (who is usually sympathetic to Wordsworth) says it is "not only far from generous, it is also disingenuous."[28] Empson echoes this conclusion by claiming that "this is very rude behavior from Wordsworth"; and Pirie says it is simply "treacherous."[29]

What makes Wordsworth's behavior doubly upsetting is that we now know his real feelings, for just as he is writing that "Note to *The Ancient Mariner*," he is also writing to Joseph Cottle, the publisher:

> From what I can gather it seems that *The Ancient Mariner* has on the whole, been an injury to the volume; I mean that the old words and the strangeness of it have deterred readers from going on. If the volume should come to a second edition, I would put in its place some little things which would be more likely to suit the common taste.[30]

Three weeks earlier he had told Cottle that the first cause of the "failure" of the *Lyrical Ballads* was simply the inclusion of *The Ancient Mariner*.[31] I suspect that Coleridge was pressured into removing much of the gothic imagery (but by no means all, for that would have made the poem incomprehensible), and then returned it to Wordsworth, who felt obliged to print it out of guilt and friendship. I don't think Wordsworth wanted to.

But then why did Coleridge make the changes between 1800 and 1817? Wordsworth was not pressuring him. Here I think it was a combination of chagrin and religious conscience. He may have been embarrassed in much the same way that any literary pundit today might be if someone dredged up an early obscene novel. It was really in 1800 a rather foolish poem—too subtle now to be understood in its original context—too disjointed to fit together. And so, in 1817, an orthodox and in a sense circumspect Coleridge (for I take the Gloss to be an extraordinary attempt to force a meaning into the poem which says just the opposite) tried to Christianize the earlier poem. William Empson has reached the same conclusion but from a different angle.

> It was not long after the nervous breakdown, and soon after preparing *Biographia* and *Sibylline Leaves*, that he gave the particularly sectarian philosophy lectures; so this is the period when he was likely to turn the spirits into angels. In 1806 he could still half agree with the crew that their dying curse was likely to induce a faction of spirits to take up their cause; but in 1815 he was pre-

---

27. This note appears on an unnumbered page following the text in volume 1 of the 1800 *Lyrical Ballads*.

28. Lowes, *Road to Xanadu*, p. 475.

29. Empson, "Introduction," p. 53, and Pirie, "Notes," p. 241, to *Coleridge's Verse*.

30. "Letter of June 24, 1799," in *The Early Letters of William Wordsworth*, ed. Ernest DeSelincourt (Oxford: Clarendon Press, 1935), pp. 226–27.

31. "Letter of June 24, 1799" in *The Early Letters*, p. 234.

tending that these spirits merely carry out the unknown plans of God, which in anyone else but God would often be called plainly unjust. Well then, no particular importance could attach to the indignation of the crew, or of anyone else. I think we should restore the drama as it was before the fatal change.[32]

Still, when you read the reviews of the 1816 revision you can see that the critics have not forgotten (as we have) the original poem. For instance there is *The Monthly Review* commentary on what we in the twentieth century have forgotten:

> 'The Rime of the Ancient Mariner' appeared at a time when, to use a bold but just expression, with reference to our literary taste, '*Hell made holiday*,' and '*Raw heads and bloody-bones*' were the only fashionable entertainment for man or woman. Then Germany was poured forth into England, in all of her sculls and numsculls: then the romancing novelist ran raving about midnight torches, to show death's heads on horseback, and to frighten full-grown children with mysteries and band-boxes, hidden behind curtains in bedrooms . . . and then sang the Ancient Mariner. . . .[33]

Perhaps we too should recognize the original context of Coleridge's poem, if only because it ties together so many of the loose ends of the 1834 (1817) edition and adds a depth of meaning otherwise neglected. It may be dangerous to read a poem in terms of its revisions, but it may ultimately be illuminating not only of the poem, but of the poet as well.

Resolution and Independence

The Ancient Mariner shares certain similarities with another outcast figure in Romanticism—Wordsworth's Leech Gatherer. Both are preternaturally old, both exert magnetic powers over young men they encounter, and both personify aspects of the artist as magician/god. In the *Rime*, however, the artist is in a sense a predator, rejuvenated not by the creation of art alone, but by tapping the sympathetic powers of his audience. If he has given wisdom to the Wedding Guest, he has taken energy in return. The Wedding Guest's energy has not simply been diffused into the air; it has flowed into the old artist and given him strength. This is not so with the Leech Gatherer, where the life-force seems to have traveled from the old man to the tyro, rejuvenating the dejected young poet while not diminishing the indomitable veteran.

Ironically, this process of energy exchange may be initially difficult to observe because we know too much about how *Resolution and Independence* was written

32. Empson, "Introduction" to *Coleridge's Verse*, p. 53.
33. *The Monthly Review* 88 (Jan. 1819): 28.

and too little of what it is about. For instance, from Dorothy Wordsworth's *Journal* we know that on 3 October 1800, she and William met a solitary old leech gatherer on the moors who had grown so weak he had taken to begging.[34] We also know that two years later, after Wordsworth had finished the fourth section of the *Intimations Ode*, he wrote the first draft of *Resolution and Independence*.[35] He entitled this poem *The Leech Gatherer*, and as his letter to Sara Hutchinson on 14 June 1802, implies, the poet-persona in the poem is himself. He reasserted the biographical connection between himself and the poet in the Fenwick note, stating, "I was in the state of feeling described in the beginning of the poem, while crossing over Barton Fell. . . ."[36]

So it has been logically assumed that the melancholia Wordsworth is describing in the first part of the *Intimations Ode* is also being described in the first thirty or so lines of *Resolution and Independence*. And, understandably, most of the criticism of *Resolution and Independence* has centered upon the character of the narrator, Wordsworth himself—or at least a suspected Wordsworth. Critics as diverse as George Meyer, W. W. Robson, William Heath, Albert Gerard, Anthony E. M. Conran, Stanley Edgar Hyman, Alan Grob, and E. E. Bostetter have all shared the assumption that the speaker is Wordsworth and that the poem is thus a poetic autobiography leading to—as the case may be—renewed interest in nature, concern with the "adjusted self," or Christian stoicism.[37]

34. This is the complete text of Dorothy Wordsworth's 3 Oct. 1800 *Journal* entry:

When Wm and I returned from accompanying Jones, we met an old man almost double. He had on a coat, thrown over his shoulders above his waistcoat and coat. Under this he carried a bundle, and had an apron on and a nightcap. His face was interesting. He had dark eyes and a long nose. John, who afterwards met him at Wytheburn, took him for a Jew. He was of Scotch parents, but had been born in the army. He had had a wife, and 'a good woman, and it pleased God to bless us with ten children.' All these were dead but one, of whom he had not heard for many years, a sailor. His trade was to gather leeches, but now leeches are scarce, and he had not strength for it. He lived by begging, and was making his way to Carlisle, where he should buy a few goodly books to sell. He said leeches were very scarce, partly owing to the dry season, but many years they have been scarce. He supposed it owing to their being much sought after, that they did not breed fast, and were of slow growth. Leeches were formerly 2s. 6d. per 100; now they are 30s.

35. According to Dorothy Wordsworth's *Journal* (4, 7, 9 May; 2, 4 July 1802) the correct date of composition is May–July 1802.

36. Wordsworth's note reads: "Town-End, 1807. This old man I met a few hundred yards from my cottage at Town-End, Grasmere; and the account of him is taken from his own mouth. I was in the state of feeling described in the beginning of the poem, while crossing over Barton Fell from Mr. Clarkson's, at the foot of Ullswater, towards Askam. The image of the hare I then observed on the ridge of the Fell."

37. The following is by no means an exhaustive list, but these are the critics who have most obviously linked Wordsworth and the persona: George Meyer, "*Resolution and Independence*, Wordsworth's Answer to *Coleridge's Dejection: An Ode*," *Tulane Studies in English* 2 (1950), 49–74; W. W. Robson, *Critical Essays* (London: Routledge & Kegan Paul, 1966), pp. 124–35; William Heath, *Wordsworth and Coleridge: A Study of Their Literary Relations in 1801–1802* (Oxford: Clarendon Press, 1970); Albert Gérard, "*Resolution and Independence*: Wordsworth's Coming of Age," *English Studies in Africa* 3 (1960): 8–20; Anthony E. M. Conran, "The Dialectic of Experience: A Study of Wordsworth's *Resolution and Independence*," *PMLA* 75 (1960): 124–34; Stanley Edgar Hyman, *Poetry and Criticism* (New York: Atheneum, 1961), pp. 103–21; Alan Grob, "Process and Permanence in *Resolution and Independence*" *ELH* 18 (1961): 89–100; and E. E. Bostetter, *The Romantic Ventriloquists* (Seattle: University of Washington Press, 1963), pp. 34–36.

One recent critic has demurred from this a priori coupling of the speaker and Wordsworth. Jeffrey Meyers, in his "Revaluation of Wordsworth's *Resolution and Independence*," asserts that the speaker is a foil, a foppish aesthete, not at all the perceptive poet described in the 1800 Preface to the *Lyrical Ballads*.[38] Meyers contends that although the speaker calls himself a "traveller" (l. 15), he is really only a wanderer, for he knows pathetically little about the life of the moors. He patronizingly says, "It is a good day" to the Leech Gatherer when he knows, at least for himself, that it is not; he asks the Leech Gatherer what he does for a living when anyone with any country-sense would know what the old man was doing. The speaker simply does not have the acute sensibility that Wordsworth had shown in *Tintern Abbey, The Prelude,* or the *Intimations Ode.* For instance, the poet says rapidly, "This must be a lonely place for an old Leech Gatherer," when just previously he has compared the Leech Gatherer to a grounded sea beast or a solitary boulder, epic similes that elsewhere Wordsworth himself asserted were supposed to show the old man's union with his natural surroundings.[39]

But the proof positive of Meyers's thesis is the poet's report of himself: that his whole life had been "lived in pleasant thought,/ As if life's business were a summer mood;/ As if all needful things would come unsought/ To genial faith" (ll. 36–39). This is simply not the thirty-two-year-old Wordsworth, whom we know from the *Prelude* and who elsewhere had suffered a good deal. For by the time Wordsworth saw the Leech Gatherer in 1800, he had suffered political, social, artistic, and personal reverses (his strained friendship with Coleridge, his affair with Annette Vallon, the not-overwhelming success of the *Lyrical Ballads*, the disappointing turn of the French Revolution). Meyers thus peels the persona away from Wordsworth, contending that the former is "unstable, melancholy, childish, anxious, irresponsible, weak, unperceptive, and egocentric," and concluding that in creating this confusion Wordsworth had detracted from the poem's central thrust.[40] But how much of this confusion Wordsworth consciously created and how much is due to our too-complete knowledge of its composition is a moot point.

However, Meyers's reading does encourage separating the other central character, the Leech Gatherer, from perhaps misleading biographical information. It may be equally informative to put aside what we have been told of the Leech Gatherer by Dorothy, and instead examine the fictionalized version created by Wordsworth. What do we know from the poem about the Leech Gatherer? One thing is clear:

38. Jeffrey Meyers, "A Re-evaluation of Wordsworth's *Resolution and Independence*," *Discourse* 11 (1968): 441–49.

39. Wordsworth comments on these epic similes at the end of the "Preface to the Edition of 1815":

The stone is endowed with something of the power of life to approximate it to the sea-beast; and the sea-beast stripped of some of its vital qualities to assimilate it to the stone; which intermediate image is thus treated for the purpose of bringing the original image, that of the stone, to a nearer resemblance to the figure and condition of the aged Man; who is divested of so much of the indications of life and motion as to bring him to the point where the two objects unite and coalesce in just comparison.

40. Meyers, "A Re-evaluation of Wordsworth's *Resolution and Independence*," p. 444.

he is not the typical Wordsworth "solitary"; he is neither the vagrant soldier of the *Prelude* nor the Old Cumberland Beggar, nor Michael nor the Solitary Reaper. He is profoundly different.

I think a case can be made that Wordsworth intended to write a vampire poem, with the Leech Gatherer as the central character. Important here is the fact that Wordsworth originally entitled the poem *The Leech Gatherer*, but changed it five years later to *Resolution and Independence* as presumably he wanted to shift the focus back to the narrator. It was not to be the usual Gothic poem like Goethe's "Bride of Corinth," Bürger's "Lenore," Southey's *Thalaba*, or the macabre staple of *The Monthly Review*; rather, Wordsworth appears to be experimenting with the psychological ramifications of the myth, just as Coleridge may have done in the *Rime*. He seems to be treating the vampire as a metaphor of the creative process with the presence of the Leech Gatherer triggering the young poet's "spontaneous overflow of powerful feelings." The energy metaphor is implicit in Wordsworth's own poetic definition—the artistic act is an *overflow* of energy. What is startling about the Leech Gatherer is that he, as almost a form in nature, revives the melancholy poet, and in doing this acts as the catalyst, not drawing in energy as had the Ancient Mariner, but reversing the flow. In this sense he is Christ-like, saying, in effect, "Drink of my energy and have creative life."

Resolution and Independence is divided into three parts: in the first, the poet feels melancholy; in the second he laments the passing of other young poets; and in the third he meets an old Leech Gatherer. The third part is the most interesting, and has never been adequately explained, possibly for the biographical reasons already mentioned. Here the speaker meets an incredibly old man who is out gathering leeches. The usual way to gather leeches is with a net, but this old man must stir the muddy waters with a stick and then, using his legs as a bait, he must wade into the shallow water, allowing the leeches to attach themselves.[41] Leeches have tiny teeth and can "bite" only something soft and pliable. Hence Wordsworth calls this "hazardous employment" (l. 101), for the hunter's bait is the hunter himself. The paradigm of host and parasite is established in the occupation of the old man.

But Wordsworth called the poem *The Leech Gatherer* for a more profound reason: he wanted us to see the deeper, although ultimately reversed, symbolism of the Eucharist. As the poet encounters the old man, he notices how incredibly old, almost timeless (ll. 55–56) the Leech Gatherer is, almost as if he were "not all alive nor dead" (l. 54). The old man neither beckons nor notices the poet; rather, the poet takes "the stranger's privilege" (l. 82) to cross over to him and initiate some small talk. Then the old man slowly "comes alive" and starts speaking. The poet becomes hypnotized in much the same way that the knight does in *La Belle Dame sans Merci* or the Wedding Guest in the *Rime*. The old man's language becomes blurred as the poet loses ordinary consciousness. Finally his senses return, and he

41. Of the many medical books detailing the collection and use of leeches, I have found the most helpful to be William Brockbank, *Ancient Therapeutic Arts: Fitzpatrick Lectures Delivered in 1950–51 at the Royal College of Physicians* (London: William Heineman, 1954), pp. 87–98.

again asks, "What do you do?" and again he is transported as the Leech Gatherer smiles and says simply that he gathers leeches. Abruptly the poet concludes:

> While he was talking thus, the lonely place,
> The old Man's shape, and speech—all troubled me:
> In my mind's eye I seemed to see him pace
> About the weary moors continually
> Wandering about alone and silently.   (ll. 127–31)

So far all we know is this: the Leech Gatherer is incredibly old, has some power over the poet once the initial contact is made, has a religious aura, and seems foreign both in language and behavior ("like a man from some far region sent" [l. 111]). He is dreamlike. What we know about him has, of course, been filtered through the hazy prism of the persona's consciousness, and like the Wedding Guest, he may not understand the significance of his Ancient Mariner. We, the audience, have to extrapolate meaning for him. Here surely it is important that just as the old man gathers leeches that come to him for succor, so he is gathering the young poet who comes to him for strength. Of course, the analogy doesn't work completely, for the leeches are captured and sent off, while the poet walks away of his own will. But I think Wordsworth is interested only in the symbolic meaning and the process of energy exchange.

This vampiric (or simply parasite and host) reading is reinforced when we examine the earlier 1802 version. In the 1807 poem Wordsworth, perhaps because originally he had made the central symbolism too obvious and too forced, deleted from the 1802 version three passages that described the old man as possibly vampiric. First, following line 56, Wordsworth omitted these lines:

> My course I stopped as soon as I espied
> The Old Man in that naked wilderness:
> Close by a Pond, upon the further side,
> He stood alone: a minute's space I guess
> I watch'd him, he continuing motionless:
> To the Pool's further margin then I drew;
> He being all the while before me full in view.

Here the poet's initiation of contact is stressed, perhaps too much. The poet crosses the threshold, as it were, of the Leech Gatherer, and in doing so is metaphorically "trapped." Second, Wordsworth cut a stanza following line 84 in which he describes the Leech Gatherer in typical vampire garb. This stanza beings:

> He wore a Cloak the same as women wear,
> As one whose blood did needful comfort lack:
> His face look'd pale as if it had grown fair.

The cloak, the blood needing revitalization, and the paleness may have made the Leech Gatherer almost a caricature, and that was not at all what Wordsworth wanted. Rather I suspect he wanted only the hint, not the statement, of the old man's strange position in the world. The one thing that Wordsworth did not want was for us to assume that the Leech Gatherer was a demonic fiend, and so he also cut these lines that follow the poet's first question about occupation: "He answer'd me with pleasure and surprise;/ And there was, while he spake, a fire about his eyes." The old man may be supernatural, but he is definitely not the red-eyed monster of folklore.

If Wordsworth did not want us to see the old man in the tradition of the demonic vampire, then why did he leave the other hints of vampirism in the poem? I think that Wordsworth rather only wanted to hint at the vampire analogy to symbolize the role of the Poet. For the real Poet in the poem is not the poet-persona (the speaker), but rather the archetypal Poet, the Leech Gatherer himself. He is the Ur-Poet, alien, outcast, wandering endlessly, unable to die, the Wandering Jew, but ironically not living off others, rather just the opposite, giving his strength to those who come into contact with him. We see the Leech Gatherer in nature acting as the seer—he is "conning" the muddy waters "as if he had been reading in a book" (l. 81). For the book of nature is his proper study, and from this study he can provide "truth" for mankind. He is also described as on a "pilgrimage" (l. 67), perhaps sent to man "by peculiar grace,/ A leading from above, a something given" (ll. 50–51). Even his own words

> . . . came feebly, from a feeble chest,
> But each in solemn order followed each,
> With something of a lofty utterance drest—
> Choice word and measured phrase, above the reach
> Of ordinary men.   (ll. 92–96)

In the sense that the Leech Gatherer reverses the vampire analogy, he is Christ-like, literally nourishing the lowly leech and figuratively giving strength to the poet manqué. For just as Christ invited men to drink his symbolic blood in the Eucharist, so the Leech Gatherer drains his own energy to give strength to man. As Stanley Edgar Hyman has said in a different context, the old man is "godlike not in power but in sacrificial attributes, a suffering saviour in fact."[42] Seeing *Resolution and Independence* in this light makes sense of the original title, *The Leech Gatherer*. It also explains the confusing ending for the poet has been strengthened, given resolution, by a process he simply cannot understand. It is true, as Professor Conran has asserted, that the poet has been in a trance, but it is the almost religious trance of art.[43] And this trance is implied in the subtle analogy of vampirism. The artist gives energy by allowing the perceiver to leech from the strength of his perception, his art. The artist thus echoes Christ's words, "He that eateth my flesh and drinketh my blood dwelleth in me, and I in him. As the living Father hath sent

---

42. Hyman, *Poetry and Criticism*, p. 113.
43. Conran, "The Dialectic of Experience: A Study of Wordsworth's *Resolution and Independence*," p. 66.

me, and I live by the Father: so he that eateth me, even he shall live by me." Hence the last lines: " 'God,' said I, 'be my help and stay secure/ I'll think of the Leech-gatherer on the lonely moor!' " (ll. 139–40). For all man needs to do to revitalize himself in times of depression is to remember the artistic experience, for in so doing he will be participating in the recharging of energy, the Eucharist of art.[44]

The Oval Portrait

Poe's *The Oval Portrait* is one of his few widely anthologized tales that have not been excessively interpreted. What little criticism there is has centered primarily on the reliability of the narrator and only secondarily on the character of the artist.[45] This is probably because the story itself is deceptively straightforward. Here, in essence, is that story: our weak narrator arrives at a castle in the Apennines, spends the evening reading a catalogue describing paintings in the room where he is sleeping. By moving a bedside candle he catches sight of an incredibly lifelike portrait of a young girl. He dozes off, wakes, and then, curious to find out more about this young beauty, reads in the catalogue that her husband was the painter and that he was so wedded to his art that he did not notice that as he was painting his wife she was growing weaker and weaker. The narrator's story ends with the end of the catalogue description; finally, just as the painter finishes his work, he exclaims, "This is indeed *Life* itself!" Enraptured, he turns from the painting to his wife, and, irony of ironies, she is dead.

Critics have noted the strong resemblance between Hawthorne's *The Birthmark* and Poe's *The Oval Portrait*, but equally striking are its similarities with *The Artist of the Beautiful*.[46] For here we have that Romantic dilemma played out once again, of the artist who is so obsessed with his art that he sacrifices his loved ones in the

44. The poem is sufficiently ambiguous to allow just the opposite conclusion—namely that the speaker is the accomplished poet who finally "resolves" to be "independent" of nature and to accept his despair dispassionately, with Christian stoicism. See, for instance, Alan Grob, "Process and Permanence in *Resolution and Independence*," pp. 89–100, and E. E. Bostetter, *The Romantic Ventriloquists*, pp. 34–36.

45. In fact there have only been two studies specifically dealing with *The Oval Portrait*, both focusing on the transformation of *Life in Death* to *The Oval Portrait*. Seymour Gross, "Poe's Revision of *The Oval Portrait*," *Modern Language Notes* 74 (Jan. 1959): 16–20, argues that Poe wisely removes the narrator's consciousness from the revision; and G. R. Thompson, "Dramatic Irony in *The Oval Portrait*: A Reconsideration of Poe's Revision," *English Language Notes* 6 (Dec. 1968): 107–14, contends just the opposite, namely that the narrator's presence is still important, but now only as it parodies the Romantic tuning-fork consciousness. The narrator, for Thompson, is a foolish dreamer who, in the tradition of Poe's earlier narrators, is not to be trusted—hence the "dramatic irony."

46. This similarity was first suggested by Arthur Hobson Quinn, *Edgar Allan Poe: A Critical Biography* (New York: D. Appleton-Century, 1941), p. 331; but I think it doubtful (especially from Poe's earlier use of the vampire myth in the 1830s) that Poe was specifically influenced by Hawthorne. Hawthorne seems to have little conscious use for the vampire analogy. *The Oval Portrait* does bear interesting resemblances, however, to Hawthorne's less-known *Prophetic Pictures*.

process of creating perfection. The portrait is as lifelike as Warland's butterfly, as beautiful as Aylmer's Georgiana. The paradox the artist doesn't recognize is that the vitality of his art drains the very life-strength of the people he loves. Hawthorne implies that this is the necessary evil in art; Poe characteristically implies nothing of the sort. His interest is only in telling a good story, a story with psychological, not moral, import.

Or so it seems. Actually, Poe's treatment may ultimately be the more metaphoric, for lurking behind his arabesque tale is another story, the myth of the vampire. This conclusion is almost inescapable when we line up *The Oval Portrait* with not only its prototype, *Life in Death*, but also his earlier tales. That Poe was familiar with vampire lore has already been substantiated, obviously in tales like *Berenice*, *Ligeia*, and *Morella*, and more subtly in *The Fall of the House of Usher*. The myth was certainly good copy, but for Poe it finally became more. The vampire tale was an ideal paradigm for love that is too demanding or, in the case of *The Oval Portrait*, art that is too life-consuming.

Before witnessing Poe's most sophisticated treatment of this vampire myth in *The Oval Portrait*, perhaps it might be best to review briefly his own use of the vampire motif prior to 1842. In *Berenice* (March 1835) we see Poe's first and rather clumsy attempt to incorporate the vampire into a tale. It seems obvious that Poe's concern here is in exploiting real historical events, and that the vampire material is just added along the way.[47] The narrator attempts to explain a relationship he has had with his cousin in which he, at first sickly and weak, grows stronger in daily contact with her. She, however, weakens and shrivels up, and as she does, her eyes and teeth become objects of incredible horror. He has metaphorically drained her of her life-blood, and in so doing he has made her desperate for energy. Perhaps fearful that she will return for his life, he kills her and rips out those potential instruments of her retaliation, her teeth.

In *Berenice* the vampire motif is really unattached to any theme and is included more for gothic stuffing than for sense, but in *Ligeia* the vampire motif is securely tied to Poe's central theme of the powers of the Will. Here another unreliable narrator must explain away a strange energy transfer. Ligeia, the narrator's inamorata, has all the physical characteristics of a vampire—no family, moves like a shadow, has marble-cold hands, pallid complexion, brilliant teeth, etc.—but what the narrator focuses on is the eyes . . . those overlarge, hypnotic eyes. ("Those eyes! those large, those shining, those divine orbs! they became to me twin stars of Leda, and I to them devoutest of astrologers.") Soon the energy exchange takes place, but this time in reverse. For as the narrator vamps the vampire, she soon grows weak and "dies." Later he takes up with Lady Rowena, whom he soon comes to despise, but no matter—he needs only her blood-energy to survive, not her love. She grows

47. Poe's main concern seems to be exploiting then-recent occurrences of grave robbing. See Killis Campbell, *The Mind of Poe and Other Studies* (Cambridge, Mass.: Harvard University Press, 1933), p. 167; and Roger Forclaz's elaboration, "A Source of *Berenice* and a Note on Poe's Reading," *Poe Newsletter* 1 (1968): 25–27.

weaker and weaker as he strengthens; finally there is that wonderfully macabre death scene where he hallucinates that Rowena is drinking wine/blood, and she soon fades from life. Not for long, for she, by entering into a vampiric symbiosis with the narrator, cannot truly die, but rather becomes initiated into the fraternity of the "living dead." Her body is reanimated, so the narrator tells us, by the first vampire, Ligeia. The end of the story, as the criticism attests, is confusing, for the metaphor of the vampire is none-too-subtly slid in behind Poe's description of the operation of the Will.

With *Morella*, written just prior to *Ligeia*, we have yet another rendition of the "La Belle Dame sans Merci" theme. Again the woman "attaches" herself to the man, again the lamiaesque descriptions of the cold hands, pallid complexion, powerful eye, *etc.*, and again, there is the narrator's final reversal of the energy drain, until he finally strengthens and she weakens. This time, as with Ligeia, the vampire lady dies, saying, "I am dying, yet I shall live," and indeed just as Ligeia returns through Rowena's body, so Morella finds "life in death" through her posthumous daughter.

In each of these stories two characters work out a lovers' balance that is destroyed as soon as one demands too much. Vampirism is only a metaphor for this process. As love gets out of control, as the rhythm is lost, one partner metaphorically starts to consume the other. *Berenice, Morella,* and *Ligeia* are all love stories in which one lover attempts too much, and so violates the psychic privacy of the other. Call it the Will, as in *Ligeia,* call it Madness, as in *Berenice,* call it any number of things, as the narrator himself does—it always works out the same. The weaker lover can be destroyed, but the love perversely endures. Like the vampire, the eccentric lover demands absolute possession even though possession finally means destruction. The narrator can never admit this, so in *Berenice* we are told Berenice is taken over by a "ghostly destroyer"; in *Morella,* the lamia-love invades the body of her daughter; and in *Ligeia* the spirit of the Will reanimates the corpse of Rowena. In all these stories the narrator's overbearing love destroys the lover while his neurotic guilt allows her to return. As quoted more fully on p. 58, D. H. Lawrence, the "first" and perhaps the best commentator on this aspect of Poe, wrote that "the desirous consciousness, the SPIRIT is a vampire."[48]

These three stories, then, form a kind of subgenre in Poe's work, each one treating a different aspect of the vampire motif. They seem to represent a progression from the simple and the obvious to the more subtle and metaphoric. *Berenice,* first published in March 1835, is the most clumsy; *Morella,* written a month later, seems to be the trying out of *Ligeia,* published September 1838. And Poe, still fascinated with the possibilities of the vampire story, used it to illustrate the warped sibling love in the *House of Usher.*

But that was not the last of Poe's attempts. In the April 1842 issue of *Graham's*

---

48. D. H. Lawrence, *Selected Literary Criticism,* ed. Anthony Beal (1932; rpt. New York: The Viking Press, 1966), pp. 331–35. This aspect of Poe's interest in the Gothic is also discussed briefly in Allen Tate, *The Forlorn Demon* (Chicago: Regnery, 1953), pp. 79–95.

Magazine a story called *Life in Death* appeared.[49] It was clearly written in a hurry and probably was a filler, for it covers exactly two pages, the space necessary for Poe to earn his four dollars. What is disturbing about its placement in the magazine is that it follows Poe's incisive review of Hawthorne's *Twice-Told Tales*, implicitly serving as a kind of exemplum. Ironically *Life in Death* does not illustrate Poe's central critical point that a tale should drive for "a certain unique or single *effect*"; rather it wanders aimlessly about. Probably, as Richard Dowell has pointed out, Poe intended to use *The Mask of the Red Death* (later *The Masque . . .*), but either it was squeezed out due to the exigencies of space, or perhaps more simply, Poe hadn't finished it in time. So, Dowell concludes,

> "Life in Death," under such circumstances, could very possibly have been an eleventh-hour replacement thrown into the breach without the "deliberate care" or revision Poe normally demanded of himself and others—another example of the editor's need to "supply a particular demand" at the expense of the artist,

which is correct; but he then oversteps the mark when he continues:

> [*Life in Death*] seems a poorly planned, hastily written tale that appeared at a very inopportune time in Poe's career. Why he felt compelled to use it must remain a matter of speculation; however, the dichotomous and often incompatible responsibilities Poe faces as artist-editor remind us that he was not a writer who always had time for meticulous composition and leisurely revision.[50]

Admittedly the tale is sloppy in places, but it is also Poe's most sophisticated handling of the vampire motif, now used not to describe eccentric love, but rather the process of artistic creation.

The major differences between *Life in Death* and the revised *The Oval Portrait* are: (1) The titles—"Life in Death" makes obvious the vampire process that "The Oval Portrait" only implies. (2) *Life in Death* has a longish introduction (about a third of the entire tale) describing how the narrator happens to be spending the night in the castle. We are told he had been attacked by bandits, had been wounded, and is now too weak to spend the night in the cold. Once inside the castle, he takes some opium to ease the pain, which sends him into a reverie from which he is "startled . . . at once into waking life as if with the shock of a galvanic battery" by seeing the portrait (p. 318).[51] There is then a great deal of extraneous

49. That Poe entitled the prototype for *The Oval Portrait, Life in Death* is obviously a key to what he intended. Darrel Abel's note, "Coleridge's 'Life-in-Death' and Poe's 'Death-in-Life,'" *Notes & Queries* 200 (May 1955): 218–20, ties Poe's concept to Coleridge's fantastic figure in *The Rime of the Ancient Mariner*. What Abel does not mention is that Coleridge's "Life-in-Death" may herself be a vampire, for recall that the Mariner must first bite his arm and draw blood before she sails over to his ship (part 3).

50. Richard W. Dowell, "The Ironic History of Poe's *Life in Death*: A Literary Skeleton in the Closet" *American Literature* 42 (Jan. 1971): 478–86.

51. *The Oval Portrait* first appeared in *Graham's Magazine* (April 1842) as *Life in Death*, and was then revised for the *Broadway Journal* (26 April 1845). The text I am using is that in *The Complete*

material comparing the smoking of opium to the drinking of laudanum, and worry over the proper dosage. This introduction introduces nothing, but allows Poe to fill up the two-page limit. It reads like stuffing, and he wisely takes it out when the tale is revised. (3) There are a number of minor word changes ("so placed it" becomes "placed it so," "an hour" for "some hours"), but the most interesting changes are two deletions. First, he dropped the epigraph—"Egli è vivo e parlerebbe se non osservasse la rigola del silentio" ("He is alive and would speak if he were not observing the vow of silence")—which has vampiric undertones; and second, in the earlier version the narrator describes the painting, saying "I could no longer support the sad meaning smile of the half-parted lips, nor the too real lustre of the wild eye" (p. 318). In the revision Poe cut the description of the weird smile and the wild eye that is so reminiscent of the earlier descriptions of Berenice, Morella, and Ligeia. (4) The original story within the story ends with the painter turning to his dead wife: "The painter then added—'But is this indeed Death?'" (p. 318). In the revision Poe cut this, having the story end,

> And then the brush was given, and then the tint was placed; and, for one moment, the painter stood entranced before the work which he had wrought; but in the next, while he yet gazed, he grew tremulous, and very pallid, and aghast, and crying with a loud voice, 'This is indeed *Life* itself!' turned suddenly to regard his beloved:—She was dead!" (p. 249)

What these changes show is Poe's final tightening of the motif, now applying it to the process of artistic creation. The narrator does not enervate the subject, as he had done in the earlier stories. Rather we have—especially in the revision—a singularly undrugged and sensible narrator who is commenting as a third party. And no longer is competitive love the subject. Instead art is the love; art itself is involved in the transfer of vitality; the process of creation is vampiric. In the early tales it was crucial to have the narrator's consciousness blotted with drugs because he must not know what the perceptive reader comes to know, namely that he is the villain, he is the too-greedy lover, he is the vampire, but here in *The Oval Portrait* the narrator is a cipher, setting the stage for the painter.

By introducing the credible narrator Poe pushes the reader toward a metaphoric understanding of artistic creation. This was not the case with *Life in Death*, in which the narrator himself is suspect. In dropping the title, the Italian epigraph, and the original ending (no longer does the painter ask whether his wife is dead, but rather states that his art is "alive") Poe removes the obvious and reinforces the vampiric analogy. The irony is still there but now it is for the reader to resolve. In doing this Poe created his most sophisticated variation on the vampire theme.

Poe's attempt was by no means the most sophisticated Romantic effort. That

---

Works of Edgar Allan Poe, ed. James A. Harrison (New York: T. Y. Crowell, 1902), 4: 245–49. Poe's deletions are listed on pp. 316–19. Page numbers will be from this edition and will follow quotations in parentheses in the text

task—and indeed it became the tour de force of all adaptations of the myth—was left to Oscar Wilde.[52] For what Wilde did was to write a parable about art in which the energies of creation don't flow as expected, namely, from object of art to artifact (*The Oval Portrait*) or from artist to audience (Wordsworth's *Resolution and Independence*) or from audience to artist (*The Rime of the Ancient Mariner*), but instead flowed from artist and artifact to subject. This is of course shockingly impossible, and to accomplish it Wilde had to splice together a number of mythic stories so that events always seem possible until, too late, we realize we have been gulled. Then, like the audience who has seen the rabbit pulled from the hat, we rush to inspect the rabbit and the hat, never thinking to look up the magician's sleeve.

The Picture of Dorian Gray

All critics agree that Oscar Wilde's *The Picture of Dorian Gray* is a moral fable about art, and as such is rich in possible analogues. Although it is a feckless question that ultimately begs the intentional fallacy, critics have been guessing who the paradoxical Dorian Gray is meant to represent. This is as hopeless a matter as it is intriguing, for aside from biographical possibilities, it is clear that the protagonist is mythic in character, and it is equally clear that an understanding of that myth may be a key to unlock many of the novel's tightly bound paradoxes. But what myths is he drawn from? Jerome Buckley and Ted Spivey contend that Dorian is a Victorian Faust and Lord Henry an aristocratic Mephistopheles.[53] Kevin Sullivan sees Dorian as a Beautiful Princess (gender here, Mr. Sullivan claims, is irrelevant), Lord Henry as the Wicked Witch, and Basil Hallward as the Fairy Godmother.[54] Frances Winwar sees Dorian as a modern-day Charmides dominating Basil, while Robert Keefe believes that Dorian is a contemporary Narcissus drawn from Ovid's *Metamorphoses*.[55] There is merit in each of these claims: Dorian does seem to make a pact with the devil; he is the "fallen prince" of the fairy tale; he is also a boyish and presumptuous student, and is so enamored with his own beauty that, like Narcissus, he becomes morally paralyzed. None of these propositions is completely satisfactory, in part because Wilde was such an eclectic and "creative" borrower that even he would have been hard-pressed to have untangled the mythic knot. Never-

52. Isobel Murray, in her "Introduction" to the Oxford English Novel edition of *Dorian Gray* (London: Oxford University Press, 1974), p. xx, contends that Poe's work seems to have been an important influence.

53. Jerome Buckley, *The Victorian Temper* (Cambridge, Mass.: Harvard University Press, 1951), pp. 234–35; and Ted R. Spivey, "Damnation and Salvation in *The Picture of Dorian Gray*," *Boston University Studies in English* 4 (1960): 162–70.

54. Kevin Sullivan, *Oscar Wilde* (New York: Columbia University Press, 1972), p. 14.

55. Frances Winwar, *Oscar Wilde and the Yellow 'Nineties'* (New York: Blue Ribbon Books, 1940), p. 164; and Robert Keefe, "Artist and Model in *The Picture of Dorian Gray*," *Studies in the Novel* 5 (1973): 62–70.

theless, in knowing this, namely that the character of Dorian Gray is wonderfully overdetermined and tangled up, I would like to suggest another possible analogue—Dorian Gray as vampire.

Dorian is not a vampire of the misty midnight, bloodsucking, extended incisors, Transylvanian variety, but rather another sophisticated adaptation of the folkloric demon. And as such he is used for serious artistic purposes, helping Wilde explore and satirize the relationships in Realism between artist, object of art, artifact, and audience. For just as the vampire enervates his victims, so too does representational art, art that attempts literally to "hold a mirror up to nature," drain metaphorical energy or attention from the artistic experience. This kind of art is reckless for Wilde in that it attempts to link the eternal opposites of art and life. Art has no business imitating anything other than "imaginative reality"; when it tries to picture life the way "it really is," the result can only be chaos and corruption. Life without the mediating influence of art is wild malefic confusion and so any art that simply mirrors this life will result in such abominations as Dorian Gray.[56]

Basil Hallward, the errant artist, explains the problem best:

> Dorian, from the moment I met you, your personality had the most extraordinary influence over me. I was dominated, soul, brain, and power, by you. You became to me the visible incarnation of that unseen ideal whose memory haunts us artists like an exquisite dream. I worshipped you.
>
> Weeks and weeks went on, and I grew more and more absorbed in you. Then came a new development. I had drawn you as Paris in dainty armor, and as Adonis with huntsman's cloak and polished boar spear. Crowned with heavy lotus blossoms you had sat on the prow of Adrian's barge, gazing across the green, turbid Nile. You had leaned over the still pool of some Greek woodland, and seen in the water's silent silver the marvel of your own face. And it had all been what art should be, unconscious, ideal, and remote. One day, a fatal day I sometimes think, I determined to paint a wonderful portrait of you as you actually are, not in the costume of dead ages, but in your own dress and in your own time. Whether it was the Realism of the method, or the mere wonder of your own personality, thus directly presented to me without mist or veil, I cannot tell. . . . I felt, Dorian, that I had told too much, that I had put too much of myself into it. (pp. 137–38)[57]

The artist has put his thumb on the scale. He has allowed his own feelings to color his art, and, worse still, he has allowed the subject of his art to be "reality" itself. This is the opposite of negative capability; it is positive interference. In the end Basil was not attempting to give an impression of Dorian Gray, but rather to capture Dorian Gray *in propria persona*. For Wilde this will never do. Art is ultimately a lie that one tells in order to tell a greater truth, but nonetheless it is still a lie. Art

56. This argument is made in detail in Houston A. Baker, Jr., "The Tragedy of the Artist: *The Picture of Dorian Gray*," *Nineteenth Century Fiction* 24 (1969): 349–55.

57. All parenthetical references to page numbers in the text are to the "authorized edition" of Robert Ross's *Dorian Gray* (Boston: John W. Luce, 1905).

is and must always be illusion. Basil was well within his rights when he painted Dorian *as* Paris or *as* Adonis, but it was when he painted him not as, but *to be* Dorian Gray that he created a monster. And this monster—rather like the Frankenstein monster—who had first been given life by the artist, then attempts to destroy not only his own maker but others as well. Basil had created something so lifelike that it needed human energies to survive. He had been able to take Realism to such an extreme that artifact and object became unified and shared the same vitality. It was Wilde's genius that he was then able to describe the monstrous result through the bold and shocking metaphor of the vampire.

I am not the first to suggest this. In fact, Edouard Roditi and Lewis Poteet have already argued that Wilde's novel is best understood in the milieu of the Gothic revival; in fact, Dorian Gray owes much to a novel by Oscar Wilde's granduncle, Charles R. Maturin's *Melmoth the Wanderer*.[58] There are numerous similarities between the two works: for instance, the decomposition death scenes and the motif of the living portraits, but there are also vampiric overtones in both novels. Melmoth is no more an actual vampire than Dorian; rather Melmoth is, as Mario Praz has said, "something of a vampire," while Dorian Gray is, as Edouard Roditi contended, "from one of the sources of the Dracula myth."[59] These Gothic protagonists share the same deathless state, the same loathing for life, the same gluttonous pleasure at the torment of others, and the same almost uncontrollable desire to destroy what is innocent and good. But Wilde's character is far more complex and his motives far more sophisticated than the creation of his granduncle. For Wilde is less concerned with making the reader's skin crawl than he is with saying something quite specific about the dynamics of artistic creation.[60]

Recognizing both the vampire tradition in English nineteenth-century literature and the position of *The Picture of Dorian Gray* in the Gothic genre, we may find it instructive to reexamine the mythic character of Dorian. We recall that the very first time Basil sees the future "subject" of his art, he experiences a strange enervation:

> I turned halfway round and saw Dorian Gray for the first time. When our eyes met, I felt that I was growing pale. A curious sensation of terror came over me. I knew that I had come face to face with someone whose mere personality

58. Edouard Roditi, *Oscar Wilde* (New York: New Directions, 1947), pp. 113–24, and Lewis J. Poteet, "*Dorian Gray* and the Gothic Novel," *Modern Fiction Studies* 18 (1971): 239–48.

59. Mario Praz, *The Romantic Agony*, 2nd ed. (London: Oxford University Press, 1951), p. 118; and Roditi, *Oscar Wilde*, p. 115.

60. Although the major "influence" on Wilde during the writing of *Dorian Gray* seems to have been Huysmans's *A Rebours*, the works of Walter Pater and Theophile Gautier seem also to have been in his mind. Pater's description of the Mona Lisa as a vampire in *Studies in the History of the Renaissance* and Gautier's vampire story *Clairmonde* may have impressed Wilde. He even quotes at length from Pater's vampiric description of the "Mona Lisa" in *The Critic as Artist*, and the references to Gautier in *The Picture of Dorian Gray* are numerous. But far more intriguing is his friendship with Bram Stoker: Stoker was a regular visitor to Wilde's home in Merrion Square, his wife Florence was a life-long inamorata of Wilde's, and Stoker may have carried letters to Wilde when he was in Paris exile. One critic even contends Dracula is Stoker's fictionalization of Wilde. See Daniel Farson, *The Man Who Wrote "Dracula"* (New York: St. Martin's Press, 1975), pp. 38, 39, 40, 60–61, 152, and 235.

was so fascinating that, if I allowed it to do so, it would absorb my whole nature, my whole soul, my very art itself. I did not want any external influence in my life. (p. 7)

This energy drain continues as Basil feels the need to see Dorian daily (p. 11), realizing all the time that "some subtle influence passed from him to me" (p. 13). Basil then attempts to recreate Dorian's beauty and charm through the alembic of art, but soon realizes that, as he says to Lord Henry, "there is too much of myself in the [painting],—too much of myself!" (p. 13). Basil realizes that the separation of artist and subject has disintegrated in the process of creation, that vitality, instead of being transferred from artist to artifact, is moving from artist to subject. In this confusion of creation Dorian Gray himself becomes the work of art, fixed forever out of time and change while the artifact (the realistic painting) becomes energized and mutable.

Wilde has devised this artistic conundrum so that blame is impossible to assess. Dorian has in a sense seduced Basil and Basil has likewise seduced Dorian.[61] It is after creation, however, that Dorian must take some responsibility, for he concludes the Faustian pact for immortality with the implicit promise of his soul. In a scene that prefigures the conclusion Basil realizes what he has done, realizes that things have gone awry, and in a burst of emotion goes to stab the painting with his palette knife. Dorian restrains him, saying, "Don't, Basil, don't! It would be murder!" (p. 33), and Dorian is right. It would be murder, for the portrait is now human, but killing Dorian would be no crime.

Lest there be any doubt as to the responsibility of the artist to divorce himself from any egotistical indulgence in the creative process, Lord Henry, a satanic mouthpiece only in the Blakean sense, claims that Basil is a "Philistine" artist.

Basil puts everything that is charming in him into his work. The consequence is that he has nothing left for life but his prejudices, his principles, and his common sense. The only artists I have ever known, who are personally delightful, are bad artists. Good artists exist simply in what they make, and consequently are perfectly uninteresting in what they are. A great poet, a really great poet, is the most unpoetical of all creatures. But inferior poets are absolutely fascinating. (p. 67)

This is a bit hyperbolic, to be sure. Henry's point is simply that a great artist keeps his hand out of the scale, letting art achieve its own balance. Basil's work has lost its balance, has become "possessed" with the artist's energy, and is thus in league with the powers of crime.

It is in Dorian's breaking the symbiosis with Basil that we see his own evil potential for draining life from others. What we realize too late is that Dorian has metaphorically "bled" his creator, leaving him weak and enervated:

61. This is especially true in the 1890 *Lippincott Magazine* version, where the overt homosexuality reinforces the symbiosis between artist and object.

> A strange sense of loss came over [Basil]. He felt that Dorian Gray would never again be to him all that he had been in the past. Life had come between them. His eyes darkened, and the crowded, flaring streets became blurred to his eyes . . . it seemed to him that he had grown years older. (p. 96)

Basil has indeed grown older; life has been drained from him, as it is soon to be with Sibyl Vane. But Basil is a willing if unknowing co-conspirator; Sibyl is not. She is totally unaware of what is happening—unaware that she is being exploited by Dorian, that she is to him, in Wilde's rather macabre pun, only a "vein."

Before her affair with Dorian, Sibyl is the complete artist—so perfectly is she able to divorce herself from her creations that they come alive with an energy all their own. She is an illusionist, a magician, a true artist. She cares not a whit for Rosalind or Cleopatra or Juliet or Ophelia, other than that they are roles to perform, characters to create. Had Basil been able to achieve this degree of "negative capability," Dorian would simply have been a subject to paint, not an expression of his ego. But Dorian, the creation of misdirected energy, has become a demon who must destroy all perfection and innocence. And so, complete in "evening cape with satin-lined wings" (p. 90), he is off batlike to bring Sibyl under his influence. He succeeds, of course, until she, like Basil, is no longer able to bring energy and concentration to her art, and instead becomes vapid and weak. Where once she had been able to "spiritualize" the audience until they felt as if they were "of the same flesh and blood" (p. 98) as the character, after her affair with Dorian she *becomes* the characters she had portrayed; she becomes Juliet to his Romeo, Ophelia to his Hamlet, no longer creating illusion but now imitating life.[62] Or, as she says,

> . . . before I knew you [Dorian], acting was the one reality of my life. It was only in the theater that I lived. I thought that it was all true. I was Rosalind one night, and Portia the other. The joy of Beatrice was my joy, and the sorrows of Cordelia were mine, also. I believed in everything. The common people who acted with me seemed to me to be godlike. The painted scenes were my world. I knew nothing but shadows, and I thought them real. You came—oh, my beautiful love!—and you freed my soul from prison. You taught me what reality really is. Tonight, for the first time in my life, I saw through the hollowness, the sham, the silliness of the empty pageant in which I had always played. Tonight, for the first time, I became conscious that the Romeo was hideous and old and painted, that the moonlight in the orchard was false, that the scenery was vulgar, and that the words I had to speak were unreal, were not my words, were not what I wanted to say. You brought me something higher, something of what all art is but a reflection. You had made me understand what love really is. (pp. 103–4)

---

62. For Wilde's discussion of the evils of imitation in art, see his "The Decay of Lying" and "The Truth of Masks" in *Complete Works*, ed. Robert Ross (New York: Bigelow, Brown & Co., 1921), 4: 8–57, 227–70.

Life and Art for Wilde may not be mutually exclusive, but certainly they are separate and distinct, and if Sibyl wants life she will have to give up illusion. She cannot have it both ways. After destroying her art Dorian discards her, claiming that the fault is hers. "You have killed my love," he whines.

> You used to stir my imagination. Now you don't even stir my curiosity. You simply produce no effect. I loved you because you were marvelous, because you had genius and intellect, because you realized the dreams of great poets and gave shape and substance to the shadows of art. You have thrown it all away. You are shallow and stupid. My God! How mad I was to love you! What a fool I have been! You are nothing to me now. I will never see you again. I will never think of you. I will never mention your name. You don't know what you were to me, once. Why, once—Oh, I can't bear to think of it! I wish I had never laid eyes upon you! You have spoiled the romance of my life. (p. 105)

Dorian, now separated from the energies of both his creator and his love, is finally alone. He becomes a creature of the night, skulking through midnight London almost literally on the prowl. Like his portrait, he lives hidden away, "shut out from the sunlight" (p. 127), behind "a pallid mask of chalk with leaden eyes" (p. 128), trapped by his own pathetic lusts, not for life, but for destruction. Like the figures on Keats's Grecian urn, he pays for eternal youth by being unable to consummate desire. He has become in effect "the spectator of [his] own life" (p. 133).

Only in the world of darkness, "of horror and misshapen joy," of "phantoms" and "grotesques," of "white fingers creep[ing] through the curtains" and of "black fantastic shapes, dumb shadows crawl[ing] into the corners of the room and crouching there," is Dorian finally secure (p. 158). He becomes enamored with perversion of all sorts, especially with aspects of the Catholic mass—

> . . . the Roman ritual had always a great attraction for him. The daily sacrifice, more awful really than all the sacrifices of the antique world, stirred him as much by its superb rejection of the evidence of the sense as by the primitive simplicity of its elements and the eternal pathos of the human tragedy that it sought to symbolize. (p. 159)

The process of regeneration through the drinking of the metaphorical blood of Christ becomes diabolic and morbid in Dorian's transvaluation. It is a new source of energy. He is entranced with "the fuming censors," the "black confessionals" (p. 117), the power of blood sacrifice. Finally Dorian succeeds in raising this perversity to an epistemology, believing that "evil [could be] simply a mode through which he could realize his conception of the beautiful" (p. 176).

To achieve this level of consciousness, Dorian needs the energies of the innocent, the blood of the lambs. Although we are never told specifically what Dorian is doing "creeping at dawn out of dreadful houses and slinking in disguise into the foulest dens in London" (p. 183), we are told that he has become "fatal to young men" (p. 181) and also a corruptor of young women (p. 182). He is not a drug addict, yet he preys on those who are. In fact, like Lord Ruthven in Polidori's novel, or Count Cenci in Shelley's drama, Dorian Gray has become a communicable disease, a plague whose mere presence forbodes evil. So Basil reports to Dorian that London society believes "that you corrupt everyone with whom you become intimate and it is quite sufficient for you to enter a house for shame of some kind to follow" (p. 183). And of course London society is correct; in fact, towards the end of the novel, Dorian becomes more than a carrier of moral infection; he becomes that infection himself.

Basil seems intuitively to understand Dorian Gray's progressive demonism, and is forever inquiring about Dorian's soul (p. 183) or Dorian's inability to pray (p. 190). Dorian realizes that Basil can only be an impediment to power and must be destroyed. And so after telling Basil his secret, Dorian stabs him "in the great vein that is behind the ear" (pp. 190–91). I would not contend that there is anything vampiric about this neck wound had Dorian not later driven the same knife through his own heart in the painting. These acts seem a metaphoric and brutally ironic image, not only of the vampire attack, but also of the staking of the vampire.

The modern reader may well be puzzled by the introduction, after Basil's death, of Alan Campbell, who is blackmailed by Dorian to clean up the mess. To the reader of the Gothic novel, however, Mr. Campbell's presence is by no means unexpected, for he appears like the supernumerary in the stage melodrama to remind us how heinous the protagonist has become. Like Basil, he reminds us that Dorian is indeed "up to the devil's work" (p. 203), but unlike Basil he is totally in Dorian's power. And as is often the case in the Gothic novel, their relationship is never explained. We do learn later, however, that Mr. Campbell would rather die than explain the power Dorian has over him. Likewise James Vane is also a set character in the genre. He is the man of honor, the avenging angel, the demon destroyer, whose inability to destroy the fiend only reinforces Dorian's satanic control of events. For Dorian has grown still more hideous, progressively more vampiric: "From cell to cell of his brain crept the one thought; and the wild desire to live, most terrible of all man's appetites, quickened into force each trembling nerve and fiber" (p. 225). It is now, as Dorian's passions for life-energy are reaching fever pitch, that Wilde attempts to extricate him from hyperbole and make him, if not sympathetic, at least human again.

Wilde does this in an almost throwaway scene near the end of the novel. Dorian, like the pathetic Frankenstein monster or the vampire in the midcentury novel, wishes he could feel passion again, wishes he could love (p. 248). And indeed he soon finds the object of his desire, a young village girl named Hetty Merton; but he realizes that his embrace would be fatal, and so he heroically spares her (p. 255). This, the central scene of pathos in the Gothic novel, is almost perfunctorily passed off by Wilde, who is after all more interested in developing paradox than in telling a scary tale. Thus the hurry-up ending and overnight conversion, complete with such commentary as Lord Henry's "death and vulgarity are the only two facts in the nineteenth century that one cannot explain away" (p. 257), or his comment to Dorian that "you are the type of what the age is searching for" (p. 263), or even Dorian's: "The soul is a terrible reality. It can be bought and sold and bartered away. It can be poisoned or made perfect. There is a soul in each one of us. I know it" (p. 261). The novel ends lamely with these bromides and witticisms because, as far as Wilde was concerned, he had constructed his China box, and there was nothing left to do but tie the ribbon and swallow the key.

The novel ends true to the constraints of both Gothic novel and vampire myth: the monster, having destroyed others, now destroys himself. With the knife, in a sense the same instrument with which he had been created, he stabs the heart of the painting, releasing the energies of decay to flood back from the work of art to the object of art. Just as the staked vampire in the current cinema turns rapidly older until he finally disintegrates to dust, so now Dorian assumes the "withered, wrinkled and loathsome visage" of the painting. The clock of time has finally caught up, and he is now in death what he never could have been in life—at last human.

It was Wilde's genius that he could juggle so many things at once with only an occasional loss of balance. He pays the price of writing a philosophical novel that is still charged today in criticism: the work often seems designed more for dazzle than for depth; the plot is hardly "well made"; the dialogue is often clogged with table talk; and the characters are cardboard. In fact, it is really not much of a novel at all, but rather an attempt to create the illusion of a fiction while all the time sharpening the axe of criticism. By making his protagonist deliberately one-dimensional and then flaunting him, as it were, before a "respectable" reading public as demonic, Wilde is showing in fiction what he considers true art to be. Dorian Gray is a myth: he is a lie. There is no Basil-like attempt to make him "real," simply because to do so would destroy illusion and defy art. And so Dorian Gray is by intention a Faust, a Narcissus, a Charmides, a fairy prince, and even a vampire.

The Sacred Fount

By the time Henry James came to tell his own vampire story, the myth had been worn almost to the bone. Both traditions of the vampire, one as nocturnal terrifier and the other as psychological analogy, had been pushed almost to parody in *Dracula* and *The Portrait of Dorian Gray*. What remained was for them to be combined—for a novel to include a truly dangerous but believable character (no perpetually demonic antagonist like Dracula or foppish, time-warped Dorian Gray), whose actions paralleled or, better yet, mimicked those of the artist. To combine these two, however entailed a shift in both point of view and narrative distance, for the reader must become involved enough in the character to be sympathetic, yet distanced enough to let certain aberrations pass uncensored. Then, finally, too late, the shock of recognition occurs, the realization that we have been a consenting party to some horror.

James achieves this believability in *The Sacred Fount* in two ways: he creates a first-person narrator who almost completely controls the flow of information, and he has this narrator operate in what seems to be an eminently sensible context. Simply put, the narrator has a theory to explain human behavior, and the novel concerns his "scientific" attempts to verify it. His theory is of the "sacred fount" and contends that in certain relationships there is an energy exchange between interacting humans, especially those of the opposite sex. Although vitality initially may flow both ways between partners, eventually the stronger member will take control until the relationship becomes parasitic or, if you will, vampiric. Then this life force flows to the dominant partner, who, seeking to consolidate his gains, will keep the weaker party supplied with just enough energy to subsist. Assuming the male finally gains control, he had best be careful, for once he depletes his partner his "sacred fount" will dry up, and he will be left weak and enervated. His partner, meantime, may decide to find a life force of her own, and will take a "lover" whom she can "live off." Although the energy may flow any number of ways, James implies that the system cannot satisfy all the participants. Like any pyramiding scheme, there will be some who sooner or later are exploited without being able to recharge. This principle of insufficiency is explained in the narrator's rather incredible metaphor: "The Sacred Fount is like the greedy man's description of the turkey as an 'awkward' dinner dish. It may sometimes be too much for a single share, but it's not enough to go around."[63] James further speculates that wit, like vitality, is a transferable commodity; hence partners can drain powers of the intellect and the imagination as well as the powers of energy.[64]

The application of this theory is what *The Sacred Fount* is about. An unnamed narrator takes a weekend trip to an elegant English country estate appropriately named Newmarch. En route he meets a Mrs. Brissenden, who seems much younger than he had remembered, and a Gilbert Long, who conversely seems much wittier. How they got this way is the organizing concern of the novel. When they arrive at Newmarch the narrator meets Guy Brissenden, who is not yet thirty, yet looks at least fifty years old. Aha, thinks the narrator, this explains why Mrs. Briss (as he coyly calls her), who is really over forty, looks twenty-five; obviously she has been sipping life from Guy, her sacred fount.

Here starts the algebraic equation that has driven some critics to distraction and many readers to sleep, for the rest of the novel entails the narrator's monomaniacal quest to learn who has been the victim of Gilbert Long. The solution, of course, rests in finding someone who was at one time witty, but who has since become dull and tedious. Who can that be—Lady John, a middle-aged unattached woman, or

63. Henry James, *The Sacred Fount* (1901; rpt. New York: Grove Press, 1953), p. 29; hereafter page numbers from this edition will appear parenthetically in the text.

64. Although some critics have contended that this energy exchange and fear of depletion resulted from James's own sexual beliefs, this view is only conjectural and never clear in the text. Cf. Leon Edel, "Introduction" to *The Sacred Fount* (New York: Grove Press, 1953), pp. xxv–xxix.

perhaps the flighty widow, May Server? To help in his quest, the narrator enlists the aid of Mrs. Brissenden and Ford Obert, a reputable artist. Ford suggests May is Long's victim because five years before, when he had painted her portrait, she seemed urbane and secure, but now, he claims, she seems addled and fey. Hence, in the narrator's analogy, someone has "tapped" the sacred fount of her intellect. Could this be the explanation for Gilbert Long's acuteness?

Only after interrogating all the principals does the narrator waiver in his enthusiasm for locating this missing link. He queries Ford about the propriety of prying into the lives of others and is assured that this is quite moral as long as he does not actually intrude into the privacy of his subject, as long as he does not play "detective at the keyhole" (p. 66). Although Lady John tells him to quit being so damnably curious, Mrs. Briss remains a staunch ally almost to the end. Then finally even she tries, as have most readers, to tell him she's had enough, that what was once fun has now become not only dull but bothersome. At the end of the novel, in a midnight peroration she informs him that Gilbert Long has been a dolt all along, that Long has been having an affair with Lady John, not May Server, and that May has in turn been having an affair with Guy Brissenden. It is the last of these affairs that has piqued Mrs. Briss and may well be the reason why (especially according to the narrator) she turns on him with such vehemence. She goes even further, however, calling him irresponsible and downright crazy. He, on the other hand, rationalizes away her behavior by asking what else could we expect from a woman who was herself "eating up her husband inch by inch" (p. 71). Thus the novel ends quite inconclusively with his comment that although she had had the last word, his inductive method and psychological theory are still intact; what he all too "fatally lacked was her tone" (p. 319).

Leon Edel, in his "Introduction" to *The Sacred Fount*, best sums up this non-ending:

> Nothing has been solved; nothing is settled. We have had an hypothesis, a series of assumptions and speculations. There have been precious few facts to go on. The reader can only take the narrator at his word; and his word has been based largely upon appearance. As for the reality—![65]

It is not the ending alone that has occasioned such wonderful critical wrath; it is the whole impenetrable book, with all its seeming nonsense. W. C. Brownell, who first read the manuscript for Scribner's, gave what for many is still the last word about this convoluted book: "It is like trying to make out page after page of illegible writing. The sense of effort becomes acutely exasperating."[66] The only person who ever claimed to really understand what was going on in the book was William Dean Howells, who said, "I have mastered the secret, though for the present I am not

65. Edel, "Introduction," p. xvi.
66. As quoted by Oscar Cargill in *The Novels of Henry James* (New York: Macmillan, 1961), p. 282.

going to divulge it," but he sagely died before being pressed into critical service.[67] For many readers Rebecca West's précis shows with gnomic concision how correct W. C. Brownell was in his early exasperation: "A Weekend guest spends more intellectual force than Kant can have used on *The Critique of Pure Reason* in an unsuccessful attempt to discover whether there exists between certain of his fellow-guests a relationship not more interesting among these vacuous people than it is among sparrows."[68]

Although everyone is sooner or later annoyed or at least puzzled with the book, almost everyone admits it is intriguing. Usually they find it intriguing for one of two reasons: either they are interested in James's continuing experiments with a narrator of dubious omniscience, or they are interested in the vampire theme of fulfillment and depletion.[69] Although these aspects have been kept apart in criticism, they are by no means separate in the book. In fact, they are inextricably linked, and it is that linkage that has proved so troublesome. For ostensibly the theme of the book is indeed, as Leon Edel first stated, the vampiric interactions between characters, but this theme is far more pervasive and includes the narrator himself.[70] I believe that James was using the narrator primarily as an authorial foil to show that just as there is energy flowing between characters, there is also energy flowing between the narrator and his subjects, or, on a different level, between the artist and his creation.[71]

That the nameless narrator is a displaced authorial voice of Henry James is almost universally accepted—it is the amount of distance between them that has been called into question. Many critics have simply accepted that James is standing foursquare behind his narrator, but recently there has been the realization that although James is writing a parable about art, the parable is ambiguous and ironic; that is to say that while the narrator is creating what he considers to be an "intellectual palace," it is really only "a house of cards." Yet even as a house of cards it is not

67. As quoted in Sidney Finklestein, "The 'Mystery' of Henry James's *The Sacred Fount*," *Massachusetts Review* 3 (1962): 753.

68. Rebecca West, *Henry James* (London: Nisbet & Co., 1916), pp. 107–8.

69. Norma Phillips, "*The Sacred Fount*: The Narrator and the Vampires," *PMLA* 76 (1961): 407, surveys the history of these two approaches.

70. Edel first used the vampire analogy in an introductory essay to the 1868 tale, *De Grey: A Romance*, in Henry James, *The Ghostly Tales of Henry James*, ed. Leon Edel (New York: Grosset & Dunlap, 1963), p. 27, where he associated it with three works: *De Grey, Longstaff's Marriage* (1878), and *The Sacred Fount* (1901). In a later "Introductory Essay" to a 1953 edition of the novel (New York: The Grove Press), pp. x–xxxii, Edel expanded his discussion of the theme of "depletion" and included two tales, *A Tragedy of Error* (1864) and *Osborne's Revenge* (1868) as well as aspects of *The Ambassadors* (1903). Again, in *Henry James: The Untried Years, 1843–1870* (New York: J. B. Lippincott Co., 1953), Edel commented at some length about the sacred fount theme and its biographical parallels in James's own life.

71. The view of the narrator as artist is shared by Cargill in *The Novels of Henry James*; James K. Folsom, "Archimago's Well: An Interpretation of *The Sacred Fount*," *Modern Fiction Studies* 7 (1971): 138–45; Jean Frantz Blackall, *Jamesian Ambiguity and "The Sacred Fount"* (Ithaca, N.Y.: Cornell University Press, 1965); and Liahna Babener, "Predators of the Spirit: The Vampire Theme in Nineteenth-Century Literature" (Ph.D. dissertation, University of California at Los Angeles, 1975), chap. 5.

without consequence, for the narrator, rather than being the Jamesian artist as Wilson Follett first proposed, is really, as Ralph Ranald has countered, the Jamesian fool—an artist, yes, but an artist manqué.[72] James is indeed creating a "jeu d'esprit," as he claimed, and the joke is on us if we take the narrator too seriously.

Although the narrator's theory is valid, his overzealous application is misplaced, for in his attempt to make sense out of what he encounters, he perforce reduces it to manageable size, and in doing this drains too much Art out of Life. Art is like a science in that it attempts to reduce relationships, yet one must proceed with care, for if the subject is reduced too far, it will perish. The narrator in *The Sacred Fount* is like the artists in Hawthorne's fiction who pry into the secrets of their characters and thereby run the risk of destroying them for the sake of "truth." James never questions the narrator's theory; as a matter of fact, he seems quite entranced by it, but the narrator's ruthless application of the vampire donnée is misguided. In the narrator's drawing of life from his subjects in order to make them conform, he becomes the psychic sponge, the artist preying on life with his fictions. As Professor Ranald comments:

> The point is then that *The Sacred Fount* is not about love as a depleting force. It is rather about the life force under the metaphor of the sacred fount, and about life struggling to be free of predatory and vampiristic entanglements: such entanglements as are represented first by the relationships among the Brissendens and the Longs and the other victims and vampires, and second, the more central relationship of the narrator to all the other characters.
>
> .   .   .   .
>
> Possibly there is a right way and a wrong way to practice art just as there were basically two kinds of love in the world of a medieval man. And what *The Sacred Fount* deals with in its surface action is the wrong kind of love— the love which is vampiristic, and which feeds upon its victims until it consumes them. It is the cupidinous love which essentially has no regard for anything outside the self.[73]

Hence on one level at least *The Sacred Fount* is James's advocacy of "negative capability"—the creator must practice a kind of sublime disinterestedness if his work is to have vitality. When he forces form onto content instead of allowing the parts to animate one another, he will suffocate what life is there and thus become a parasite on his own imaginative creation. Unfortunately, there is no way to prove this other than to do to the narrator exactly what he does to the other characters. We must become "Paul Prys" peeping in the keyhole to observe his private actions. There are no *ficelles* in this work to guide us through the labyrinth, no maps, no

72. Wilson Follett's argument was made in "Henry James's Portrait of Henry James," in the *New York Times*, 23 Aug. 1936; while a more recent view of the narrator as fool is in Ralph Ranald, "*The Sacred Fount*: James' Portrait of the Artist Manqué," *Nineteenth Century Fiction* 15 (1960): 239–48.
73. Ranald, "*The Sacred Fount*: James' Portrait of the Artist Manqué," pp. 243–44.

convenient signposts. We also get no help at all from the "real artist," for James decided not to include *The Sacred Fount* in the New York Edition, and hence wrote no critical preface. There is also no specific mention of the work in the *Notebooks*.[74] All we have is an offhand comment in a letter he wrote to Mrs. Humphrey Ward explaining the novel's irresolution and his lack of interest in pursuing it.[75] So the critic is truly on his own.

James may have intended all this and it may well be why he included the fantastic scene in the art gallery, for here inside the work of fiction is precisely the problem faced outside the work. The central characters of the novel view a painting of a young man "with a pale, lean, livid face and a stare, from eyes without eyebrows, like that of some withered old world clown." The young man holds in his hands a mask "such as might have been fantastically fitted and worn" (p. 55), a mask with the features of a normal human face. What does it mean? We are never told. Gilbert Long supposedly has an interesting interpretation, but alas, since our knowledge is limited to what the narrator can tell us and since the narrator never overhears Gilbert's views, we must remain ignorant. May Server thinks that the mask represents death and the figure is life, but the narrator, ever out to needle her, counters with just the reverse interpretation. Ford Obert, the artist, who really should be the intelligent commentator, never offers his complete interpretation, so we are left here inside the book as we are outside the book—every critic for himself.

All we have for certain are clusters of images (images of sacrifice, of hunting, of

74. In the *Notebooks* we do get a sense of James's general plan:

The notion of the young man who marries an older woman and who has the effect on her of making her younger and still younger, while he himself becomes her age. When he reaches the age that she was (on their marriage), she has gone back to the age that he was.—Mightn't this be altered (perhaps) to the idea of cleverness and stupidity? . . . The two things—the two elements—beauty and "mind," might be correspondingly, concomitantly exhibited as in the history of the two related couples—with the opposition, in each case, that would help the thing to be dramatic.

The Notebooks of Henry James, ed. F. O. Matthiessen and Kenneth B. Murdock (New York: G. Braziller, 1961), pp. 150–51.

75. After James dismisses *The Sacred Fount* as not "worth discussing" in a letter to Mrs. Humphrey Ward, he adds that he wrote it as a joke, a "jeu d'esprit":

Alas, for a joke it appears to have been round about me here, taken rather seriously. It's doubtless very disgraceful, but it's the last I shall ever make! Let me say for it, however, that it has, I assure you, and applied quite rigorously and constructively, I believe, its own little law of composition. Mrs. Server is not "made happy" at the end—what in the world has put it into your head? As I give but the phantasmagoric I have, for clearness, to make it evidential, and the Ford Obert evidence all bears (indirectly,) upon Brissenden, supplies the motive for Mrs. B's terror and her re-nailing down of the coffin. I had to testify to Mrs. S's sense of a common fate with B. and the only way I could do so was by making O. see her as temporarily pacified. I had to give a meaning to the vision of Gilbert L. out on the terrace in the darkness, and the appearance of a sensible detachment on her part was my imposed way of giving it. Mrs. S. is back in the coffin at the end, by the same stroke by which Briss is—Mrs. B's last interview with the narrator being all an ironic exposure of her own false plausibility, of course. But it isn't worth explaining, and I mortally loathe it!

This unpublished letter, dated 15 March 1901, is in the Clifton Waller Barrett Library at the University of Virginia, and contains James's most precise comments about the book. It is—to say the least—as confusing as the book, but the imagery is fascinating.

collecting, of paying, etc.) and the characters' names. As is so common in James's work, these names often provide a temporary buttress against confusion. Newmarch, the elegant country estate conspicuously without proprietors, implies a kind of ghostly world, elegant yet haunted with strange life. Everything is clean but macabre: it is a "new march" to somewhere, but we are never told where. In addition the narrator's very namelessness—he is never addressed by any first name, surname, or nickname—reinforces the impersonality of it all. Lady John, a strange, androgynous figure, seems totally unconnected to any of the other characters, as does Gilbert Long. Admittedly Mr. and Mrs. Brissenden do "belong" together, but their life in the novel is totally separate, in fact, even hostile. Additionally there are characters like Ford Luttley and Lady Froome who pass like shadows across the stage, never talking, just showing us their backs. But May Server's name and personality are developed, for she is the critical link in the narrator's theory; all is centered around whom she "may" be "serving," i.e., who is "feeding off" her.

The indeterminacy of so much of the story, the positive eeriness of the setting, and the anonymity of the characters are indeed reminiscent of James's other ghost stories. For twenty years he had been writing such tales as *The Turn of the Screw*, *Owen Wingrave*, *Sir Edmund Orme*, *The Beast in the Jungle*, *Maud Evelyn*, and *The Altar of the Dead*; and *The Sacred Fount* continues his interest in this genre. It was here in the ghost story, as R. P. Blackmur noted, that James finally found the symbols and images to picture psychological truths in all their vagueness and ambiguity.[76] As is often the case in the ghost story, the only things we can be certain of are the narrator's states of consciousness; everything else is transitory and spectral. Just as there is no objective agreed-upon meaning in the painting of the man and the mask, there is no real sense of what most of these characters represent or what, if anything, they are doing. What makes *The Sacred Fount* such a haunting work is that we can never even be sure who the ghosts are. We don't really know that any of the characters are vampires; we know only that the narrator thinks they are. Still, as James K. Folsom comments:

> Whether or not vampirism exists in fact, it indubitably exists in the mind of the narrator. It is stated early in the book as an axiom which might serve as a useful metaphorical shorthand to explain the relation of man to woman. . . .
> Who these vampires are becomes constantly more difficult to discover. Only two things gradually become clear: first, the narrator becomes increasingly convinced that vampires are operative in the world of Newmarch; second, given the narrator's definition of vampires, we as readers become conscious that there is at least one vampire in the book, and that this vampire is none other than the narrator.[77]

Typically James hides his ghost story between the lines of an otherwise dispas-

76. R. P. Blackmur, "*The Sacred Fount*," *Kenyon Review* 4 (1942): 328–52.
77. Folsom, "Archimago's Well: An Interpretation of *The Sacred Fount*," p. 140.

sionate treatise on human interactions: the narrator is indeed a "psychic vampire." For instance, when May Server is described by Ford Obert as "darting from flower to flower . . . clinging for a time to each" (p. 61), the narrator intercedes, saying that it is not May but himself who is darting into the lives of others: "Oh, she didn't at all 'dart,'" I replied, "just now at me. I darted much rather, at her" (p. 61). Indeed he is quite right, for he has made emotional forays into the psychic territories of others; he has made them so quickly that we are often unaware of what has happened until too late. He has "fed" his ego on the Brissendens, on Gilbert Long, on Ford Obert, on Lady John, and even on May Server, whom, ironically, he claims to be protecting. From beginning to end the narrator is "on the pounce" (p. 75), a sadistic parasite who, once he has latched onto his victims, "lets them off" (p. 15) when he pleases or "adds them to his collection" or "little gallery" (pp. 22, 104). When he wants them to accede to his wishes, he seems to have preternatural powers; he holds Guy Brissenden spellbound, "forcing him to meet my eyes" (pp. 112, 126) while he has his way. He has an overly acute sensitivity (pp. 125, 127) and is continually aware of the slightest changes in his victims' constitutions. Although he claims that this behavior is all harmless (pp. 114–15), and that he can quit at any time, Mrs. Brissenden knows better. She knows how potentially lethal he can be once he has attached himself to his victim.

What little sense of his past we have (we know nothing about the pasts of any of the other characters except such trivia as the fact that May Server had two sons) comes in one of his few pensive moments. As twilight falls on Newmarch he reminisces:

> There was a general shade in all the lower reaches—a fine clear dusk in garden and grove, a thin suffusion of twilight out of which the greater things, the high tree-tops and pinnacles, the long crests of motionless wood and chimnied roof, rose into the golden air. The last calls of birds sounded extraordinarily loud; they are like the timed, serious splashes, in wide, still water, of divers not expecting to rise again. I scarce know what odd consciousness I had of roaming at close of day in the grounds of some castle of enchantment. I had positively encountered nothing to compare with this since the days of fairy-tales and of the childish imagination of the impossible. *Then* I used to circle round enchanted castles, for then I moved in a world in which the strange "came true." It was the coming true that was the proof of the enchantment, which, moreover, was naturally never so great as when such coming was, to such a degree and by the most romantic stroke of all, the fruit of one's own wizardry. I was positively—so had the wheel revolved—proud of my work. I had thought it all out, and to have thought it was, wonderfully, to have brought it. Yet I recall how I even then knew on the spot that there was something supreme I should have failed to bring unless I had happened suddenly to become aware of the very presence of the haunting principle, as it were, of my thought. (pp. 128–29)

These oft-quoted lines are central, for they not only reestablish the gothicism of James's story but also give the narrator an eerie timelessness reminiscent of Melmoth or Ruthven or Varney. In the scene that follows we watch him in operation. As the sky darkens he starts his prowl, this time stalking May Server like a cat after a wounded bird or a hunter after a fawn (p. 130). He finds her alone in a nearby woods, but as he is unable to initate any rapprochement, he waits patiently for her to turn and approach him. When she does, he is confident of his "victory." He soon has her in his spell (p. 134), weak, enervated:

> I saw as I had never seen before what consuming passion can make of the marked mortal on whom, with fixed beak and claws, it has settled as on a prey. She reminded me of a sponge wrung dry and with fine pores agape. Voided and scraped of everything, her shell was merely crushable. So it was brought home to me that the victim could be abased, and so it disengaged itself from these things that the abasement could be conscious. (pp. 135–36)

But does he take pity on her, knowing she is already weak? No, rather he toys with her, plays with her (p. 143). As he keeps his eyes on hers (p. 147) she dissembles still more. When he has had his fill, he simply walks off to stalk new prey, this time Guy Brissenden.

Clearly these vampiric attacks and intrusions into the privacy of others are hyperbolic expressions of social interaction. *The Sacred Fount* is a ghost story, yes, but it is also a novel of manners in which each nuance is elevated to crucial importance. On one level it is all a game, humorous sport, the Charles Addams child playing in the basement with his chemistry set. The narrator is the mad scientist gloating over his new discoveries (p. 162); he is the hunter hot on the scent of new game (p. 173); or he is the sportsman waiting for the toss of the ball into his court (pp. 179–80). But he is also the arranger, the artist, if you will, coordinating, exhibiting, creating a society between people. In this respect he both gives and takes life. It is here that the narrator has his greatest delight, and it is here that we may glimpse the artist in passing. Reflecting smugly on how he has created a "system" to investigate social behavior, he comments:

> This was a possibility into which my imagination could dip even deeper than into the depths over which it had conceived the other pair as hovering. These opposed couples balanced like bronze groups at the two ends of a chimney-piece, and the most I could say to myself in lucid deprecation of my thought was that I mustn't take them equally for granted merely because they balanced. Things in the real had a way of not balancing; it was all an affair, this fine symmetry, of artificial proportion. Yet even while I kept my eyes away from Mrs. Briss and Long it was vivid to me that, "composing" there beautifully, they could scarce help playing a part in my exhibition. (pp. 182–83)

But he goes too far. It is one thing to construct an imaginary castle for personal habitation; it is quite another to force one's friends to live there. The narrator becomes so obsessed with his *idée fixe,* so concerned about having all his characters fit into his masterplan, that he intimidates them into compliance. Then, once they seem to be behaving "properly," he intrigues without necessity, plots without concern. It is finally Mrs. Brissenden who acts as the dhampire, crushing his "superstructure" (p. 230), and in so doing, destroys him.

She does this in one of the strangest meetings in the fiction of a writer who loved nothing more than strange meetings. The narrator is summoned to meet Mrs. Brissenden at midnight in the deserted banquet hall. She arrives full-flushed, well-nourished, as if from some energizing repast (p. 240). According to the narrator's theory she is strong because she has just been "feeding off" her husband. Earlier we have been told that when "Mrs. Briss had to get her new blood, her extra allowance of time and blooms somewhere; [and] from whom could she so conveniently extract them as from Guy himself" (p. 29). After some initial banter about the midnight hour (p. 242) and a discussion of the behaviors of various people (a conversation which has the narrator and Mrs. Briss, as well as the reader, thoroughly confused), Mrs. Brissenden launches her fearsome attack. Not only does the narrator talk too much and bother others with his pettifoggery (p. 262), but worse, still, she tells him his theory is all wrong—his "intellectual palace" is only a "pack of cards" (p. 262). Gilbert Long, she claims, is as witless now as he ever was; likewise May Server has not changed a bit. It has all been in the narrator's mind, all a figment of a deranged imagination.

The narrator's reaction is extraordinary, for he squirms about, almost as if he fears being psychologically staked, or worse still, being vamped by the character he himself has initiated. In fact, Norma Phillips, in *"The Sacred Fount:* The Narrator and the Vampires," makes precisely this claim:

> The vampire theme of fruition and depletion, far from being illusory or superficial, is fundamental to the whole conception of the novel in that it is the very means by which the collapse of the narrator is effected. Mrs. Brissenden's growth in subtle awareness and in fineness of perception, to the point where she can even turn these newly acquired weapons against her teacher, is achieved by her having filled her receptacle at the sacred fount of his acute consciousness. The changes in the narrator, his own apprehension that something is the matter with him, all that portion of the action thus falls logically into place, nor is it surprising that his first scruples about prying into the secrets behind other relationships, scruples which he himself later realizes to have been somehow connected with Mrs. Brissenden, should come to him as he senses her independent eagerness to continue the pursuit and learn more.[78]

Still, we must be careful in accusing Mrs. Brissenden, for most of what we know about her is dependent on the narrator's now disintegrating consciousness. Although he describes her as fat and bloated, as if she has just gained life by draining

78. Phillips, "The Sacred Fount," pp. 411–12.

her husband, this is not necessarily so. As a matter of fact, as the novel progresses, we can believe less and less of what the narrator has to say. We can more likely believe the other characters, especially when the narrator is quoting them verbatim. So when Mrs. Brissenden actually says to him, "I think you are crazy" (p. 278), or that he is "horrid" (p. 298), or, better still, that he acts like an "incubus" (p. 310), we can more readily believe her than his implications about what she has been saying.

In any case, by the end Mrs. Brissenden is victorious. He retreats and moves elsewhere for sustenance. He has found not only "a mind on which he cannot feast," as Professor Folsom contends, but one that will feast on him if he is not careful.[79] She has cost him what he repeatedly calls "my perfect palace of thought," and she has saved herself from his infernal sorties to her own "sacred fount." He rationalizes all this away by believing that Mrs. Briss is jealous because her husband Guy is sharing what little life he has left with May Server. Furthermore, he desperately claims that his theory is still intact, for Mrs. Briss is still consuming what is left of her husband. But it won't work—we've been fooled long enough. We realize at the end what he has not understood; he is finished, he can no longer find life-sustenance at Newmarch. The novel ends on his typically forced rationalization; "I *should* certainly never again, on the spot, quite hang together, even though it wasn't really that I hadn't three times her method. What I too fatally lacked was her tone" (p. 319). By now, however, we know that he lacks more than her "tone"; he lacks her life; and as he himself ironically realizes, this lack will prove fatal.

Why "fatal"? Is this merely the hyperbole of a human tuning fork who can only ring when struck? Or is it rather a just description of a narrator without a story, a painter without a canvas? The Newmarch weekend is indeed over, and with it his hope of orchestrating characters into some kind of symphonic order. He admits almost as much by comparing himself to Ludwig II of Bavaria, "the exclusive king of his Wagner opera" (p. 296). For, like Ludwig, who built those incredibly complex Bavarian castles and lush opera sets, the narrator has indulged his eccentricities to the nth degree, but unlike Ludwig, he lacks the creative passion to make them continue. He is instead the artist manqué, the artist boffo, who must now search for other players—a vampire on the prowl for new victims.

Much in *The Sacred Fount* is reminiscent of the other treatments of the vampire as artist. Partly this is because there are only so many ways to tell the story, but it is also because James seems aware of the previous retellings. Martha Banta, in her discussion of James's gothicism, has noted that he often seems influenced by Poe's "emotionally heightened grotesques," as well as his "Dupinesque" types, and although she does not specifically mention *The Sacred Fount*, both modes apply.[80] James's narrator bears particular resemblance to the enraptured artist in Poe's *The Oval Portrait*, where the protagonist, "lost in reveries . . . would not see that the

79. Folsom, "Archimago's Well," p. 142.
80. Martha Banta, "The House of the Seven Ushers and How They Grew: A Look at Jamesian Gothicism," *Yale Review* 57 (1967): 56–65.

tints he spread upon the canvas were drawn from the cheeks of her who sat beside him." This same "economy of sight" is also practiced by Poe's narrators in *Berenice, Ligeia,* and *Morella,* in which the narrator erects a "palace of imagination" to hide his obsessive fixations. So too James's narrator erects a "perfect palace of thought" (p. 311). These nameless narrators in both James and Poe depend on our willingness to suspend disbelief until, too late, we become willing co-conspirators in their heinous appetites.

As James's narrator may resemble Poe's, his imagery is perhaps unconsciously reminiscent of Coleridge's, for when the narrator reports May Server's enervation, "She fixed me with it [her "lovely grimace"] as she has fixed during the day forty persons, but it fluttered like a bird with a broken wing" (p. 133), or when May sinks "in confused collapse" beside him "as if discouraged by the sight of weariness that her surrender had let out" (p. 135), we may be reminded of the symbiosis between Geraldine and Christabel. For in the narrator's mind, at least, she is the lap-winged dove caught in his nets, and his comparison of May's pathetic grimace to the fluttering of the injured bird may well recall the bird in Bard Bracy's dream (*Christabel,* ll. 531–36).

Additionally, the relationships between the narrator and the other characters may have something of the Ancient Mariner/Wedding Guest interaction. The narrator is forever holding his partners with his eye, a fact that James K. Folsom compares with the fairy tale motif of the vampire story.[81] Although the "glittering eye" and the "skinny hand" are not there, the process of transfixing is still intact. The narrator is compelled to speak, and the Wedding Guest, or in this case the guests at Newmarch (including us), are compelled to listen. More importantly, however, in the telling of the tale, the narrator gains a vitality, an enthusiasm, that although short-lived, is similar to what the Ancient Mariner achieved.

I would not contend that any of these influences are direct, but only that by the turn of the century a series of images had become standardized to such a point that James could use them without explanation. One sees how important this could be when comparing James to Hawthorne, for Hawthorne was fascinated with the same theme, the unpardonable sin, i.e., emotional cannibalism, but Hawthorne never found an appropriate mythic context. The notion of psychic bondage, of parasitic relationships, is prominent in many of Hawthorne's novels: witness, for example, Chillingworth in *The Scarlet Letter,* Coverdale in *The Blithedale Romance,* Holgrave in *The House of Seven Gables,* and Kenyon in *The Marble Faun,* but the process is never really worked out specifically in vampiric imagery. Hawthorne has the subject but not the language. Hawthorne even explored the theme of the artist as vampire as well as art as enervation, in such tales as *The Prophetic Pictures, The Birthmark,* and *The Artist of the Beautiful,* but once again, while the spiritual trespassing is evident, the vampire is not. A case could be made for reading *Ethan Brand* as a story about spiritual vampirism, for the protagonist is eternally wander-

81. Folsom, "Archimago's Well," p. 140.

ing, seeking life to plunder, and finally ends like Varney, consumed in fire, but Ethan Brand seems more a leech than a consistently demonic figure.[82] James's predators, while not necessarily more successful in literature, are certainly more traditional in gothic imagery.

In a sense, *The Sacred Fount* is the last nineteenth-century attempt to use the vampire myth to explore complex relationships involved in society and art. Perhaps the enduring quality of the myth in both literature and popular culture attests to our recurring need for a nonscientific vocabulary to describe destructive aspects intrinsic in certain relationships. James seems to have acknowledged this need. If we set *The Sacred Fount* in this psychological context, James seems not to have "chawed more than he bit off" (as Henry Adams's wife contended), but rather bitten off quite a bit and then chewed it exceedingly fine.

Looking back over a century of interest in coupling the vampire story with the process of artistic creation, we find no consensus, no "Romantic view," instead only a welter of adaptations. What they all have in common is the interchange of energy. Expressed schematically the interchange might look something like this:

ARTIST	WORK/PROCESS	+ ENERGY GAINER	− ENERGY LOSER
Coleridge	*The Rime of the Ancient Mariner,* 1798, rev. 1800, 1817, "Audience for artist's sake"	The Ancient Mariner, the artist-teller of the tale	The Wedding Guest, the audience, the listener to the tale
Wordsworth	*Resolution and Independence,* 1802 (entitled *The Leech Gatherer,* 1800). "Art for artist's sake."	The speaker, the melancholy poetic persona	The Leech Gatherer (The Ur-Poet)
Poe	*The Oval Portrait,* 1842 (entitled *Life-in-Death,* 1842). "Subject for the sake of the artifact."	The artifact, the painting	The object, the sitter
Wilde	*The Picture of Dorian Gray,* 1890, rev. 1891. "Art for the sake of the subject."	Dorian Gray, the subject of Basil's art.	The artist (Basil) and the object of art.

82. For an interpretation of Hawthorne's characters as vampires, see Babener, "Predators of the Spirit," chap. 4, "The Vampire Motif in the Fiction of Nathaniel Hawthorne."

James	*The Sacred Fount,* 1901. "Art for the object's sake"	The "scientific" theory of the Sacred Fount.	The artist manqué, the narrator and the subjects—Mrs. Brissenden, May Server, et al.

In each work the vampire story is used to dramatize the struggle of creation—a struggle between artist, audience, work of art, object of art, and even the artist himself. When this struggle succeeds, as it does in *The Rime of the Ancient Mariner* and *Resolution and Independence*, energy is properly transferred, but when it fails, as it does in *The Oval Portrait, The Picture of Dorian Gray,* or *The Sacred Fount,* the energy destroys order and chaos results.

Epilogue: D. H. Lawrence and the Modern Vampire

"Oil and Blood"

In tombs of gold and lapis lazuli
Bodies of holy men and women exude
Miraculous oil, odour of violet.

But under heavy loads of trampled clay
Lie bodies of the vampires full of blood;
Their shrouds are bloody and their lips are wet.

—W. B. Yeats

Although it is really beyond the chronological limits of this study, I would be remiss not to mention a few of the modern adaptations of the vampire myth. For although the interest in describing human energy transfer in terms of this analogy has waned (as transactional psychology has provided a more comprehensive vocabulary), the vampire is still alive and well. To illustrate, I will discuss in detail one modern adaptation—D. H. Lawrence's characterization of the Brangwen women as lamias—but first we need to review the Victorian plight of this Romantic figure.

In mid-Victorian literature the vampire went underground, so to speak, became the subject of throwaway prose, and so has been lost for study; we have *Varney the Vampyre* and not much else. The vampire appeared occasionally in serious fiction, most notably in Dickens's portrayal of the solicitor Vholes in *Bleak House*, and Quilp, the hideous monster, in *The Old Curiosity Shop*. Vampirism also figures in such works as Wilkie Collins's *The Dream Women*, Walter de la Mare's *Seaton's Aunt*, Bulwer-Lytton's *A Strange Story*, Robert Louis Stevenson's *Olalla* and *Thrawn Janet*, as well as H. G. Wells's *The Flowering of the Strange Orchids* and Conan Doyle's *The Adventure of the Sussex Vampire*, but it is tangential at best. The old vehemence is lost as the vampire becomes domesticated and intellectualized. There are only two Victorian vampire poems: Kipling's "The Vampire" (1897) and James Clerk Maxwell's "The Vampyre" (1845)—both memorable for nonliterary reasons. Maxwell went on to become one of the world's greatest physicists, while *A Fool There Was* was made from Kipling's poem, launching the career of Theda Bara and the whole world of Hollywood "vamps."

These works, like most of their counterparts in our century, rarely attempted to use the myth as anything other than gothic stuffing. There are recent exceptions, to be sure, as seen in the works of such modern "Romantics" as W. B. Yeats, James Joyce, Randall Jarrell, and Richard Wilbur. Yeats's "Oil and Blood" uses the vampire to contrast the sterility of royal pomp with the feral vitality of folklore. In *Ulysses* the vampire becomes a metaphor to discuss the energy exchange between father and son, artist and art, priest and penitent.[1] The theme of lovers transfusing each other with life is the concern of Randall Jarrell's "Honensalzburg: Fantastic Variations on a Theme of Romantic Character," while in Richard Wilbur's "The Undead" the vampire appears as a sympathetic figure, an exile from mortality, almost a poet among outcasts. Additionally, Virginia Woolf and F. Scott Fitzgerald used the myth to portray characters who enervate those they come in contact with, while more recently novelists like Desmond Steward and Anne Rice have used the monster to portray the forces of fascism and decadence.[2] But these works are all the exceptions; for the last hundred years the vampire has more usually been exploited by hacks, merchandised by hucksters, and vulgarized into parody.

Still, one adaptation stands out. Of all the modern Romantics, it was D. H. Lawrence who best understood what the earlier poets had found intriguing and who was able to provide the myth a fresh adaptation. He did this by choosing to explore a repeated event in all our lives—the act of falling in love, of having to battle for selfhood, of having to protect one's independence while giving up one's isolation. When this process goes awry, as it often does for Lawrence, the lovers may become vampires to each other. Instead of merging into a holistic unity, the separated partners may strive to consume what they cannot control.

Although Lawrence used the vampire myth in various contexts, I should like to focus on just one scene in his middle novels, *The Rainbow* and *Women in Love*.[3] This scene is so often repeated that it becomes a leitmotif unifying various subplots. The scene is simple: two young people meet and enter into what is described as a "battle for life itself." Their relationship deepens until one of the members, usually the woman, demands too much and starts to "suck" her partner dry. If he is weak she will devour him; if he is strong, they both will survive.[4]

1. Michael Seidel, "*Ulysses*' Black Panther Vampire," *James Joyce Quarterly* 13 (1976): 415–27.

2. Mr. Ramsey, in Virginia Woolf's *To the Lighthouse*, is vampiric in the sense that he drains life from others (chap. 7) as are the ghostly Duncan Shaeffer and Lorraine Quarrles in F. Scott Fitzgerald's *Babylon Revisited*; see my "*Babylon Revisited*: Chronology and Characters," *Fitzgerald/Hemingway Annual* (Detroit, Mich.: Gale Research, 1979), pp. 155–61. For a more modern treatment, see Desmond Stewart, *The Vampire of Mons* (New York: Harper and Row, 1976); Anne Rice, *Interview with the Vampire* (New York: Knopf, 1976), and other works cited in note 50, chap. 4.

3. Vampirism is a critically neglected aspect of Lawrence's literary criticism and fiction, yet it is obvious in such works as *The Ladybug*, although more subtle in others, especially in *Sons and Lovers* (Paul and Miriam) and *Lady Chatterley's Lover* (Clifford Chatterley).

4. Lawrence's reductive view of women has of late been examined and reexamined, often more to prove sociological arguments than to provide literary insight: see Simone de Beauvoir, *The Second Sex* (New York: Bantam Books, 1961), p. 204; Kate Millett, *Sexual Politics* (Garden City, N.Y.: Doubleday and Co., 1970), and Norman Mailer, "The Prisoner of Sex," *Harper's Magazine* 242 (March 1971): 70. For an examination of this type of female in Lawrence's short stories, see Kingsley Widmer, *The Art of Perversity* (Seattle: University of Washington Press, 1962), chap. 2, "The Destructive Women." And for

Once again the best explanation of this process outside these novels occurs in the famous piece on Edgar Allan Poe which Lawrence wrote after the publication of *The Rainbow* and during the revisions of *Women in Love.*[5] First Lawrence explains the psychology of human interaction:

> The central law of organic life is that each organism is intrinsically isolate and single in itself.
>
> The moment its isolation breaks down, and there comes an actual mixing and confusion, death sets in.
>
> This is true of every individual organism, from man to amoeba.
>
> But the secondary law of all organic life is that each organism only lives through contact with other matter, assimilation of new vibrations, non-material. Each individual organism is vivified by intimate contact with fellow organisms: up to a certain point.[6]

But if that "certain point" is passed, if the struggle for contact becomes too frenetic, then one lover may seek to dominate or, in Lawrence's terms, to "know" the other. When this happens, the "life membranes" of the weaker begin to rupture as the lovers vibrate to such a pitch that "the nerves begin to break, to bleed as it were, and a form of death sets in" (SCAL, p. 331). As with Lawrence, Poe usually has the female (Morella, Ligeia, Berenice) acting as the devourer, even though she is often introduced to the demonic pleasures of eccentric love by her male consort. Lawrence next explains what happens when the lovers lose their psychic independence:

---

a more complete view of the destructive female in Lawrence's fiction, see Charles Rossman, "'You are the call and I am the answer': D. H. Lawrence and Women," *The D. H. Lawrence Review* 8 (Fall 1975): 258–68. To the best of my knowledge, Lawrence first uses the lamia motif in *Sons and Lovers* with the characterization of Miriam Leivers, who is described by Mrs. Morel as "one of those who will want to suck man's soul out till he has none of his own left." Here is a typical scene between Paul and Miriam:

> She seemed to want him, and he resisted. He resisted all the time. He wanted now to give her passion and tenderness, and he could not. He felt that she wanted the soul out of his body, and not him. All his strength and energy she drew into herself through some channel which united them. She did not want to meet him, so that there were two of them, man and woman together. She wanted to draw all of him into her. (chapter 8)

5. Lawrence was reading and writing about Poe during the composition of *Women in Love* and possibly during *The Rainbow* as well. His first essay on Poe was written between 1917 and 1918 in Cornwall and appeared in the *English Review* for 1919. It does not include the references to Poe's lovers as vampires. However, the 1923 book version does, so it seems reasonable to assume that between 1918 and 1922 Lawrence is thinking about the specific analogy of the lover as vampire, perhaps as a result of his own fiction. For the 1919 version see Armin Arnold, ed., *The Symbolic Meaning* (New York: Viking Press, 1964), pp. 105–20.

6. "Edgar Allan Poe," *Studies in Classic American Literature* as included in *D. H. Lawrence: Selected Literary Criticism*, ed. Anthony Beal (New York: Viking Press, 1966), p. 331. Hereafter this edition will be referred to in the text as SCAL in parentheses with page numbers. Lawrence's novels will also be cited parenthetically in the text by abbreviated title and page numbers from the following editions: R, *The Rainbow* (New York: Viking Press, 1961); WL, *Women in Love* (New York: Viking Press, 1960) and Prol., "Prologue to *Women in Love*" in *Phoenix II: Uncollected, Unpublished and Other Prose Works by D. H. Lawrence*, ed. Warren Roberts and Harry T. Moore (New York: Viking Press, 1968).

It is easy to see why each man kills the things he loves. To know a living thing is to kill it. You have to kill a thing to know it satisfactorily. For this reason, the desirous consciousness, the *spirit*, is a vampire.

One should be sufficiently intelligent and interested to know a good deal *about* any person one comes into close contact with. *About* her. Or *about* him.

But to try to *know* any living being is to try to suck the life out of that being. . . .It is the temptation of a vampire fiend, is this knowledge. (SCAL, p. 335)

Lawrence attempts to illustrate this process in *The Rainbow*. From the very first Anna Lensky is described in terms that while not precisely vampiric, are nonetheless in the Gothic tradition of the possessed child. She has "unblinking" (R, p. 38), "resentful black eyes" (R, pp. 27, 38), "wild fierce hair" (R, p. 37), is called a "changeling," "bewitched" (R, p. 28), "a wild thing" (R, p. 93), and a "savage" (R, p. 80); and although she goes to church she cannot abide the rosary (R, p. 100) or for that matter the service itself. She even has all the lamia's serpentine attributes: "a little darting forward of the head, something like a viper" (R, p. 62); "she hissed forward her head" (R, p. 65), yet she is also her father's darling, loving to cuddle up next to him in his chair or on the gig. Naturally enough it is with her stepfather Tom that she initiates the first of her "encounters."

On two occasions Lawrence hints of her potentially demonic nature and the weird symbiosis between father and daughter. First he mentions that Anna never sleeps with her eyes completely shut: "The little Anna clung around her mother's neck. The fair, strange face of the child looked over the shoulder of her mother, all asleep but the eyes and these wide and dark . . . " (R, p. 38); "The child was asleep, the eyelids not quite shut, showing a slight film of black pupil between. Why did she not shut her eyes?" (R, p. 75)[7] Then, when he describes Anna's response to her father's death, Lawrence seems to be pulling out all the stops to show the vampiric nature of all family relationships, even subtly incestuous ones.[8] "When Anna heard the news [that her stepfather was dead], she pressed back her head and rolled her eyes, as if something were reaching forward to bite at her throat." (R, p. 247). Are we to believe that there may have been some diabolical relationship between them, some sublimated energy flow between father and daughter? The analogy, if indeed I am reading this correctly, is as bold as it is apt, and prepares us to understand the other relationship with a man Anna has, namely with her stepcousin Will.

7. That vampires sleep with their eyes open, see for instance, Nancy Garden, *Vampires* (New York: J. B. Lippincott Co., 1973), p. 64; Montague Summers, *The Vampire: His Kith and Kin* (1928; rpt. New Hyde Park, N.Y.: University Books, 1960), chap. 3; and Basil Cooper, *The Vampire in Legend, Fact and Art* (Secaucus, N.J.: Citadel Press, 1974), chap. 3. This is a crucial bit of lore, for since the vampire is always seeing, he will know who is attempting to destroy him.

8. While it is true that Tom and Anna are not related by blood, their relationship is psychologically incestuous. Lawrence believed that neurosis was primarily caused by incestuous desires. Since vampires first attack those whom they loved best, usually the first victim is a spouse or relative, hence incest becomes a part of the vampire superstition. For Lawrence's views on incest, see "Parent Love" in *Fantasia of the Unconscious*.

The Anna/Will relationship is both a condensation and a prefiguring of male-female interactions to come. It starts abruptly: they meet, become spellbound, and kiss. Here is their first kiss (as it will later be repeated), with the male as aggressor.

> Her breast was near him; his head lifted like an eagle's. She did not move. Suddenly, with an incredibly quick, delicate movement, he put his arms round her and drew her to him. It was quick, cleanly done, like a bird that swoops and sinks close, closer.
>
> He was kissing her throat. She turned and looked at him. Her eyes were dark and flowing with fire. (R, p. 112)

Paradoxically it is Will, the eagle-vampire, who is being caught in Anna's Circesque web, for the participants will soon reverse roles. As in the Poe stories, the female takes control; slowly the male wastes away, becoming dependent on her for life itself until she realizes he has become only a husk and must be cast off. The echoes of Poe can be heard in Lawrence.

> His [Will's] hovering near her [Anna], wanting her to be with him, the futility of him, the way his hands hung, irritated her beyond bearing. She turned on him blindly and destructively, he became a mad creature, black and electric with fury. The dark storms rose in him, his eyes glowed black and evil, he was fiendish in his thwarted soul.
>
> There followed two black and ghastly days, when she was set in anguish against him, and he felt as if he were in a black, violent underworld, and his wrists quivered murderously. And she resisted him. He seemed a dark, almost evil thing, pursuing her, hanging on to her, burdening her. She would give anything to have him removed. (R, p. 148)

Yet when she needs his energy he is there and willing:

> He could not bear to think of her tears—he could not bear it. We wanted to go to her and pour out his heart's blood to her. He wanted to give everything to her, all his blood; to the last dregs, pour everything away to her. He yearned with passionate desire to offer himself to her, utterly. (R, p. 151)

His death wish comes to fruition before even he is aware of what has happened. In "Anna Victrix" she finally literally has her man: "He did not understand, he had yielded, given way. There was no understanding; there would be only acquiescence and submission, and tremulous wonder of consummation" (R, p. 153). But in her victory, like the praying mantis, she has destroyed her mate. He fights back, but too late: "Dark and destroyed, his soul running with blood, he tasted of death" (R, p. 168). He has become subservient to her. She has made him bleed (R, p. 166) and, as with the vampire of lore, he has been consumed in fire.[9] Now with the male docile, submissive, enervated and bled, the new female generation can begin.

9. Will's death by fire is implied in his reaction to Anna's victory dance (R, p. 181). After this, Will is "born again," and now, like the vampire of folklore, he prowls the evenings for victims of his own. He

Ursula, the result of their dark union, draws life and energy from her battling parents, and in so doing pacifies them as Anna had done for Tom and Lydia. Here starts the first variation on the vampire theme, for Ursula will replay that role, with some modification, that her mother and grandmother had played before her. She must now find a man, a livelihood of her own. The man she finds is Anton Skrebensky, a slight, indolent, intellectual, aristocratic Middle European.

Ursula is as "fated" to meet Anton as her mother had been to meet Will, but Anton is not the man Ursula's father finally became. He is spineless from the start, pallid, already enervated, and so it is not long before we see what is becoming the central act of the male-female relationships, the infamous kiss.

> Then his mouth drew near, pressing open her mouth, a hot, drenching surge rose within her, she opened her lips to him, in pained, poignant eddies she drew him nearer, she let him come farther, his lips came and surging, surging, soft, oh soft, yet oh, like the powerful surge of water, irresistible, till with a little blind cry, she broke away.
>
> She heard him breathing heavily, strangely, beside her. A terrible and magnificent sense of his strangeness possessed her. (R, pp. 297–98)

Ursula soon realizes he is in her power, realizes she can "live off" him and indeed proceeds to do so: "she reached him her mouth and drank his full kiss, drank it fuller and fuller" (R, p. 302).

> Looking at him, at his shadowy, unreal, wavering presence a sudden lust seized her, to lay hold of him and tear him and make him into nothing. Her hands and wrists felt immeasurably hard and strong, like blades. He waited there beside her like a shadow which she wanted to dissipate, destroy as the moonlight destroys a darkness, annihilate, have done with. (R, p. 319)

. . . .

---

finds one, a shopgirl, Jeannie, and the process of eccentric love continues. As they are walking into the dark night,

> He was alert in every sense and fibre, and yet quite sure and steady, and lit up, as if transfused. He had a free sensation of walking in his own darkness, not in anybody else's world at all. He was purely a world to himself, he had nothing to do with any general consciousness. Just his own senses were supreme. All the rest was external, insignificant, leaving him alone with this girl whom he wanted to absorb. He did not care about her except that he wanted to overcome her resistance, to have her in his power, fully and exhaustively to enjoy her. (R, p. 227)

Once their eyes meet, "he seemed to hold her in his will" (R, p. 227). Then the inevitable kiss:

> So he came at length to kiss her, and she was almost betrayed by his insidious kiss. Her open mouth was too helpless and unguarded. He knew this, and his first kiss was very gentle, and soft, and assuring, so assuring. So that her soft, defenceless mouth became assured, even bold, seeking upon his mouth. And he answered her gradually, gradually, his soft kiss sinking in softly, softly, but ever more heavily, more heavily yet, till it was too heavy for her to meet, and she began to sink under it. She was sinking, sinking, his smile of latent gratification was becoming more tense, he was sure of her. (R, p. 228)

She escapes, leaving him both despondent and exhilarated, to turn like his Uncle Tom to his work and to his daughter for sustenance.

She seemed to be destroying him. He was reeling, summoning all his strength to keep his kiss upon her, to keep himself in the kiss.

But hard and fierce she had fastened upon him . . . destroying him, destroying him in the kiss. And her soul crystallised with triumph, and his soul was dissolved with agony and annihilation. So she held him there, the victim, consumed, annihilated. She had triumphed: he was not any more. (R, p. 320)

Finally, as a sign of complete mastery she is able not just to annihilate but resurrect as well:

Her heart was warm, her blood was dark and warm and soft. She laid her hand caressively on Anton's shoulder.

"Isn't it lovely?" she said, softly, coaxingly, caressingly. And she began to caress him to life again. For he was dead. And she intended that he should never know, never become aware of what had been. She would bring him back from the dead without leaving him one trace of fact to remember his annihilation by. (R, p. 321)

She has drained him and revived him, made him a coreless, bloodless initiate of the walking dead ("To his own intrinsic life, he was dead. And he could not rise again from the dead. His soul lay in the tomb" [R, p. 326]). Since he is enervated, he can no longer furnish her life and so she turns, as Lawrence's characters will later do in *Women in Love*, elsewhere.[10]

Six years pass before Anton is strong enough to return. Away from Ursula in Africa, he has been revived, but it will prove a short, unhappy revival, for once again

He kissed her, with his soft, enveloping kisses, and she responded to them completely, her mind, her soul gone out. Darkness cleaving to darkness, she hung close to him, pressed herself into soft flow of his kiss, pressed herself down, down to the source and core of his kiss, herself covered and enveloped in the warm, fecund flow of his kiss, that travelled over her, flowed over her, covered her, flowed over the last fibre of her, so they were one stream, one

10. Ursula's relationship with Winifred Inger is also desultory. Lawrence realized that the rightful opponent of all love struggles is the opposite sex, just as it almost always is in the vampire myth—the possible exceptions being Coleridge's *Christabel* and LeFanu's *Carmilla*. Yet he also realized that there is an onanistic desire to regenerate without opposition, without passing the confines of one's own sex. In one almost throwaway scene that occurs between Ursula and the melancholy Maggie Schofield, Lawrence hints of a possible symbiosis growing between them. Maggie, jealous for Ursula's attention, tries to separate Ursula from her brother Anthony, by inviting her for a walk in the woods. They wander off into the park at Belcote. They settle beneath "a big tree with a thick trunk twisted with ivy [where] Maggie took out a book, and sitting lower down the trunk began to read Coleridge's 'Christabel.' Ursula half listened. She was wildly thrilled" (R, p. 415). Why "Christabel," and why is she "thrilled"? Because, I suspect, Lawrence knew what A. H. Nethercot has to remind the twentieth-century reader, namely that Geraldine was a lamia preying on Christabel (see chap. 2). Lawrence here uses the literary allusion to show the possible similarity of the affairs, for in Coleridge's poem Christabel meets Geraldine under an old oak tree covered with ivy. But unlike Christabel, Ursula escapes for the moment at least, as Anthony, the noble knight of the piece, arrives to break the spell.

dark fecundity, and she clung at the core of him, with her lips holding open the very bottommost source of him. (R, p. 447)

What little life he has regenerated flows here to Ursula as she, the predator, consumes him. Once again we watch his slow demise:

She waited, every moment of the day, for his next kiss. She admitted it to herself in shame and bliss. Almost consciously, she waited. He waited, but, until the time came, more unconsciously. When the time came that he should kiss her again, a prevention was an annihilation to him. He felt his flesh go grey, he was heavy with a corpse-like inanition, he did not exist, if the time passed unfulfilled. (R, p. 450)

. . . .

He felt like a corpse that is inhabited with just enough life to make it appear as any other of the spectral, unliving beings which we call people in our dead language. . . . He felt as if his life were dead. His soul extinct. The whole being of him had become sterile, he was a spectre, divorced from life. He had no fullness, he was just a flat shape. (R, p. 457)

Then, finally, he is shattered:

His drawn, strangled face watched her blankly for a few moments, then a strange sound took place in his throat. She started, came to herself, and, horrified, saw him. His head made a queer motion, the chin jerked back against the throat, the curious, crowing, hiccupping sound came again, his face twisted like insanity, and he was crying, crying blind and twisted as if something were broken which kept him in control.
    "Tony—don't," she cried, starting up. (R, pp. 466–67)

In keeping with the vampire myth, the victim does not physically die, but rather becomes an active participant in the process that destroys him. She, the lamia, the devourer, has made him party to her appetites, only to have the balance of horror reverse as he now turns on her. At last Skrenbensky becomes "an incubus upon her" (R, p. 471), desperately attacking back.

This is a situation that cannot endure. This is the situation where, in Lawrence's words, the lovers' vibration has risen to such a pitch that the nervous membranes must break, and indeed they do. In a scene that could come from Lewis's *The Monk* or Maturin's *Melmoth the Wanderer*, Lawrence has Ursula, like a hideous Goya character, devour her mate.[11] On the moonlit Lincolnshire coast among the dunes, she consumes him:

She prowled, ranging on the edge of the water like a possessed creature, and he followed her. . . . And she seized hold of his arm, held him fast, as if

11. This omophagic scene is more ghoulish than vampiric for the ghoul preys upon living people, sucking brains and spinal fluid as well as blood. The ghoul has never been human and usually acts in response to some external command. Often in folklore the two are mixed, so that the vampire/ghoul drinks the blood and eats the flesh, as is metaphorically happening here with Ursula and Skrebensky.

captive, and walked him a little way by the edge of the dazzling, dazing water.

Then there in the great flare of light, she clinched hold of him, hard, as if suddenly she had the strength of destruction, she fastened her arms round him and tightened him in her grip, whilst her mouth sought his in a hard, rending, ever-increasing kiss, till his body was powerless in her grip, his heart melted in fear from the fierce, beaked harpy's kiss. The water washed again over their feet, but she took no notice. She seemed unaware, she seemed to be pressing in her beaked mouth till she had the heart of him. Then, at last, she drew away and looked at him—looked at him. He knew what she wanted. (R, pp. 478–79)

. . . .

"Have you done with me?" he asked her at length, lifting his head.

"It isn't me," she said. "You have done with me—we have done with each other." (R, p. 480)

And indeed they have. She has had her fill. There is no more love between them, no energy flow, no possibility for flux, no life, no blood.

This then is the circle at its greatest circumference—just at the moment of bursting. It is the discordant coda that ends this movement of Lawrence's symphony of human affairs. The rhetoric of horror has reached a wondrously percussive crescendo. We listen for some final harmony, some resolution in the novel, but there is none. We expect, for instance, that Ursula will carry Anton's child to term (if indeed she is really pregnant), that it will be born female, and that this new female will be able to return to the balanced world of her maternal grandmother.[12] But no, there is to be no child. Instead we are given Ursula's gratuitous vision of the rainbow, an ephiphany of sorts, a faint half-hope for new generation. Here biographical reality dashed fictional resolution, for *The Rainbow* was banned as obscene: World War I was more than a year old, Lawrence was dejected, quarrelsome, and despondent, and what seemed Ursula's hopeful vision was to prove possibly an illusion. For in Lawrence's next novel, *Women in Love*, the cycle simply continues; the same themes are recapitulated until with the entry of a "real man," Birkin, there is at last the faint hint of genuine resolution.

Human relationships begin in *Women in Love* by precisely repeating the one that concluded *The Rainbow*: namely predatory female attempting to devour debilitated male. We know from the Wagnerian pattern of composition that Lawrence invented Ursula's affair with Skrebensky to prepare us for her success with Birkin; it

12. I am not alone in believing this: see Mark Kinkead-Weekes, "Eros and Metaphor: Sexual Relationship in the Fiction of D. H. Lawrence," *Twentieth Century Studies*, 1 (1969): 11. Lawrence's problems with endings, both in *The Rainbow* and *Women in Love*, has been much discussed, most notably in David Daiches, *The Novel and the Modern World*, rev. ed. (Chicago: University of Chicago Press, 1960), pp. 168 ff.; F. R. Leavis, *D. H. Lawrence: Novelist* (New York: Knopf, 1956), p. 172; Alan Friedman, "Suspended Form: Lawrence's Theory of Fiction in *Women in Love*" in *Twentieth Century Interpretations of Women in Love* (Englewood Cliffs, N.J.: Prentice Hall, 1969), pp. 40–42.

was then Lawrence's task to prepare Birkin for Ursula.[13] He did this by introducing an Ursula figure without redeeming features, almost an Elizabethan humor character, in the figure of Hermione. To rearrange Lawrence's own analogy of describing characters on a continuum or as allotropic states of the same ego, Hermione is one extreme, coal dust to what will become Ursula's future diamond.[14] In both cases, however, the theme is carbon—the man-destroying woman.

When we first meet Birkin in the "Prologue" to *Women in Love* (the discarded opening chapter), he is remarkably like Skrebensky—"hollow and ghastly to look at," while Hermione is waging the inner battle between Eros and Thanatos, on one hand wanting to consume, on the other wanting to be consumed but never wanting to consummate. While she lusts for Birkin she also despises him.

> She wanted him to take her, to break her with his passion, to destroy her with his desire, so long as he got satisfaction. She looked forward, tremulous, to a kind of death at his hands, she gave herself up. She would be broken and dying, destroyed, if only he would rise fulfilled. . . . And she hated him, and despised him, for his incapacity to wreak his desire upon her, his lack of strength to crush his satisfaction from her. If only he could have taken her, destroyed her, used her all up, and been satisfied, she would be at last free. She might be killed, but it would be the death which gave her consummation.
> (*Prol.*, p. 100)

As *Women in Love* opens, Birkin is just at the moment of collapse; her "deadly half-love" has almost drained him dry. "He became more hollow and deathly, more like a spectre with hollow bones. He knew that he was not very far from dissolution" (*Prol.*, p. 103). This is, of course, the precise description of Skrebensky, and we may well have the feeling we have met him before. It is here, however, that Ursula enters—Ursula who has blood and strength sufficient to revive Birkin from Hermione's deathly onslaught.

All this formulaic recapitulation of the vampire motif is lost in Lawrence's final version, for this chapter never made it to print. It is understandable why Lawrence excised this "Prologue," for the rhapsodic descriptions of homosexuality are maudlin and unsubstantiated, and Birkin is such a fop as to be unsympathetic, but the deletion is nonetheless unfortunate.[15] For this chapter is an important causeway between *The Rainbow* and *Women in Love*, preparing us for Birkin's battle with Hermione by reminding us of Skrebensky's duel with Ursula. It reminds us how truly dangerous Lawrence felt the predatory female could become if not resisted.

13. For an explanation of the composition of *The Rainbow* and *Women in Love* see Mark Kinkead-Weekes, "The Marble and the Statue," in *Imagined Worlds, Essays on Some English Novels and Novelists in Honor of John Butt*, ed. Maynard Mack and Ian Gregor (London: Methuen, 1968), pp. 371–418.

14. "Letter to Edward Garnett, June 5, 1914" in *The Collected Letters of D. H. Lawrence*, ed. H. T. Moore (New York: Viking Press, 1962), p. 282.

15. See George Ford, "An Introductory Note to D. H. Lawrence's 'Prologue' to *Women in Love*," *The Texas Quarterly* 6 (Spring 1963), 96–97.

Hermione is not merely as Julian Moynahan has asserted in passing, "like a kind of vampire figure"—she *is* a vampire figure.[16] In no female characterization so far has Lawrence been more insistent on the analogy. Hermione is serpentine: "coiled to strike" (WL, p. 10), "like a pythoness" (WL, pp. 35, 290); she is the "spectre" (WL, p. 289) with the "phosphorescent face" (WL, p. 131), literally "craving" (WL, p. 11) Birkin, attempting first to transfix him with her hypnotic stare (WL, p. 16) and then possess him (*passim*). She is indeed, as Birkin diagnoses, "the woman wailing for her 'demon lover'" (WL, p. 36).[17]

Although at the beginning of *Women In Love* Hermione is full-fleshed and healthy, Birkin's refusal to enter any sort of rapprochement soon deprives her of the possibility of drinking at his "sacred fount." She becomes pale and weak, now all the more desperate for his strength. In a scene almost as gothic as Ursula's sucking life from Skrebensky, Lawrence pictures Hermione's death-agonies:

> Hermione looked at him along her narrow, pallid cheeks. Her eyes were strange and drugged, heavy under their heavy, drooping lids. Her thin bosom shrugged convulsively. He stared back at her, devilish and unchanging. With another strange, sick convulsion, she turned away, as if she were sick, could feel dissolution setting-in her body. . . .
>
> She suffered the ghastliness of dissolution, broken and gone in a horrible corruption. And he stood and looked at her unmoved. She strayed out pallid and preyed-upon like a ghost, like one attacked by the tomb-influences which dog us. And she was gone like a corpse. (WL, p. 82)

She is literally wasting away, "sick, like a *revenant*" (WL, p. 83; DHL's italics), almost "unconscious, sunk in a heavy half-trance" (WL, p. 83), until finally "she suffered sheer dissolution like a corpse, and was unconscious of everything save the horrible sickness of dissolution that was taking place within her body and soul" (WL, p. 85). All sustenance denied her, she even "seemed to grip the hours by the throat, to force her life from them" (WL, p. 91). Lawrence graciously did not pursue the temporal applications of the vampire myth, as it could only produce imagery beyond even his ability to sustain; but still the reader gets the point— Hermione bleeds everything, not just organic life, but life in the abstract as well.

The analogy of energy flow and blood transfer is by no means circumscribed by the vampire imagery. In fact, Lawrence is so intent on using it to describe the interactive process between overly demanding female and weak male that he makes it part of the fugal organization of many subsidiary scenes. Thus Minette's fascination with the bleeding hand (WL, pp. 63–64), the "Blutbruderschaft" or the intermingling of Birkin's and Gerald's blood (WL, p. 198), or the hemorrhaging death

16. Julian Moynahan, *The Deed of Life: The Novels and Tales of D. H. Lawrence* (Princeton, N.J.: Princeton University Press, 1963), p. 72.

17. The demon lover in *Kubla Khan* has caused considerable critical investigation, of which the vampiritic explanation is only one of many. See Nicolas K. Kiessling, "Demonic Dread: The Incubus Figure in British Literature" in *The Gothic Imagination*, ed. G. R. Thompson (Pullman: Washington State University Press, 1974), p. 37. For more on Lawrence's use of *Christabel* see note 10.

of Mr. Crich (WL, pp. 209–10) are all variations on this theme of human interaction with blood as a common image.[18] So too in a sense is the macabre death scene of Diana Crich and her rescuer at the "Water-Party." For here in an imagistic epitome is the predatory female not draining blood, but rather throttling life from the male: "These bodies of the dead were not recovered till towards dawn. Diana had her arms round the neck of the young man, choking him. 'She killed him,' said Gerald" (WL, p. 181). And, of course, Gerald is correct.

All of these scenes, scenes that appear at first so extraneous, are included to prepare us for, and provide accompaniment to, the major vampiric action of the novel—the battle for life between Gerald and Gudrun. Early in the novel we are introduced to Gerald as a man's man, unlike Skrebensky or Will or even Birkin. Throughout he exerts his power over both man (the colliers) and beast (the mare at the railroad tracks, the rabbit), but from the outset he is no match for Gudrun; "he would be helpless in the association with her" (WL, p. 114). The more he struggles to dominate her, the more potent she becomes, the more lamia-like, the more fatal: "Gudrun looked at Gerald with strange, darkened eyes, strained with underworld knowledge, almost supplicating, like those of a creature which is at his mercy, yet which is his ultimate victor" (WL, p. 234). Ironically, his power makes him all the more vulnerable, as Lawrence details in another controlling analogy for interpersonal dynamics—electricity. Gerald is indeed a generator of fearsome current, but this current, like blood flow, cannot be stopped up, and especially cannot be redirected back against itself without disastrous consequences.

The battle for this current, this blood-life, becomes most intense, as we have seen before, in the kiss, the kiss of death. In a scene reminiscent of Ursula's and Skrebensky's seaside death embrace, Gudrun and Gerald meet under the colliery railroad bridge. It is here that Gerald, like Will Brangwen and Anton Skrebensky, initiates the perverse eucharist.

> His arms were fast around her, he seemed to be gathering her into himself, her warmth, her softness, her adorable weight, drinking in the suffusion of her physical being, avidly. He lifted her, and seemed to pour her into himself, like wine into a cup.
>
> "This is worth everything," he said in a strange, penetrating voice.
>
> So she relaxed, and seemed to melt, to flow into him as if she were some infinitely warm and precious suffusion filling into his veins, like an intoxicant. Her arms were round his neck, he kissed her and held her perfectly suspended, she was all slack and flowing into him, and he was the firm, strong cup that receives the wine of her life. (WL, p. 323)

From this encounter Gerald first draws strength, gains access to reserves of energy otherwise unknown—but to do so he becomes "possessed," a creature of the night,

---

18. There is also the suggestion of a blood bind—almost a marriage ritual performed by the clawing rabbit—between Gerald and Gudrun in chap. 18; see Eliseo Vivas, *D. H. Lawrence: The Failure and Triumph of Art* (Evanston, Ill.: Northwestern University Press, 1960), pp. 250–54.

endowed with "senses . . . almost supernaturally keen" (WL, p. 333), able to travel through the darkness to his lover with "occult carefulness" (WL p. 334). In the chapter "Death and Love," which Mark Schorer aptly retitled "Love as Death," Gerald, the night stalker, sneaks into the sleeping Brangwen household. He makes his way to Gudrun and once he is by her bedside, Gudrun realizes that his mysterious powers have flowed from her, and that somehow she must stop the flow before he attacks. "He was inevitable as a supernatural being. When she had seen him, she knew. She knew there was something fatal in the situation, and she must accept it. Yet she must challenge him" (WL, p. 335). And challenge him she does, with all the wiles of her sister, all the inherited cunning of her mother and grandmother. She has given him appetites for energy that will never be sated. She has made him dependent on her for his life:

> As he drew nearer to her, he plunged deeper into her enveloping soft warmth, a wonderful creative heat that penetrated his veins and gave him life again. . . . All his veins, that were murdered and lacerated, healed softly as life came pulsing in, stealing invisibly into him as if it were the all-powerful effluence of the sun. His blood, which seemed to have been drawn back into death, came ebbing on the return, surely, beautifully, powerfully.
>
> He felt his limbs growing fuller and flexible with life, his body gained an unknown strength. (WL, p. 337)

By the time they arrive in the Tyrolean Alps, however, Gudrun has almost been destroyed by the obscene monster she helped create. Gerald has become too demanding, too dependent. Finally with the "bat-like" (WL, p. 413) Loerke's assistance, she "turned aside, breaking the spell" (WL, p. 404), refusing Gerald her life. Then one night he is sent to bed—in Lawrence's rather horrid pun—without his dinner: "When he slept he seemed to crouch down in his bed, lapped up in his own strength, that yet was hollow. And Gudrun slept strongly, a victorious sleep" (WL p. 407).

It is now all over but the actual dying. Deprived of his life support, Gerald physically shrivels up, as had his predecessor Anton Skrebensky. But Anton was made lucky by his own weaknesses; he was able to escape his own appetites for blood energy by separating himself from Ursula. Gerald, the mechanical man, is not so resourceful. He cannot escape; he is so brittle he cannot bend, only break. Death is the only choice, and so like his literary predecessor, Emily Brontë's Heathcliff, he burns himself out, he consumes himself, he dies in a sense of starvation.[19]

19. Lawrence had first read Brontë's *Wuthering Heights* in 1906 (Rose Marie Burwell, "A Catalogue of D. H. Lawrence's Reading from Early Childhood," *D. H. Lawrence Review* 3 [Fall 1970]: 204). Anton buys a copy of it for Ursula soon after they meet (R, p. 293). This may be Lawrence's ironic joke, for Heathcliff is described as if he were a vampire sucking life from the Earnshaws and Lintons. The final kiss scene at Thrushcross Grange, Heathcliff's digging up of Catherine's grave, his offer to drink Edgar's blood for her sake, and his strange death (almost a kind of suicide) all reinforce Nelly Dean's final question: "Was he a ghoul or a vampire?" (chap. 34). Gerald acts like Heathcliff—powerful, clingingly devoted, heroically demonic, and perhaps Lawrence is comparing his death to Heathcliff's. For more, see chap. 4.

In the end only Ursula and Birkin remain. They are the only ones in this generation who have achieved the literal and figurative marriage of opposites. They have "struggled into being" primarily because Birkin has refused to mix blood with Ursula. She may have been bled (WL, p. 183), but she has never bled him.

> He knew that Ursula was referred back to him. He knew his life rested with her. But he would rather not live than accept the love she proffered. The old way of love seemed a dreadful bondage, a sort of conscription. What it was in him he did not know, but the thought of love, marriage, and children, and a life lived together, in the horrible privacy of domestic and connubial satisfaction, was repulsive. He wanted something clearer, more open, cooler, as it were. The hot narrow intimacy between man and wife was abhorrent. The way they shut their doors, these married people, and shut themselves into their own exclusive alliance with each other, even in love, disgusted him. (WL, p. 191)

So they battle it out, not for control but for balance, to become "like two poles of one force, like two angels, or two demons" (WL, p. 191). Even though Ursula wants "to drink him down—ah, like a lifedraught" (WL, p. 257), to quaff him "to the dregs" (WL, p. 258), he will never give in. Ursula, in a scene of ironic description, furiously calls him an "eater of corpses" (WL, p. 299), but the description better fits her. Birkin is neither eater nor eaten: he is the unfusable, unmergeable, unconsumable, independent man. Birkin is the hero of the piece, and as such he sets the pattern for a masculine figure that will become dominant in Lawrence's fiction from here on. As Charles Rossman has noted, *Women in Love* is a decisive turning point in Lawrence's treatment of character, for in it he makes a transition from strong women who destroy men to positive men who destroy women. The male, starting with Birkin, wins the "fight for phallic reality" and the women become not the destroyers but (at best) the source of his strength; not lamias, but acolytes. The female role is still not one of equality; as a matter of fact, with the exception of Constance Chatterly, it is still lopsided, but now in the other direction.[20]

Lawrence never returns to the vampire myth again, for he never returns to this view of the female. He has taken both the character-type and the myth about as far as they can go before disintegrating into self-parody. Still, when the analogy works, as I think it does best with Ursula and Skrebensky, it is marvelously effective, and readers who have complained about Lawrence's excessive hyperbole may simply have misunderstood his mythopoetic design. For Lawrence defanged and otherwise tempered the macabre aspects of the vampire while still asserting the validity of the process of energy transfer, and it is this psychological process, minus the gothic machinery, that he repeats again and again in *The Rainbow* and *Women in Love* to show what happens when the "struggle into being through love" goes awry.

20. Rossman charts the rise of the Birkin-type male and catalogues his female help-mates, "'You are the call and I am the answer': D. H. Lawrence and Women," pp. 282–306.

Appendix: *Varney the Vampyre*

The text of *Varney* I will condense is from the Dover edition (New York: Dover Publications, 1973), but the same text can be found in the Arno Press edition (New York: Arno Press, 1970), 3 vols. Page numbers will appear in parentheses after quotations.

While sleeping in Bannerworth Hall "fair Flora" Bannerworth is molested and beaten by a stealthy attacker. Her screams arouse the household: brothers Henry and George, her loving mother, and Robert Marchdale, a family friend. Although Dr. Chillingworth, skeptical local medic, diagnoses an insect bite, the Bannerworths suspect a vampire. The tall and cadaverous Sir Frances Varney, a nearby neighbor, offers to buy Bannerworth Hall from the distraught Bannerworths, but is refused. That night the molester again returns. By day Varney annoys them with offers, while by night the vampire molests fair Flora. Now Charles Holland, a dashing young artist who loves Flora, arrives, as does his uncle, the generous Admiral Bell, and the dimwitted Jack Pringle. They join forces with the Bannerworth boys to protect Flora, who is growing progressively weaker from the attacks ("a lily now instead of a rose"). It soon becomes clear to all that Varney is the vampire, and although the young men valiantly protect Flora, Varney eludes them, finally even capturing Charles Holland. In each scuffle Varney remains an absolute gentleman; he hates what he must do, he is sorry to bother them, but he must have the house and he must have Flora. When the boys pester him with challenges to duel, he is always courteous in accepting, making only a few polite demands. With the crusty Admiral Bell his politeness is not always reciprocated:

> "Well," said the admiral, [to Varney] when they were fairly under the tree, upon the leaves of which the pattering rain might be heard falling; "well—what is it?"
>
> "If your young friend, Mr. Bannerworth, should chance to send a pistol-bullet through any portion of my anatomy, prejudicial to the prolongation of my existence, you will be so good as not to interfere with anything I may have about me, or to make any disturbance whatever."
>
> "You may depend I sha'n't."
>
> "Just take the matter perfectly easy—as a thing of course."
>
> "Oh! I mean d— easy."
>
> "Ha! what a delightful thing is friendship! There is a little knoll or mound of earth midway between here and the Hall. Do you happen to know it? There is one solitary tree growing near its summit—an oriental looking tree, of the fir tribe, which, fan-like, spreads its deep green leaves across the azure sky."
>
> "Oh! bother it; it's a d—d old tree, growing upon a little bit of a hill, I suppose you mean?"
>
> "Precisely; only much more poetically expressed. The moon rises at a quarter past four to-night, or rather to-morrow morning."
>
> "Does it?"
>
> "Yes; and if I should happen to be killed, you will have me removed gently to this

mound of earth, and there laid beneath this tree, with my face upwards; and take care that it is done before the moon rises. You can watch that no one interferes."

"A likely job. What the deuce do you take me for: I tell you what it is, Mr. Vampyre, or Varney, or whatever's your name, if you should chance to be hit, wherever you chance to fall, there you'll lie."

"How very unkind." (pp. 181–82)

This duel is interrupted by the local mob, which is out to "burn, destroy and kill" the vampire, and so Varney takes his French leave, fleeing to Monk's Hall, where he has incarcerated Charles Holland, Flora's lover.

That night the Hangman of London arrives at Bannerworth Hall to extort money from Varney, for the Hangman knows how Varney became a vampire. It seems that the Hangman had once hanged Varney, and then delivered the body to a young medical student who, in the tradition of Victor Frankenstein, had him "revived." The Hangman joins the menfolk in protecting Bannerworth Hall, when, lo and behold, who should come running around the house but Varney, who has, it seems, been looking for treasure. Dr. Chillingworth tries to apprehend Varney, but the vampire pulls out a pistol and shoots him at point-blank range. But wait! the skeptical doctor is not dead. Varney has used blanks because, as we soon learn, Dr. Chillingworth was the young medic who revived him in London and Varney never forgets a kindness.

Meanwhile the mob has been fanatically exhuming the recent dead, finding that indeed some of the coffins are empty. They storm Varney's house, and Varney greets them: "If you honor me with this visit from pure affection and neighborly good will, I thank you." But alas, their intentions are otherwise. They ransack his mansion and set it afire; Varney escapes in the smoke. The Bannerworths now decide they have had enough, and are set to move. Varney notifies Admiral Bell that he is still willing to buy, and a breakfast meeting (appropriately the only kind Varney ever has to discuss "business") is arranged. In one of his rare outbursts of emotion Varney loses his temper with the curmudgeonly admiral and drops a table leaf from beneath the admiral's elbow, causing the good sailor, breakfast and all, to go tumbling to the floor. Varney asks politely to be excused and hurries off.

Meanwhile back at Bannerworth Hall: Charles Holland has been freed by Varney from Monk's Hall in return for silence and a promise not to seek vengeance. Marchdale, the family friend, who has been scheming to get the booty that Varney is seeking, has met a timely death from a highly localized storm, and Varney has explained that the hidden treasure is what he and Marmaduke Bannerworth, Flora's father, had gotten from killing a gambling partner. This is the crime for which he was hanged in London, the hanging death that was reversed by the young Dr. Chillingworth. In an aside Varney now claims that he would have been revived anyway by the moonlight, but he appreciates any gesture of kindness. As the Bannerworths prepare to depart, Varney promises that he will leave "fair Flora" alone.

Just as everyone seems to have made peace with Varney (except, of course, the mob, which is acting more and more like a character with a crazed mind of its own), a tall and cadaverous Hungarian nobleman arrives. He has extraordinary habits; for instance, he will drink only claret wine, "for it looks like blood and yet may not be it." He is looking for Varney, but the mob, thinking that anyone wanting Varney must be a vampire—"Birds of a feather *do* flock together," we are told—kills him, only to have him later revived by the moonlight. We are never told why the Hungarian wants Varney, but there are hints of blackmail. During all this Varney is being pursued over hill and dale by the brickthrowing mob, until exhausted, he reaches the door of a country cottage. He opens the door and falls faint at the feet of none other than "fair Flora" who is doing her evening's embroidery. Politely he tells the assembled Bannerworths of his perils, and continues to explain the disposition of the ill-gotten booty, including how the Bannerworths can find the deed to their country home. All agree he is a fine fellow, especially after he confesses that he never sucked blood from fair Flora: "I solemnly aver, that my lips never touched her, and that, beyond the fright, she suffered nothing from Varney, the vampyre" (p. 392). This is nonsense, because Flora has been bled and has the marks to prove it; but no matter, we can believe what we want. The Bannerworths believe Varney has been unfairly treated, and hide him from the mob, in Flora's boudoir. Meanwhile, when Dr. Chillingworth surreptitiously goes to examine the mysterious portrait of Marmaduke, someone tall and cadaverous steps out from behind the portrait, knocks him down, and escapes into the night with the painting.

It later happens that a few miles away a tall and cadaverous Baron Stolmuyer of Saltsburg is negotiating to buy Anderbury-on-the-Mount, a gloomy mansion built on a promontory overlooking the sea—a mansion that has an underground passageway from the cellar down through the rock to the beach. A man in black (presumably the Hungarian nobleman who had been previously looking for Varney) attacks the baron on the beach, but the baron kills him and stuffs his body into an ice well that is inside the underground passageway. Later that night the light of the moon shines through a crack in the door and the body seems to be reviving.

Meanwhile we learn that Marmaduke's fortune was hidden in the lining of the portrait; that Charles Holland will wed fair Flora; that the body of the man in the ice well was found and removed to the "boneyard" (still more moonlight); and that the baron is implicated in the killing, but could not care less. He cares for only one thing—the hand of a beautiful young virgin in wedlock—and any virgin except Flora Bannerworth will do.

The baron finds such a candidate in Helen Williams, the daughter of a scheming mother who rivals the worst of Dickens's evil parents. After some haggling, a deal is struck: Helen is to be the baron's wife, even though she is still in love with young James Anderson, who is presently sailing the seas. The baron is still bothered by the nagging memory of the man in black, who is laid out in the "boneyard" preparatory to being interred, and so goes to make sure that the job is really finished. It has not been finished, for by the time the baron arrives, the body has slunk out of the coffin to be more directly in the moonlight. The baron is about to administer the killing stroke when the revived corpse battles back and escapes into the night.

The Bannerworths, meanwhile, have completed the move to Deerwood, their country estate near Anderbury. An anonymous letter arrives telling them that Varney will never again molest them and they can rest easy. Dr. Chillingworth is in no mood to rest easy, as he is still concerned about recovering the family fortune. Who should now be rescued from a shipwreck by Jack Pringle (the Admiral's dim retainer) but James Anderson, who becomes friends with the Bannerworth ensemble. Mr. Anderson is understandably befuddled when he learns that Helen is to marry the emaciated baron and desperately tries to get word to her, but is thwarted by the treacherous mother. Finally, believing that nothing can be done, he and Flora and Charles and Henry and Jack Pringle and the admiral arrive at the wedding. The bride is on time, but the bridegroom is late:

> Minute after minute thus passed, and Mrs. Williams, who was attired in a richly-flowing garment of white silk, embroidered with flowers, began to be in a most particular fidget.

"Where could be the baron—good God! where is the baron?" and some one or two said, "D—n the baron!" When suddenly the door at which the bride had entered was again flung open, and two servants in rich liveries made their appearance, one standing on each side of it. Then there was heard approaching a slow and measured footstep, and presently attired in a court suit of rich velvet Baron Stolmuyer of Saltsburg appeared in the hall, and marched up to the table.

He had but just time to execute half a bow to the assembled multitude, when Admiral Bell called out in a voice that awakened every echo in the place,—

"It's Varney, the vampyre, by G—d!" (p. 538)

There follows a battle worthy of the Marx brothers, which concludes with Varney's heaving James Anderson like a bowling ball along a table of confectionaries until he finally rolls into the lap of Mrs. Williams. Varney runs down the underground passageway and escapes. All ends happily, however, for James Anderson marries Helen, Mrs. Williams courts the admiral but is spurned and then rendered destitute by the wedding expenses, and Varney really does at last leave the Bannerworths alone. For the next two hundred thousand or so words he spends his time molesting others.

In chapter 127 the scene switches to London. An invalid, Colonel Deverill, rich, tall, and cadaverous, comes to the boarding house of the greedy Mrs. Meredith and her three unmarried daughters. That night the screams of a neighborhood girl are heard, as well as footsteps on the roof. The girl claims that her blood was sucked; her father is confused and furious; and so a check is made of the guests in Mrs. Meredith's boarding house. "Was the invalid Colonel disturbed?" "No, not much." After Mrs. Meredith succeeds in matching up her unwilling daughter with the colonel, a friend asks if a high-ranking military man might attend the wedding. Mrs. Meredith eagerly says yes. The wedding day arrives—sure enough, the high-ranking guest is Admiral Bell, and at the wedding breakfast he recognizes Colonel Deverill as Varney, just as the neighbor's girl recognizes him as the nocturnal intruder. In the melee Varney escapes, leaving Mrs. Meredith, as he has earlier left Mrs. Williams, to pay the wedding expenses. Clearly *Varney's* working-class audience understood both the public embarrassment of the bride as well as the financial distress of her parents.

In the next extended episode Varney rescues Captain Frazer and his family from an overturned coach. "Will he come for dinner?" "No, but breakfast will be fine." That night Miss Stevens, Fraser's sister-in-law, is bitten on the arm, and at the inquest Varney suggests that perhaps a large dog was responsible. The group, including Varney, soon goes to Bath to relax; Varney hears of a rich old dowager whom he robs and kills, leaving behind some of the loot that is too heavy to carry. When he does return, he finds it missing, and is pursued by a mob across the rooftops. Exhausted, he slips into a garret where an old sick sailor is resting. The mob has him cornered, but Varney shouts "Fire!" and in the ensuing confusion escapes. The nephew of the late dowager is caught with some of the booty, and is charged with murder. Varney is unconcerned and proposes to Miss Stevens, who is pressured by the Frasers to accept. The wedding is all arranged, but wait—here come the police with the old sick sailor. It is Admiral Bell, and to make a short episode shorter, Varney escapes.

A change of scene (Naples, Italy), new characters (a young man, Jose, and his girlfriend, Fiametta), but the same tall, cadaverous stranger. Without explanation, Jose and the stranger fight. The stranger stumbles and is seemingly killed. Jose goes to fetch a monk to perform the last rites, but the moonlight revives the body and by the time the monk arrives the cadaverous stranger is back on his feet. The stranger kills the monk, dons the habit, and claiming he desperately needs virgin blood, heads for the local convent where Juliet, an unwilling maiden, is being pressured to take the vows rather than to marry Jules, the man she loves. The monk a.k.a the cadaverous stranger, tells the Mother Superior he can handle the problem, and in private tells Juliet that Jules is dead and that his last wish was that Juliet take him, the monk, as her husband. Juliet is rather weak and almost assents, when who should arrive but the police and (not Admiral Bell!) Jose, Fiametta, and Jules. "That's the man who killed the monk!" But too late—Varney the Vampyre escapes in the confusion.

Next comes a throwaway episode of a few chapters in which Varney's body is washed ashore at night and discovered by a good fisherman. "A little more light—a little more light, if you please" (p. 704), Varney asks politely as he is dragged up the beach. Varney is invited home, where that night the fisherman's daughter is attacked and Varney is pursued, shot, and later revived in the moonlight. Now the scene shifts abruptly and without warning to Naples. Here Varney saves the life of Count Polidori (yes, Polidori, the man who first gave life to the literary vampire is rescued by his fictional protagonist) by chasing off a band of thugs. Polidori takes Varney home to receive the thanks of the requisite daughter Isabella. Varney tells a lot of lies to get into her good graces, and, as the count feels a certain responsibility towards his savior, the wedding is soon planned. On the wedding day who should arrive but her brother and soldiers and witnesses who all recognize the groom as the monk killer, a.k.a the monk, a.k.a Varney, but this time Varney does not escape in the ensuing confusion. Rather, claiming he'll find some witnesses to clear himself, he simply "quitted the palace in a gondola, and never reappeared" (p. 722).

In chapter 166 Varney finally returns to England where he is robbed by highwaymen and left for dead, only to revive under the light of the moon. He is weakened and so needs the blood of a young virgin. He finds such a young lady, is almost apprehended by the same highwaymen who first attacked him, but finally escapes. These chapters do little more than return Varney to his native sod, and show that he is pathetically dependent on others. They also make it clear that although Varney can be nasty, there are people like these highwaymen or Mr. Marchdale, Mrs. Meredith, Mrs. Williams, or the Hangman, who are worse. Varney is victimized by others as well as by his own uncontrollable thirsts, but these characters simply exploit others for financial gain. Varney would never do that. The author (whoever he may be at this point of the tale) explains it best:

> Can it be true, and if so, how horribly strange, that a being half belonging to a world of spirits, should thus wander beneath the cold moon and the earth, bringing dismay to the hearts of all upon whom his strange malign influence is cast!
>
> How frightful an existence is that of Varney the Vampyre!
>
> There are some good points about the—man, we were going to say—and yet we can hardly feel justified in bestowing upon him that title,—considering the strange gift of renewable existence which was his. If it were as, indeed, it seemed to be the case, that bodily decay in him was not the result of death, and that the rays "of the cold chaste moon" were sufficient to revivify him, who shall say when that process is to end! and who shall say that, walking the streets of giant London at this day, there may not be some such existences? Horrible thought that, perhaps seduced by the polished exterior of one who seems a citizen of the world in the most extended signification of the words, we should bring into our domestic circle a vampyre!
>
> But yet it might be so. We have seen, however, that Varney was a man of dignified courtesy and polished manners; that he had the rare and beautiful gift of eloquence; and that, probably, gathering such vast experience from his long intercourse which had extended over so many years, he was able to adapt himself to the tastes and the feelings

of all persons, and so exercise over them that charm of mind which caused him to have so dangerous a power.

At times, too, it would seem as if he regretted that fatal gift of immortality, as if he would gladly have been more human and lived and died as those lived and died whom he saw around him. But being compelled to fulfill the order of his being, he never had the courage absolutely to take measures for his own destruction, a destruction which should be final in consequence of depriving himself of all opportunity of resuscitation. (p. 734)

Has there ever been a better description of the Byronic Hero—the man who loathes himself as he is loathed by others?

The next episode in Varney's eventful career is an exemplum of this paradoxical life of being both hound and hounded, attacker and attacked. The elderly Mr. and Mrs. Lake and their son arrive in London with Annetta, a lovely rich young lady. A short and grouchy Mr. Blue soon arrives at their hotel as well as a tall and cadaverous Mr. Black. During the night Annetta is attacked (sucking sounds are heard), and Mr. Blue is suspected and asked to leave. Mr. Black and Mr. Lake agree to stand guard, but Mr. Black lures Mr. Lake away. A scream is heard and when Mr. Lake returns he finds Mr. Blue with a gun and Mr. Black in a swoon. This time Mr. Blue is forcibly ejected. Mr. Lake, however, is the one really trying to exploit Annetta—for he wants his son to marry her for her money. He schemes with his son to pretend that the younger Lake act like a vampire, frighten Annetta, and then in the confusion appear as himself to save her. The scheme works until the make-believe vampire enters Annetta's room to find the real vampire furiously at work. The real vampire is wounded, escapes out the window, and is found to be none other than Mr. Black. But Mr. Black, alias Baron Stolmuyer, Colonel Deverill, the Monk, etc., is our Varney and of course a little moonlight does wonders. The next day he writes to Annetta that he won't bother her anymore, and warns Messrs. Lake to leave her alone. Varney then informs Annetta's true love, a Lieutenant Rankin, that he had better rescue her, which of course the lieutenant does. Later we learn that Mr. Lake has kidnapped Annetta from his brother, the good Lord Lake, who was earlier disguised as none other than Mr. Blue. The guilty Lakes are arrested. Varney has done a good deed!

This good deed seems to have a profound effect on Varney, for he now dreams of escape from his eternal bondage. In a vision he is told that death by drowning (death presumably out of the revivifying rays of the moon) is the only release. But alas, although Varney throws himself off a ship and seems to drown, his body floats to the surface, is washed ashore, and found by Edwin and Charles Crofton. The Crofton boys, thinking the body dead, take it to the "boneyard" where Will Stevens, the sexton, greedily eyes the large finger rings. That night as Will prepares to cut the rings off, the moonlight streams through the cracks of the vault, and Varney is revived. He is as furious to be alive as Will is terrified to have him so. When the Croftons hear of his recovery, they invite him to Crofton Grange to recuperate. Varney accepts, and en route sees a rider fall from a horse. Although Varney is torn whether to help or not, he finally decides to be true to his diabolical nature and leave the rider to suffer. This rider, we later learn, is the young Mr. Ringwood, who is coming to court Clara Crofton, the requisite young woman. To literally make a long story short, that night Clara's screams are heard, as are steps on the rooftops; on her deathbed Clara describes Varney and dies. Night vigils are now set up to protect Emma, the other sister. The doctor diagnoses a vampire attack, for he has just read an article by a Dr. Chillingworth on vampires. Later that night Varney appears and is frightened off.

Meanwhile back in the graveyard Will Stevens notices that the recently deceased body of Clara Crofton is not in her coffin. He hears ghosts who chant, "Awake, sister, be one of us," and Will, terrified, calls for the Reverend Beven. The Reverend, who should, of course, protect his flock by leading the charge against the vampire, claims this is all a dream and should be forgotten. But Ringwood insists that he cannot take the chance that fair Clara will be possessed, and so volunteers to stand guard. That night he sees Clara rise from the coffin in the moonlight; he entreats her to stay, but instead she runs off while he is clobbered from behind by a man in black.

Meanwhile in town a sixteen-year-old girl is attacked; the schoolmaster deduces a vampire; Sir George Crofton realizes that it must be his late daughter; the Reverend Beven, who is up on his Gothic novels, says it can all be explained by natural causes; and the townspeople say they don't care, they want vengeance. Soon all parties converge on the "boneyard," Clara is discovered fresh-faced, blood trickling from her mouth, Sir George goes berserk, the Reverend still says it's all imaginary, but the mob knows better. They want this demon destroyed. They capture Clara and plan to burn her, but (thanks to Varney?) one of those highly localized storms occurs, making burning impossible so it is suggested that she be taken to a crossroads and staked. All agree, and with a shriek it is done—Clara is given eternal rest.

Ironically poor Varney, who really needs the rest, is still doomed to live. Later that night he passes by Clara's crude grave and sadly fills it in. Also out this night is the Reverend Beven. They meet:

> Mr. Beven did not at the moment recognize in the form before him the man who had been the guest of Sir George Crofton, and from whom it was supposed had sprung all the mischief and horror that had fallen upon the family, at the Grange.
>
> "Who are you?" he cried; "can you give me information of an outrage that has been committed hereabouts?"
>
> "Many," said Varney.
>
> "Ah! I know that voice. Are you not he who was rescued from the sea by the two sons of Sir George Crofton?"
>
> "Well?"
>
> "Now I know you, and I am glad to have met with you."
>
> "You will try to kill me?"
>
> "No, no—peace is my profession."
>
> "Ah! you are the priest of this place. Well, sir what would you do with me?"
>
> "I would implore you to tell me if it really be true that—that—"
>
> Mr. Beven paused, for he disliked to show that the fear that it might be true there were such creatures as vampyres, had taken so strong a hold of him.
>
> "Proceed," said Varney.
>
> "I will. Are you then a vampyre?"
>
> "A strange question for one living man to put to another! Are you?"
>
> "You are inclined to trifle with me. But I implore you to answer me. I am perhaps the only man in all this neighborhood to whom you can give an answer in the affirmative with safety."
>
> "And why so?"
>
> "Because I question not the decrees of Heaven. If it seems fit to the great Ruler of Heaven and of earth that there should be ever such horrible creatures as Vampyres, ought I his creature to question it?" (pp. 844–45)

Varney accepts this Neoclassical argument and takes an immediate liking to the man who is supposed to be his destroyer. Beven says he can help ("Have you tried prayer?" he queries. "Prayer?" answers Varney), and Varney promises to reform.

They return to the Reverend's house where Varney beds down under his cape in the study. Next morning Sir George arrives for consolation, and is told that Varney is sleeping inside. Sir George will not be restrained and dashes past Beven, breaks down the door, heaves back the cape, but . . . no Varney. However, Varney has left a note detailing his life (he has been an acquaintance of Charles I, a henchman to Oliver Cromwell, an accidental killer of his own son, plus the participant in a number of incidents which involved the daughters of widows, etc.). Alas, the journal breaks off abruptly as Varney realizes that he must now act to set things aright. A week later Beven reads of an adventurous Englishman who climbed to the top of Mount Vesuvius and flung himself into the molten rock crying to his guide:

> "You will make what haste you can, from the mountain, inasmuch as it is covered with sulphurous vapours, inimical to human life, and when you reach the city you will cause to be published an account of my proceedings, and what I say. You will say that you accompanied Varney the Vampyre to the crater of Mount Vesuvius, and that, tired and disgusted with a life of horror, he flung himself in to prevent the possibility of a reanimation of his remains." (p. 868)

And that is pretty much the end for Varney, as well as for the vampire in nineteenth-century literature—at least until he is revived decades later in the moonlit prose of Bram Stoker's *Dracula*.

Index